Made to Work

Made to Work analyses the conditions of mobile knowledge work (MKW) in contemporary worklives, contrasting and drawing parallels among three highly significant sectors of the knowledge economy: academia, information communication technology (ICT) management, and digital creative start-up work.

It introduces the concept of 'corollary work' to characterise the elusive work underpinning the configuration of workers, informational, technological, relational and infrastructural resources in (re)producing liveable worklives.

It ultimately illuminates the myriad strands of corollary work that enable MKW to take place and contributes to emergent debates on how exploitation, at least in the domain of MKW, can be named, resisted and creatively subverted. In so doing, it opens up a conversation about the complex ways in which contemporary worklives are 'made to work', and about potential interventions to bring about more just worklife conditions in the future.

Breda Gray is Senior Lecturer in Sociology, University of Limerick (Ireland).

Luigina Ciolfi is Professor of Human Centred Computing at Sheffield Hallam University (UK).

Aparecido Fabiano Pinatti de Carvalho is Associate Researcher at the Institute of Information Systems and New Media of the University of Siegen (Germany).

Changing Mobilities

Series Editors: Monika Büscher, Peter Adey

This series explores the transformations of society, politics and everyday experiences wrought by changing mobilities, and the power of mobilities research to inform constructive responses to these transformations. As a new mobile century is taking shape, international scholars explore motivations, experiences, insecurities, implications and limitations of mobile living, and opportunities and challenges for design in the broadest sense, from policy to urban planning, new media and technology design. With world citizens expected to travel 105 billion kilometres per year in 2050, it is critical to make mobilities research and design inform each other.

Cycling
A Sociology of Vélomobility
Peter Cox

Sea Log
Indian Ocean to New York
May Joseph

Material Mobilities
Edited by Ole B. Jensen, Claus Lassen and Ida S. G. Lange

Brazilian Mobilities
Edited by Maria Alice de Faria Nogueira and Camila Maria dos Santos Moraes

Made to Work
Mobilising Contemporary Worklives
Breda Gray, Luigina Ciolfi and Aparecido Fabiano Pinatti de Carvalho

For a full list of titles in this series, please visit www.routledge.com/Changing-Mobilities/book-series/CHGMOB.

Made to Work

Mobilising Contemporary Worklives

Breda Gray, Luigina Ciolfi and Aparecido Fabiano Pinatti de Carvalho

Routledge
Taylor & Francis Group
LONDON AND NEW YORK

First published 2020 by Routledge

2 Park Square, Milton Park, Abingdon, Oxon OX14 4RN
605 Third Avenue, New York, NY 10017

Routledge is an imprint of the Taylor & Francis Group, an informa business

First issued in paperback 2021

British Library Cataloguing-in-Publication Data
A catalogue record for this book is available from the British Library

Library of Congress Cataloging-in-Publication Data
Names: Gray, Breda, author.
Title: Made to work : mobilising contemporary worklives / Breda Gray, Luigina Ciolfi, Aparecido Fabiano Pinatti de Carvalho.
Description: Abingdon, Oxon ; New York, NY : Routledge, 2020. | Series: Changing mobilities | Includes bibliographical references and index.
Identifiers: LCCN 2019057561 (print) | LCCN 2019057562 (ebook) | ISBN 9780367109325 (hbk) | ISBN 9780429023958 (ebk)
Subjects: LCSH: Knowledge workers–Social aspects. | Knowledge economy. | Information services industry–Employees. | Knowledge management.
Classification: LCC HD8039.K59 G73 2020 (print) | LCC HD8039.K59 (ebook) | DDC 331.7–dc23
LC record available at https://lccn.loc.gov/2019057561
LC ebook record available at https://lccn.loc.gov/2019057562

ISBN: 978-0-367-10932-5 (hbk)
ISBN: 978-1-03-217264-4 (pbk)
DOI: 10.4324/9780429023958

Typeset in Times New Roman
by Wearset Ltd, Boldon, Tyne and Wear

Contents

Note on authors

Breda Gray is Senior Lecturer in Sociology, University of Limerick (Ireland). She has published extensively on gender, migration, work, identity and emotion in international peer-reviewed journals including: Mobilities; Work, Employment and Society; Sociology; British Journal of Sociology; The Sociological Review, International Migration Review; Gender, Place and Culture; International Review of Social Research; and the European Journal of Cultural Studies. She is co-editor of Special Issue of Mobilities on mobile methodologies and editor of Special Issue of Irish Journal of Sociology on transnationalism.

Luigina Ciolfi is Professor of Human Centred Computing at Sheffield Hallam University (UK). An experienced scholar in the fields of HCI and CSCW, she researches the understanding, practicing and designing of digital interactive systems from a sociotechnical perspective. She has published her work in journals such as Human Computer Interaction, Mobilities, Personal and Ubiquitous Computing, CoDesign, CSCW Journal, and in prestigious conferences such as EUSSET ECSCW, and ACM CSCW, Designing Interactive Systems, and CHI. She is co-author (with Eva Hornecker) of *Human-Computer Interactions in Museums*. She is a Member of EUSSET and Senior Member of the ACM.

Aparecido Fabiano Pinatti de Carvalho is Associate Researcher at the Institute of Information Systems and New Media of the University of Siegen (Germany). His interests span, amongst others, Computer Supported Cooperative Work, Human-Computer Interaction, Ubiquitous and Mobile Computing, and Mobile and Nomadic Work Practices. He has published several relevant articles on related topics in prestigious international journals and conferences – such as JCSCW, IEEE Access, EUSSET ECSCW and ACM CSCW – and served as a guest editor for the JCSCW Special Issue on *Work Practices, Nomadicity and the Mediational Role of Technology*. He is a professional member of the EUSSET and the ACM, and has been serving as a EUSSET Competence Network Co-Chair since early 2018.

Preface

As researchers on this study and authors of this book, we see ourselves as both observers and participants, constantly seeking to identify patterns while recognising many as personally familiar, and always producing the social world of which we speak. As academics, of course we share much with the accounts of the academic study participants, but there are also crossovers with the worklife patterns of non-academic participants. In writing up this multi-stranded study, we try to adopt an orientation of 'with-ness' as we travel alongside these fellow mobile knowledge workers, in exploring worklife practices, possibilities and potentials. Yet, there are also times when this is a study 'of' mobile knowledge work – when mobile knowledge work is made an object of study. This objectifying move is self-conscious as we try to identify emergent patterns and examine how they are upheld and reproduced by particular sociomaterial knowledge/power relations and practices. As such, we are positioned both inside and outside the study while totally implicated with it insofar as both the study and this book enact mobile worklives as a particular reality. Of course we are indebted to all those workers who shared their experiences with us and whose worklives shape the narrative, issues and quandaries addressed in this book.

Over more than ten years of collaboration on this study, we have been involved in myriad intersecting processes and practices, involving diverse people, objects, places and infrastructures, as well as shifting purposes and agendas. An account of these alone could form the basis for a manuscript, so we reflect on only a few of them here. Initiated in the Department of Sociology at the University of Limerick (UL), the project developed into a collaborative effort with the Department of Computer Science and Information Systems in 2008, enabled by a five-year funding grant through the Government of Ireland and supported by the EU Regional Development Fund, the Irish Social Science Platform (ISSP), the Department of Enterprise, Trade and Innovation and the Higher Education Authority. The project also received funding support from the University of Limerick and the UL Institute for the Study of Knowledge in Society (ISKS). The research team was established including: Breda Gray and Luigina Ciolfi as joint Principal Investigators, postdoctoral researcher, Anthony D'Andrea, and PhD scholars, Fabiano Pinatti and Lisa Wixted.

The five-year life of the fieldwork included numerous relocations between continents and countries, as well as recruitment via videoconferencing and multiple international seminars involving academic mobility and live video links. Through project-related journeys and connections, the interdisciplinary team developed a knowledge base in common and marshalled mobile concepts and theoretical debates to develop an overall project framework. The input of all those international scholars who took part in the project advisory seminar series, workshops and special issue journals was particularly significant in this regard. Of course, the study would never have gotten off the ground without those manifold longer-term and complex sociomaterial practices ranging from research design, funding applications, team recruitment, set-up and conduct of fieldwork, to data analysis, work-in-progress workshops, international collaborative events and presentations at international conferences. All of these practices and processes in intersecting and complex ways shape the content and form of this book.

The experience of co-writing this book involved the three authors in navigating many intersecting mobilities: three different countries, many coinciding collaborations, projects, people and networks, as well as the general sense that the book presented a great practical (as well as intellectual) challenge. Besides writing, reading and refining our argument, analysing data and structuring the book, the end product relied on extensive corollary work. For example, a dedicated infrastructure, including a shared online folder, collected and categorised all materials, countless emails were exchanged, and meetings took place via a virtual meeting room – always with the same URL, now a familiar address. Interestingly, the service used for these virtual meetings brands itself as a tool for the kinds of worklives we describe: 'It … no longer matters where your team sits. And by what office, coffee shop or home your team collaborates from. Whereby brings people together no matter where they are' (https://whereby.com/information/brand). The effortless, light and agile work culture pitched by Whereby's branding slogan is not so simple though. It requires multiple reconfigurations of effort and even then – at least from our perspective and those of workers in our study – never even approximates this promise of ease and agility. For us, getting to 'our meeting room' involved the coordination of diverse mobilities, places, time zones and worklives. During the two years of writing, emails were exchanged and conversations held between Brazil (more specifically in Clementina and Araçatuba), Boston, Lancaster, Sheffield, Dublin, Limerick and Siegen.

Despite the geographic movement of this work across continents, countries and regions, it did matter when and where we sat and worked from, and how. We got together in 'writing rooms' across many material places: in August 2018, at a rented apartment in Manchester, Lui and Breda called Fabiano in Germany. When he joined them via video call, he was surrounded by boxes, having just moved house. After the call, Breda and Lui had to check out of the apartment, and spent the rest of the day working at Waterstones bookstore café on Deansgate. Although the table was too small, it had the distinct advantage of a nearby electrical socket. They took it in turns to charge their laptops. Halloween 2018 was spent at work in a hotel in Limerick, discussing drafts and fieldnotes, with Fabiano joining via Skype, while the city outside grew hazy with firecracker smoke. St Patrick's Day weekend 2019 found the three of us together in Manchester. A large pendulum swinging from the ceiling in the hotel lobby where we were working reminded us that the planet was still moving as we sat down to share progress, exchange feedback and revise timelines. In yet another hotel room the following day, the coffee machine worked hard to sustain the work. It was a wet, grey Sunday more suited to rest than to going through large wads of data transcripts. Interruptions included student emails requesting assignment extensions, colleagues seeking confirmation of dates, journal reminders of review reports, friends and family checking in re arrangements on return. These interruptions prompted a discussion of 'productivity' as articulated by study participants and links with some aspects of our own worklife practices.

Alongside the myriad manifestations of movement and connection between people, places, times, productive efforts and labours of love, we also moved across disciplines to find a common ground and a common voice. This meant revisiting concepts and debates numerous times to help configure our theoretical framework and analytic approach. We have made ourselves to work together in constantly emergent sociomaterial configurations while writing about how our participants do the same. As we draw together all of these comings and goings, connections and disconnections, encounters and environments in this book, our aim is to show how contemporary mobile knowledge work is made to work. We do this from the perspectives of workers themselves. By doing so, we demonstrate the many ways in which they also are 'made to work'. Looking to the future, we question the sustainability of these worklife practices and ask whether we want to sustain them, given the growing burden of corollary work involved. Are these the ways and conditions in which worklives are best made?

Acknowledgements

First and foremost, we would like to thank all the participants who made this research possible. Without their time, insights, goodwill and cooperation, this book would not have been possible. We warmly thank Anthony D'Andrea and Lisa Wixted who were part of our research team and actively contributed to the data collection and initial analysis stages of this project. Special thanks go to Liam Bannon, who served as a consultant during the lifespan of the project, provided feedback on some aspects of the book and has supported this project from start to finish. We are also grateful to all those participants in the Nomadic Work/Life Seminar Series, who gave their time to join us in Limerick and to explore and discuss conceptual, theoretical and methodological aspects of our research: Michaela Benson, Kate Boyer, Barry Brown, Tim Cresswell, Barbara Czarniawska, Doris R. Eikhof, Al James, Kate Kenny, Detlev Lück, Gloria Mark, Katie Milestone, Elaine Moriarty, Misha Myers, Mark Perry, Henrike Rau, Justin Spinney, Carsten Sørensen, John Urry (*in memoriam*), and Jo Vergunst. A special thanks to all the colleagues who, as work on this book progressed, kindly provided us with valuable feedback through informal conversations, discussions at joint workshops, and by reviewing early chapter drafts: Liam Bannon, Anne Cronin, Ingrid Erickson, Airi Lampinen, Ellie Lockley, Íde O'Carroll, Seán Ó Riain, Daniela Petrelli, Annie Rogers, Chiara Rossitto, Simona Spedale, and Norman Su. Breda would like to thank Anne-Marie Fortier, Monika Büscher and the Centre for Mobilities Research at Lancaster University for hosting her as Visiting Scholar in Spring Semester 2018. We would also like to acknowledge colleagues in the Department of Sociology, the Department of Computer Science and Information Systems, the Interaction Design Centre and the Institute for the Study of Knowledge in Society at the University of Limerick.

Abbreviations

A	Academic
CSCW	Computer Supported Cooperative Work
DC	Digital Creative
EI	Enterprise Ireland
HCI	Human-Computer Interaction
ICT	Information and Communication Technology
ICTM	Information and Communication Technology Manager
IxD	Interaction Design
MKW	Mobile Knowledge Work
MKWr	Mobile Knowledge Worker
STS	Science and Technology Studies

Introduction

Most of the world's workers today are bound to specific workplaces, and are engaged in monotonous, or physically demanding work. Moreover, only a minority of workers, at 13 per cent across 142 countries, report being engaged by the work they are doing (Schwartz & Porath, 2014). It is also true to say that most organisational forms remain predominantly 'bureaucratic and hierarchical in nature' (Langfred & Rockmann, 2016, p. 634). Yet, we are witnessing a de-institutionalisation, dispersal and individualisation of work in advanced capitalist economies as more forms of work are made amenable to such arrangements. 'Mobile knowledge work' (MKW) is at the forefront of this trend. Mobile and flexible work arrangements intertwine with mobile devices and networked connectivity to align with the 'new spirit of capitalism', which relies on workers 'being mobile, enthusiastic, versatile, [and] having potential to be autonomous …' (Boltanski & Chiapello, 2005, p. 112). Indeed, MKW is widely celebrated for its agility, flexibility and weightlessness, as well as its promise of self-expression and happiness. In this book we investigate emergent practices of mobile worklife by foregrounding first-person accounts of how MKW is practiced and accounted for by mobile knowledge workers (MKWrs) themselves. The book examines the overlooked but ceaseless practices of crafting liveable worklives in three emblematic sectors of MKW: academia, Information Communication Technology (ICT) management, and digital creative work. These relatively privileged work sectors exemplify particular aspects of these trends which are spreading, albeit in different forms, across nearly all sectors of the labour market.

Based on our analysis of MKWrs' accounts, we propose the term *corollary work* to capture all the elusive work undertaken as workers as well as informational, technological, relational and infrastructural resources are entangled in the making of liveable worklives. We call it 'corollary' because it is the inevitable and practical consequence of MKW; it naturally follows from and is already presupposed by it. The Latin term 'corolla', from which corollary stems, means 'little garland' (Dictionary.com, 2019). As a wreath of interwoven leaves or flowers, the garland metaphor evokes the incessant weaving together of multiple capacities out of which MKW takes form. Although we propose the term *corollary work* to refer to those worklife practices beyond what might be commonly designated MKW tasks, we argue that neither corollary work nor MKW can be defined in advance, but unfold together in everyday life. However, *corollary work* can be distinguished by its production of those conditions and capacities necessary to MKW, even if these are often hard to disentangle. It includes, but is not confined to, (re)creating and sustaining workplaces, varying forms of anticipatory and reflexive 'time work', and the interconnected quest for (and performance of) work productivity, self-expression and passion through 'identity work'. Although this work materialises the conditions necessary to and through which MKW is *made to work*, it tends to go unnoticed.

Relatedly, the intimacy of the relationship between work and life for participants in our study, and the ways in which work is lived through life and vice versa, led us to adopt the term '*worklife*' (without a hyphen, or slash) as best reflecting the tenor of our findings. The term worklife emphasises their entanglement while at the same time enabling us to be alert to those specific contexts and circumstances in which differentiation rises up in the midst of this joining of work and life (Ingold, 2007). Boundaries get made and unmade, but these contextual, contingent and contested practices of (un)boundarying cannot be assumed in advance. If, with Ingold, we conceive of life 'as the creative potential of a world-in-formation', then work is in life and is endlessly caught up in its 'current of continual generation' (Ingold, 2007, p. S31).

Today's digitalised work environment is implicated with the promotion of entrepreneurialism and self-employment, alongside the rise of the 'gig economy', portfolio careers, on-demand business models and 'entrepreneurial academics' (Bauder, 2015; Fleming, 2017; Gregg, 2018; Meyer, 2003; Teichler, 2017; Vostal, 2015). Organisational norms and structures, taken for granted in the post-WWII global North, are being 'upended for new, more flexible arrangements variously instantiated across telecommuting, home-working, co-working, shared offices, hot-desking, and mobile working forms' (Erickson, Jarrahi, Thomson, & Sawyer, 2014, p. 5). Moreover, as higher education internationalises and universities compete for 'world-class' status (Lynch, 2006; Menzies & Newson, 2008; Müller, 2014; Slaughter & Leslie, 1997; Storme, Faulconbridge, Beaverstock, Derudder, & Witlox, 2017; Vostal, 2015; Ylijoki, 2003), mobility is gaining significance as a form of academic 'network capital' (Urry, 2004). These trends intersect with and are shaped by global economic instability, heightened labour market precarity, diminishing worker rights, growing levels of personal debt and accompanying anxieties (Adkins, 2017; Fleming, 2017; Kalleberg, 2009; Shibata, 2019).

Yet, recent policy, media and corporate discourses celebrate the positive aspects of mobile working, constant connectivity and 'associated entrepreneurial and creative values' (Taylor & Luckman, 2018, p. 2). One example is the goal of the *Mobile Minds* project, born out of the World Economic Forum. This project examines 'the global impact of remote work as it relates to both the mobility of the 21st century workforce and workplace' (Global Mind Project, 2019).[1] It promotes remote and mobile work for business as a means of achieving cost savings, productivity, agility and scalability, access to talent and improved retention (Olubunmi, Dey, & Sutton, 2017). The assumed social and cultural benefits include the mitigation of global traffic and connecting of people from different locations around the world (ibid.). Notably absent from this account is any reference to the costs or benefits for workers. Neither are the sociomaterial conditions under which 'mobile minds' are cultivated or harnessed addressed. By erasing the embodied, material conditions that underpin the organisation of mobile minds, workers themselves fall off the agenda of global competition for skilled workers. But it is not only the embodied material lives of MKWrs that are invisibilised. So also are all those workers engaged in the offshored work of manufacturing the tools and resources that underpin MKW, as well as the more proximate domestic and care work, without which the work dedication of MKWrs would be impossible.[2]

Globalised policy discourses of mobile work and workers circulate as fashionable 'packages of ideas and management' that gain enough momentum to 'travel' as 'global ideas' and take on the status of 'best practice' (Orlikowski & Scott, 2008, p. 464). So, even for relatively privileged MKWrs, the promise of autonomy, flexibility and self-fulfilment through mobile work and connectivity, comes into tension with those aspects of worklife that are rapidly disappearing, such as secure employment, designated office space and specified working hours (Taylor & Luckman, 2018). Although these disappearing working conditions, often associated with Fordism, might be seen as limiting, they are sometimes viewed with nostalgia in the face of the worklife demands of hypermobility. Mobility is 'sold' then as freeing and emancipatory, but its effects are often oppressive, restrictive and burdensome. It is in and through these contradictory discourses, practices and unequal conditions that MKW is *made to work*.

A Google search for the term 'made to work' offered the Merriam Webster definition of 'made-work': 'work *designed to provide employment* as distinguished from work that is *inherently necessary or permanently valuable*' (Merriam-Webster.com, 2019; emphasis added). As a de-institutionalised and individualised mode of work, MKW requires the mobilisation of economic, social and material resources in the designing and making of employment (for self and in some cases for others). Barad proposes the concept of 'intra-action' rather than 'interaction' to indicate that it is through 'specific agential intra-actions that the boundaries and properties of the "components" of phenomena become determinate and that particular embodied concepts become meaningful' (2003, p. 815). When work is mobile it needs to be 'made-work' in the intra-action of workers and tools, technologies and environments as well as through the ongoing cultivation of productive and passionate worklife dispositions. Google also threw up the 'Ludwig.guru Write Better English' examples of 'I made it to work'.[3] These included:

> I don't know how I did it, but **I made it to work** every day. (*New York Times*)

> **I made it** clear **to** him that my **work** was the only thing I really loved. (*New York Times*)
>
> Mr. McLaughlin, who began his teaching career in the Bronx with Teach for America, always bicycled **to work**, so "**I made it** a point **to** live in apartments that were a reasonable distance from my school," he said. (*New York Times*)
>
> **I made it** my mission **to work** hard and earn enough money to own my home, drive a nice car, send my kids to college, travel well, and retire comfortably. (*Huffington Post*)
>
> That's because **I made it** my job **to work** for free for these firms, whether they realized it or not. (*TechCrunch*)
>
> (Ludwig.guru, 2019)

These phrases refer to 'a world in the making, not a world already made' (Ingold et al., 2016, p. 7). They variously point to: the movement involved in making it to a workplace; making communication work; place making through commuting practices and deciding to live close to work; the making of a lifestyle through work; and the making of work through 'free labour' (Hesmondhalgh, 2010). For Ingold, 'making is a never-ending task of world-weaving, a correspondence of material movement and ambient vision' (Ingold et al., 2016, p. 7). Relationality is central to practices of 'making'. For example, the mobilisation of the term 'made to work' above involves myriad relations between technologies, vehicles, roads, workplaces, home places, travel, and notions of the past, present and future. The 'I' in all of the examples, is 'continually rediscovering itself through its continual responsiveness to the flow of material-discursive practices' (Hultin, 2019, p. 102). It is constituted in its resonance with the movements of this flow, its ability to see, listen, feel, join and participate as it flows along (ibid.).

In our study, workers tell us how they do things and all those relational practices that 'make' worklife possible and liveable at any one moment in time. The term *made to work*, or the continuous *making to work*, emphasises 'making' as a capacity that is realised in the entangled practices of workers, places, artefacts, policies and technologies. Through the corollary work that mobilises the interactive capacities of these diverse actors, MKW is *made to work*. We expand on this theme of 'made to work' and 'making to work' in Chapter 1, and so move on in the next section to outline the interdisciplinary debates (sociological, feminist and computer supported cooperative work) relating to mobility and mobile work that inform our study and this book.

Mobility and mobile work: interdisciplinary debates

Our analysis of MKW draws on and bridges two broad strands of work on mobilities, emanating from sociology and computer supported cooperative work (CSCW). Sociologists have described the term mobility as an 'evocative keyword', that is suggestive of productivity yet freedom, adaptability yet independence, and pervades business strategy, advertising, technology development and government policy (Hannam, Sheller, & Urry, 2006). In *New Keywords* (Bennett, Grossberg, & Morris, 2003), it is attributed with expressing the 'different, sometimes contradictory meanings underlying our most fundamental beliefs about progress, freedom, individuation and power' (Berland, 2003, p. 217). Contemporary mobility studies emphasises the significance of networks and flows in materially transforming and remaking the social, not least via emerging infrastructures of mobility (Urry, 2000). Of course, 'mobility can do little on its own until it is materialised through people, objects, words and other embodied forms' (Chu, 2010, p. 15). As such, mobility studies incorporates the study of *motility*, which refers to 'the capacity of entities (e.g. goods, information or persons) to be mobile in social and geographic space' (Kaufmann, Bergman, & Joye, 2004, p. 750). Thus, the mobility lens highlights the ways in which fields of possibilities are mobilised relative to movement (ibid.). For example, which worklives are agile enough to shift direction in response to speeded-up worklife opportunities and threats?

Feminists have a long history of challenging the gendered valorisation of mobility and autonomy which has the effect of invisibilising or hypervisibilising the immobilities and forced mobilities of some groups (see Chapter 1). In particular, they draw attention to the unequal colonial, patriarchal and classed power relations that underpin idealisations of mobility (Ahmed, 2004; Felski, 1995; Gray, 2004, 2006, 2013; Grewal, 1996; Grewal & Kaplan, 1994; Kaplan, 1996; Skeggs, 2004). Such idealisations equate men and masculinity with challenging and expansive movement in public and urban spaces and women and femininity with familiar, domestic spaces and restricted movement (Hanson, 2010). In response to such critiques, contemporary mobility studies is concerned with the 'power and politics of discourses and practices of mobility in creating both movement and stasis' (Hannam et al., 2006, p. 3). This book documents MKWrs' sociomaterial practices of mobility with particular reference to their relatively privileged labour market positioning and the gendered dimensions of MKW.

Some scholars point to the 'romance' of mobility (Büscher, 2014) and the 'cultural myths' that ideologically reproduce representations of mobile work and the 'office of the future' (Humphry, 2014, p. 355). For example, the globalised knowledge sectors of advanced economies are, according to Presskorn-Thygesen, marked by a 'moral injunction to be mobile, flexible and constantly on the move' (2015, p. 747). Indeed, the normalisation of online work cultures in the past three decades reinforces this injunction (Gregg, 2011). The mobility imperative also circulates in technology-focused literature, such as computer science, which assigns value to gaining control over surroundings, tools, and the unpredictability associated with constantly changing locations and workplaces (Churchill & Munro, 2001; Kleinrock, 1996; Perry, O'Hara, Sellen, Brown, & Harper, 2001; Wiberg & Ljungberg, 2001). This romance of mobility shapes management attitudes and worker career aspirations with terms such as 'old', 'stationary', 'fixed', 'heavy' and 'slow' being associated with passé office-like settings and set against representations of mobility as 'new', 'flexible', 'free', 'light' and 'fast'.

If this mobility/stasis dualism structures how work is represented, it is also inscribed in 'the materiality of technologies' designed to facilitate frictionless mobility (Humphry, 2014, p. 357). The assumption is that physical mobility spurs creativity and freedom to chase inspiration for productivity. Less attention is paid to the work that goes into forging the conditions that make mobility possible. For example, connectivity is integral to some corporate strategies, including the promotion of cloud infrastructures that underpin telework, remote work and other mobile activities (IBM, 2019; Brinker and Schwartz, 2018). They also shape MKWrs' practices as these intra-act with locational, temporal, organisational and cultural distances (Erickson et al., 2014), the storing and managing of information (Nelson, Jarrahi, & Thomson, 2017) and maintenance of information flows (Nash, Jarrahi, Sutherland, & Phillips, 2018).

The field of CSCW addresses many similar concerns to those of mobility studies. Its focus is not just on technology per se, but on the role of digital tools and infrastructures in mediating human practices. It strives both 'to understand the nature and requirements of cooperative work' and to design 'computer-based technologies for cooperative work arrangements' (Schmidt & Bannon, 1992, p. 11). As 'more a bazaar than a cathedral' (Schmidt & Bannon, 2013, p. 347), CSCW is informed by a variety of theoretical frameworks, including those of sociology and sociology of work, organisation theory, science and technology studies (STS), and by studies of the social organisation and structures underpinning work (Gerson & Star, 1986). It is underpinned by a critique of system-driven models underlying coordination technologies (such as office automation tools), which often ignore the situated nature of work and the background work practitioners do in making coordination technologies work (Schmidt & Bannon, 1992, p. 349). The challenge is to design computing systems that support not only the execution of a computational model of tasks, goals and procedures, but also the sociomaterial practices of getting work done.

Two decades ago, Luff and Heath located mobility at the heart of CSCW noting that 'individuals rely upon their own mobility, and the mobility of particular artefacts, to support collaboration' (1998, p. 305). This work addresses the management of mobile (collaborative) work across locations (Bellotti & Bly, 1996; Koehne, Shih, & Olson, 2012; Olson & Olson, 2014) as well as the relationship between mobile work, technical and informational infrastructures (Brown & O'Hara, 2003; Ciolfi & de Carvalho, 2014; Erickson et al., 2014; Jarrahi & Sawyer, 2017; Nelson et al., 2017; Perry et al., 2001; Rossitto, Bogdan, & Severinson-Eklundh, 2014; Su & Mark, 2008). Common to this work is a view of digital technologies as multifaceted and never obvious because digital mediation is problematised and never taken for granted as a general 'enabler', or a resource.

The term 'nomadicity' emerged in CSCW in the 1990s to address how mobile work is achieved. It originally referred to system supports (via nomadic computing and communications) providing ‘capabilities and services to the nomad’ moving from place to place (Kleinrock, 1996, p. 353). The associated term ‘digital nomads’ describes professionals freed from time and location constraints, thanks to mobile intelligent devices and high-speed communication networks (Makimoto & Manners, 1997). By way of overcoming assumptions that workers are freed from time and location constraints, and that mobile digital devices and networks are always enabling, nomadicity has been extended to capture the impact of myriad technological, spatial, organisational and personal circumstances (Bogdan, Rossitto, & Eklundh, 2007; Bogdan, Rossitto, Normark, Adler, & Eklundh, 2006; de Carvalho, 2013; de Carvalho, Ciolfi, & Gray, 2011, 2017; Mark & Su, 2010; Perry et al., 2001; Rossitto, 2009). This approach grounds technology use in particular contexts as it takes on different meanings as interacted with, interpreted and practiced (de Carvalho, 2013). The focus is on the entanglement of humans, artefacts and processes through unfolding worklife practices (de Carvalho, 2014).

The two disciplinary perspectives of sociology and CSCW are increasingly aligned in their concern with untangling the ‘imbroglio of technology, social practices and intersecting social, physical, virtual, communicative and imaginative mobilities of nomadic work’ (Büscher, 2014, p. 230). Together, they provide lenses for investigating questions and issues relating to MKW. The capacity of work to be mobile and done across multiple locations, and sometimes on the move, is now commonplace as some worklives are ‘sociomaterially’ constituted as mobile (Suchman, 2002). Indeed, the new convergence between the physical movement of people, vehicles and things; information production, storage and retrieval; wireless distributed computing and ‘smart cities’, as well as the rise of surveillance and tracking technologies, make these sociotechnical and cultural transformations urgent topics of enquiry (Sheller, 2014, p. 795). This book grounds these debates in the everyday worklife practices of MKWrs and unravels the myriad intersecting forms of *corollary work* that channels the flow of MKWlives. In the section that follows we briefly review debates about the post-Fordist restructuring of advanced capitalist economies and introduce our study location of a city region in post-Celtic Tiger Ireland.

Locating our study in relation to the post-Fordist restructuring of work and the post-Celtic Tiger economy

Numerous theoretical perspectives have emerged in recent decades to explain what is variously called a ‘knowledge’, ‘smart’, ‘new’ or ‘network’ economy. These include: ‘the information age’, a ‘post-industrial’ era, ‘globalisation’, ‘late capitalism’, ‘disorganised capitalism’ and ‘post-Fordism’. Our discussion is informed primarily by post-Fordist debates that foreground changing work arrangements, practices and subjectivities. These debates address what is sometimes characterised as a transition (albeit uneven) from a capitalist development phase based on nationally bound, industrial economies, organised by mass production and consumption (Fordism), to a new formation or phase of capitalism characterised by 'very different economic, societal and political norms' (post-Fordism).

When portrayed in terms of a transition from Fordism to post-Fordism, a linear shift or rupture is suggested. However, it is more accurate to say that contemporary capitalism involves the simultaneous coexistence of pre-Fordist (sweatshops; forced labour), Fordist (factory and other manufacturing work), and post-Fordist work arrangements (cognitive and affective work, financialisation and platform-based work).[4] Although Fordism may no longer form the dominant paradigm in the global North, it has not disappeared. Instead, the codification of industrial production processes during the 1980s and 1990s has enabled much of this work to be exported to lower cost production sites in the south and east.[5]

Post-Fordism is linked with an expansion in women's employment and the idea that labour market participation is a moral duty and marker of good citizenship, including good motherhood (Ekinsmyth, 2011; Luckman, 2015; McDowell, 2008, 2012; McRobbie, 2007, 2010). These trends are attributed to a number of factors including: the end of the Fordist 'family wage'; the dual income imperative (Conor, Gill, & Taylor, 2015)[6]; the growing educational attainment of young women (McRobbie, 2007, 2011); new opportunities in the knowledge economy for educated women; and a related rise in low-paid work for those women (often migrant) now doing the (social reproduction) work previously done by 'home makers' (McDowell & Christopherson, 2009, p. 336). As 'enterprising femininity' (Gray, 2003) is increasingly valorised, women are positioned as ideal entrepreneurial subjects (Gill & Scharff, 2011; McRobbie, 2007, 2009, 2011; Ringrose & Walkerdine, 2008).[7] This emphasis on entrepreneurial subjects requires professional women with families 'to undergo a "splitting" of identifications — being "men" in the public sphere while cordoning off their roles as women in the private sphere' (Rottenberg, 2014, p. 166).[8] Questions arise therefore about the changing relationship between gender, paid labour and the home as 'the relations of work to life are (…) currently undergoing substantial and radical revision' (Adkins & Jokinen, 2008, p. 139).[9] These debates are taken up in our discussion of women MKWrs' accounts in the chapters that follow.

Studies of the globalised high-tech industry, epitomised by Silicon Valley, suggest that it is the seedbed of a 'new masculinity' nurtured by a deeply masculine environment (Cooper, 2000; Massey, 1995). Technical skill and brilliance are highly valued (ibid.), and workplace cultures are marked by long working hours and uninterruptable availability to work teams (Frenkel, 2008). While Silicon Valley men adhere to a gender-egalitarian ideology and welcome women colleagues, they do so only as long as these women accept the norms of this new masculinity (Bardzell & Churchill, 2011; Cooper, 2000).[10] This globalised work culture puts greater pressure on women to conform to masculine norms and play down any care-giving activities, if not delegate them altogether (Frenkel, 2008).

Post-Fordist economies are most often associated with advanced capitalist states. However, Brenner argues that while this state scale is not being eroded, it is being 'rearticulated and reterritorialized in relation to both sub- and supra-state scales' (1998, p. 1). Although global cities are central 'sites of post-Fordist forms of global industrialization' there has been a turn towards all major urban regions as sites for achieving global competitive advantage (ibid.). More recently, the role of second-tier cities has gained significance in analyses of national economic performance across Europe (Brady, 2016). Although the relatively centralised Irish state has been somewhat ambivalent about developing this policy direction, some initiatives have been developed via its National Spatial Strategy 'Gateways' policy in the 2000s and subsequent efforts to implement this (Brady, 2016).

As economic development strategies increasingly emphasise high-tech regional economies, we decided to locate our study in a second-tier regional city context in Ireland.[11] Regional city economies are deemed key sites of economic development through collaborative networks and their potential for knowledge transfer and innovation (James, 2013). Because innovation and knowledge diffusion are organised by regional/city-based agglomerations of ICT, creative industries and higher education (ibid.), a configuration that characterises the regional/city area in which we conducted this study, our choice of study cohorts included these sectors.

The start of the study coincided with the economic crash of 2008 and demise of the 'Celtic Tiger' economy (1998–2007). During the Celtic Tiger years, GDP per capita in Ireland rose from about 60 per cent of the EU average to over 120 per cent of the average (Russell, McGinnity, Callan, & Keane, 2009). Key factors underpinning this rapid economic growth included the attraction of high-tech FDI (Foreign Direct Investment), a strong educational and ICT infrastructure, Ireland's English-speaking population, and its membership of the Single European market (Paus, 2012).[12] Economic growth in the 1990s was underpinned by 'a partial move toward a European-style combination of industrial policy, social investment and social partnership' (Ó'Riain, 2014, p. 4). Although these early Celtic Tiger years involved relatively stable economic development, this approach was 'trumped by financialisation in the 2000s' (Ó'Riain, 2014, p. 286). A financial and property bubble was created by state-supported market liberalism, 'Anglo-American financial globalisation' and the 'Irish and European banking and property systems' (ibid.).[13] This bubble combined with weak regulation contributed to the 2008 economic crisis, which heralded a 10 per cent reduction in employment between 2008 and 2014 (Boyle, 2017). While there were cutbacks in public sector jobs including academia, the ICT sector continued to grow throughout the recession (Bobek & Wickham, 2018, p. 19). Recessionary trends were reversed in late 2013 and, as the economy began to recover, so did employment (ibid.).

The Celtic Tiger economy saw women's employment rise by 52 per cent reaching an employment rate of 60.4 per cent in 2010, while men's employment rate increased by only 33 per cent in the same period (Russell, McGinnity, et al., 2009, p. 6).[14] As employment and dual earner households grew rapidly during the economic boom, Russell, O'Connell and McGinnity (2009) found work–life conflict to be higher for women than for men, for those with higher educational qualifications, and among employees with young children.[15] These findings are reflected in James' study of the IT sectors in Cambridge and Dublin between 2006 and 2008. Women workers in Dublin 'generally exhibit[ed] greater levels of work-life conflict' and negative work-to-home spillovers than their counterparts in Cambridge due to long commutes, high childcare costs, limited opportunities for flexible work arrangements and the absence of paternity leave (James, 2013, pp. 21–22). Childcare provision was left to the market despite the exponential growth in labour market participation of mothers with young children (Devitt, 2016; Gallagher, 2012).

Following the economic crash, the same economic model remained in place and was pursued even more vehemently. Public sector salaries were subject to progressive tiered pay cuts of between 8 to 21 per cent between 2009 and 2014 and embargos on employment were implemented (Roche, 2017).[16] Amongst other things, the government's 'Smart Economy' policy focused on 'enhancing productivity per person by investing in human capital; [and] incentivising innovation and commercialisation' (Government of Ireland, 2008, p. 33).[17] The knowledge sectors of ICT and creative industries have continued to grow since 2008 and higher education has been restructured to harness it more closely to national economic goals, including a shift towards private sources of funding and pressures to internationalise (Brennan, Enders, Valimaa, Musselin, & Teichler, 2008; Courtois, 2018; Grummell, Devine, & Lynch, 2009; Irish Higher Education Strategy Group, 2011).[18] Of course, the specificities of regional and national culture as well as the Irish economy shape our findings. Yet, the sectors under investigation and their regional configuration have much in common with those of other advanced economies and are known for their globalised work culture (Frenkel, 2008). As such, we see the analysis presented in this book as informing debates about shifting work arrangements and their implications for MKWrs across advanced capitalist contexts.

Studying MKW: framing assumptions and concepts

The book is informed by an in-depth study of MKWrs in a city/regional hub in Ireland. High-tech city/regional hubs are central to post-Fordist processes of production in which knowledge diffusion, learning and innovation are assumed to emerge via agglomerations of ICT, creative industries and higher education (James, 2013; Walby, Gottfried, Gottschall, & Osawa, 2007). ICT industries tend to be the flagship sector located 'at the vanguard of new working practices' (James, 2013, p. 7). Academic institutions also play a central role as resources (or more proactively as generators) of new knowledge, and play an increasingly entrepreneurial role in transforming 'academic knowledge into economic and social utility' (Brennan et al., 2008, p. 47). The creative industries, described as 'paradigms of entrepreneurial selfhood' (Ross, 2008, p. 32), make up the third key sector and are deemed central to 'wealth and job creation and the generation and exploitation of intellectual property' (Henry & Johnston, 2007, p. 212). Even as unemployment rose and recession set in after the 2008 economic crash, creative work maintained its exceptional status (Adkins, 2013). Our study population was chosen on the basis that these sectors are emblematic of contemporary knowledge work (Walby et al., 2007) and are closely associated with mobile, autonomous and flexible forms of work (Gill & Pratt, 2008; Massey, 1995).

A total of 56 participants made up our study sample: 48 MKWrs (24 women and 24 men) across the three sectors of ICT managers (ICTMs), digital creatives (DCs) and academics (As); and a further eight key regional and national development agency actors (one woman and seven men).[19] Each of the three cohorts (ICTMs, DCs and As) included 16 participants (eight women and eight men). The age profiles of participants range from the mid-20s to the mid-50s. While there was no correlation between age and degree of digital and technical competence, it is important to note that older participants began careers before the ubiquitous spread of digital connectivity and mobile devices, and so their worklives are shaped by the memory of different work contexts, practices and cultures. Most of the participants were white Irish with a few of European or North American origin but living in Ireland on a long-term basis. Participants worked in different positions or under different job titles in each sector (see Appendix for demographic details). For example, Academics (As) included full/part-time lecturers and researchers and worked in Computer Science and Engineering disciplines (11) as well as in Humanities and Social Science disciplines (five). The DCs' jobs span those of web designer, graphic designer, digital entrepreneur and internet marketing specialist. Finally, those in the ICTMs' cohort held positions such as CEO, CTO and managing director. The ICT companies included software development (including specialised software, such as scientific software); telecommunication networks development and management; IT systems design and support; and IT consultancy.

Although some aspects of the work of ICTMs and academics involve individual work, their wider work context includes teams and institutional agendas, so that organisational resources and cultures shape their work to a large extent. For ICTMs, a key component of their work is the management of others (i.e. colleagues and clients). Yet, many of them set up companies on their own, or in partnership with one other, and all of them are individually responsible for developing strategy and ideas. Academic roles involve relationships with colleagues, students, managers and funders, but also include significant individual work (such as research and teaching preparation). In contrast, DCs are mainly solo workers, with only three in the study cohort collaborating with one or two business partners.

In-depth interviews[20] (in some cases two interviews) were conducted with all study participants. The focus of the interviews was on how their worklives are *made to work* in the matrix of sociomaterial relations and practices through which MKWlives emerge and become recognisable as such. Our semi-structured interview protocol included questions about the daily practices of their worklives, including examples of a typical day and atypical day, the significance of particular places, times and artefacts, particularly technologies, their career trajectories and aspirations, paying particular attention to gender. Nearly all interviews took place in the workplace, which for digital creatives was often the participant's home.

ICT companies, high-tech start-ups and universities are each characterised by different product and productivity discourses and practices. ICT companies deliver goods such as software packages, digital services and customer support. DCs produce one-off bespoke digital solutions (e.g. websites, graphics, etc.), or even innovative new platforms, but also work to prepare the market for innovation (and, therefore, for future products and services). The University's core business is about education and research. Its 'products' include course delivery, increasingly measured via quantified (and commodified) student satisfaction surveys, research outcomes (i.e. funding, publications, impact, etc.), and knowledge transfer measured more and more in relation to economic and/or societal impact indicators. Product in these sectors is the (sometimes unanticipated) outcome of a complex mix of processes and expertise so that even when it is an artefact (i.e. a software package), the product is an immaterial one, subject to constant changes, updates and dependent on expertise in support of it. The significance of profitability and profit, passion, interest and creativity are differently emphasised and articulated across these sectors and also in the ways that participants in one sector view and represent workers in another.

The overall study was carried out as part of the Nomadic Work/Life in the Knowledge Economy (NWL) project, a Government of Ireland[21] funded research project concerning mobility, technology, gender and work developed in one city/regional hub in Ireland. It involved a five-year collaboration (2008–2013) between the Departments of Sociology and Computer Science and Information Systems at University of Limerick. This collaboration capitalised on 'emergent synergies' between the sociologies of work, mobility and gender and the fields of CSCW, human-computer interaction (HCI) and ubiquitous computing (Büscher, 2014). As well as benefiting from these synergies, this book seeks to synthesise those aspects of scholarship on mobile work that tend to get separated out into these different domains of scholarship.

A qualitative approach to how MKW is *made to work* enabled an open-minded inductive investigation of the patterning of study participants' worklife practices. It allowed us to trace the practices through which workers generate, join, flow along with and become blocked by locations, places, digital infrastructures, mobile devices and other artefacts animating and enacting worklives in relationship with colleagues, family, friends and others. All participants were recruited via public advertisements and snowballing in the city region in which the study took place. In the case of members of the academic sector, the research also involved shadowing[22] and time-space diaries.[23] As for the DCs, an analysis of presence on social networking platforms complements the interview data. In this book we draw only on the interview data (using pseudonyms and anonymising all other names referenced, as well as place and company names) in order to achieve data consistency across the three cohorts. Interview length ranges from one to two hours (average one and a half hour). Interviews were audio recorded and transcribed afterwards using the *Intelligent Verbatim* level of granularity, where most mumbling expressions (e.g. 'ums' and 'ers'), filler phrases (e.g. 'you know') and stumbles are omitted, but everything else is transcribed as said.

The findings presented and discussed in this book are based on an inductive thematic analysis of the interview data (Braun & Clarke, 2012). Data analysis began at the fieldnote stage when observations were noted and connections made. This continued at the transcription stage when initial themes were identified. Individual transcripts were coded and recoded following repeated readings and coding across all transcripts. These codes were then reviewed in research team meetings to clarify and agree interpretations and inferences. Systematic data analysis involved the flagging of differences across disciplines and constant reference to our original questions and ontological assumptions in arriving at overall findings. Particular attention was paid to how 'conditions of possibilities to think, act, and become in certain ways' came about (Hultin, 2019, p. 96).

The workers' accounts cannot be separated from the enactments in which they are produced, i.e. those enactments 'among researcher-data-participants-theory-analysis' (Hultin, 2019, p. 101). We attend therefore to how these accounts are produced in the 'flow of material-discursive practice' (ibid.). We look to the term 'sociomateriality', which has gained some currency in recent years as a way of moving beyond viewing technology, work and organisation as separate phenomena, to inform our analysis. The sociomaterial approach is underpinned by the assumption that the social and material are 'constitutively entangled' (Orlikowski, 2007, p. 1437). As such, it adopts a *relational* rather than a *being* ontology. Although the latter views the world as made up of ontologically distinct entities, the former starts from the assumption that there are no separate beings or entities. Instead, actors and categories are assumed to be relational enactments, or material configurations through which the world becomes (Barad, 2007; Hultin, 2019). Informed by wider debates in actor-network theory (ANT) (Latour, 2007; Law & Hassard, 1999; Mol, 2010) and scholarship that attempts to overcome the subject/object dualism (Barad, 2007; Suchman, 2002, 2007), the sociomaterial approach starts from the position that human bodies, the arrangements of place and environment, physical objects and technologies are inextricably intertwined with discourse, interaction and practices in reproducing everyday life.

By focusing on practices, the consequential role played by both humans and nonhumans (including natural objects and technological artefacts) in producing social life are highlighted (Feldman & Orlikowski, 2011). The world takes on a particular order through an ecology of connected practices which perform 'social and material relations together' (Feldman & Orlikowski, 2011, p. 1248). Heterogeneous elements are ordered through practice within and between multiple discourses and unequal power relations to achieve provisional outcomes at any particular moment in time (Gherardi, 2016, p. 684). Bodies, artefacts, discourses, policies, institutions, technologies and norms entangle and are performed through this ecology of practices. As such worklives are not entities but enactments unfolding – in processes of becoming. For example, the worklives examined in this book are performed in the intra-action of various capacities from the kitchen table to EU start-up funding policy, and from FaceTime calls with partners to regional and local digital infrastructures.

The sociomaterial approach 'grants equal status to the humans and more-than-humans linked within a practice' (Gherardi, 2016, p. 693). In doing so, it treats the social and the material in the same register (Orlikowski, 2007). However, because this equivalence makes everything an 'actant', Ingold (2016) argues that this approach loses the sense of what 'life' is. He goes on to state:

> I would define life as the name for what is going on in the field of relationships within which organic forms emerge, develop and are held in place – that is what I understand as a life process.
>
> (Ibid.)

Because our starting point is the accounts of workers themselves, their lives are not rendered equivalent with material forms. Rather we consider the ways in which these lives are shaped within the field of worklife relationships. We also attend to how shifting capitalist work arrangements reconfigure life and work. For example, life is constructed as 'a resource for reproducing labour outside of the point of production' in Fordist arrangements. This requires the division of work and life into distinct spheres of production and social reproduction, public and private (Adkins & Dever, 2014a). In contrast, many see post-Fordist arrangements as dissolving these divisions (Adkins & Dever, 2014a; Gill & Pratt, 2008; Hardt & Negri, 2000, 2004; Morini & Fumagalli, 2010; Weeks, 2007). For example, Hardt and Negri suggest that

> life is no longer produced in the cycles of reproduction that are subordinated to the working day; on the contrary, life is what infuses and dominates all production. The excess of value is determined today in the affects, in the bodies crisscrossed with knowledge, in the intelligence of the mind, and in the sheer power to act.
>
> (1999, p. 367 cited in Fleming, 2014, p. 884)

From this perspective capitalism permeates 'life projects, making human capital no different to any other resource' (Fleming, 2014, p. 883) such that life process and practices are increasingly subject to capitalist rationalities of calculability.

We keep Ingold's notion of moving life processes to the fore by privileging what is going on in the field of worklife relationships through which mobile workers emerge and come to see themselves as such (Ingold et al., 2016). So, while assuming workers and technologies to be 'constitutively entangled' (Orlikowski, 2007, p. 1438), we distinguish between them and privilege human accounts in order to represent MKWlives in process. Work is not just about the conditions and relations of production, but those of life (social reproduction) politics, and culture too, even as these are incorporated in contemporary capitalist processes. Worklife practices comprise 'configurations of always already interrelated, reiterated sociomaterial practices' (Suchman, 2007, p. 257), which shift and change through ongoing repetition. As such, our analysis attends to how worklives unfold into mobile worklives. It also addresses how the power dynamics and the effects of pre-existing (and sedimented) practices, not least those of Fordist and post-Fordist capitalism and related inequalities, shape these becomings (Mutch, 2013).

Because worklife practices are narrated in the retrospective context of the interview, they are accounted for at a temporal remove from worklife as 'lived'. Worklife practices as recounted in interview data take on a different status than those potentially accessed via observation and discussion on the spot. However, because we are interested in how workers inhabit and practice becoming MKWrs, we attend to the possibilities and conditions under which worklife materialises in their accounts. Worklife is not a performed *being* but a performed *doing*. This doing involves the corollary work of forging 'ongoing connections, disconnections, and reconnections between countless actors' (Felski, 2011, p. 578). As 'anything that modifies a state of affairs by making a difference' (Felski, 2011, p. 582), an actor takes on this status through its relations with other phenomena to produce particular effects (ibid.). So, for example, a laptop can modify a state of affairs as a participant in a chain of events that influences and shapes an event or outcome (ibid.). The laptop or mobile phone as a technological tool is not an already known, passive intermediary or channel, but an actor and component of the *corollary work* that configures and reconfigures practices, their meanings and effects. Because they are so closely tied up with practices, such artefacts incite attachments, so that we form intimate relationships to them and those practices we associate with them. Through such attachments and the promise of self-expression and fulfilment that accompanies them, the corollary work of MKWrs is sustained. Yet, even as MKWrs 'become as enactments in material-discursive practices … [they] are never fully constituted … there is always space for reworking and resisting' (Hultin, 2019, p. 102).

Informed by all of the above debates, we see worklives as bound up with all those material forms, artefacts, spaces and times through which mobile worklives are becoming. The sociomaterial practices of *corollary work* require constant micro-negotiations and dynamic translations to make and sustain the connections necessary in making of MKWlives. By opening up questions about the sociomaterial constitution of worklife through MKW, we give concrete texture to the *corollary work* that makes MKW possible. In Chapter 1 we take up the question of work, what it means, and how we might distinguish between MKW and the corollary work that we argue is its consequence, but also its precondition. This chapter reviews the many ways in which work and work contexts are mobilised and discussed in this book. The following chapters provide textured accounts of the many different aspects of corollary work and its centrality in the making of MKW. These range from complex and shifting sociomaterial practices of place making (Chapters 2 and 3), to the nuanced practices of time work and their different configurations across sectors (Chapters 4 and 5), to those practices that cultivate and sustain productive MKWlife dispositions and performances (Chapter 6), to the generation of passionate attachments to MKW by making it a labour of love (Chapter 7).

Notes

1 The Mobile Minds White Paper, produced in collaboration with remote.com in 2017, noted that: 53 per cent of workers in India prefer to work from home; 37 per cent of all workers work remotely at least occasionally in the US up from 9 per cent in 1995; 54 per cent of workers in the UK engage in remote work; and between 10 and 20 per cent of managers work remotely in developing countries (Olubunmi et al., 2017, p. 3). These figures include both aspirations and practice and so overstate the prevalence of teleworking, or mobile working. Evidence from the EU and Ireland suggests much lower figures. The European Council recognises mobile work as an emerging trend and negotiated the *European Framework Agreement on Telework* in 2002 as a step in 'modernising' the organisation of work across EU member-states (Eurofound, 2010). Yet, despite these optimistic expectations, the *Telework in the European Union* report indicated that the rate of teleworking in Ireland was 4.2 per cent of the workforce, with the European average standing at 7 per cent (ibid.).

2 As Boltanski and Chiapello argue, the capacity for movement, not only in geographical space, but between people, within mind spaces and between ideas 'is the essential quality for "big" people, so that "small" people find themselves characterised first and foremost by their fixity (their rigidity)' (2005, pp. 445–446), or by forced movement.

3 The website https://ludwig.guru/ is host to the Ludwig.guru 'Write Better English' app. It has +15 million users in 200 countries and defines itself as 'the first sentence search engine that helps you write better English by giving you contextualized examples taken from reliable sources'.

4 The French regulationist tradition locates the capitalist mode of production driven by the accumulation of capital at the centre of its analysis with economic development relying on both a regime of accumulation and a mode of regulation (Aglietta, 1979; Lipietz, 1987, 1992). A regime of accumulation refers to those economic regularities that enable processes of capitalist accumulation, including the norms of work organisation, exchange, management and the market (Amin, 1994). A mode of regulation is made up of those formal (institutionally sanctioned e.g. via legal or policy means, industrial codes) and informal rules (including norms and habits) that define social relationships and through which the accumulation regime is secured (Amin, 1994; Jessop, 1992; Nielsen, 1991). Because there is an inherent instability in each regime of accumulation, restructuring can be triggered. This leads to the emergence of a new regime of accumulation accompanied by an emergent if unpredictable mode of regulation. In this framework, therefore, structural crisis tendencies drive the process of economic development (Wigfield, 2001), even if the particular dynamics that give rise to crises are much contested (Jenson, 1990; Jessop, 1992; Leborgne & Lipietz, 1988). Regulation theory is developed in another direction by Hardt and Negri who argue that, instead of market deregulation, regulations are proliferating and come together in the supranational political-juridical form of Empire. It is made up of unruly globalised flows of people, information and wealth that escape

monitoring and governance by metropolitan centres (Balakrishnan, 2000). Drawing on Foucault's notion of biopower – 'a form of power that regulates social life from its interior, following it, interpreting it, absorbing it, and rearticulating it' (Hardt & Negri, 2000, pp. 23–24), they see Empire as underpinned by 'the plural multitude of productive, creative subjectivities of globalization' (Hardt & Negri, 2000, p. 60). These theorists, along with others in this tradition (Lazzarato, 1996, 1997; Virno, 2004; Virno & Hardt, 1996), see the antagonic relationships between workers and capital as central to capitalist arrangements but the ways in which these antagonisms play out are shaped by the regime of accumulation (Hardt & Negri, 2000; Negri, 1979; Weeks, 2005).

Alongside the regulation theoretical perspectives discussed above, flexible specialisation theorists advance a more indeterminate account of post-Fordist economic restructuring as shaped by multiple factors and contextual conditions. The rapid fragmentation and 'dismassification' of consumer markets contribute to the transformation of Fordist production processes into a post-Fordist technological paradigm defined as 'flexible specialization' (Piore & Sabel, 1984). In response to these markets and technological changes, labour markets and organisational arrangements became more flexible leading to unprecedented transformations in workplace time/space (Lash & Urry, 1994) and increasingly flexible geographies of production (Harvey, 1991). Flexible manufacturing technologies and work practices enable small batch production of customised goods, which are best achieved via flexible specialisation. Work organisation is linked to a geographic clustering of production as, for example, in Silicon Valley, because proximity is assumed to build trust and enable rapid responses to market conditions (Sabel, 1994). Piore and Sabel (1984) point to a disintegration of the job hierarchies characteristic of mass production, alongside a dissolution of centralised power and authority. Contra this position, Tomaney (1994) argues that the flexible specialisation thesis neglects the potential for work intensification and unanticipated effects of these restructuring processes. Others argue that the optimism expressed by flexible specialisation theorists hides the growth of precarious and casual contracts, self-employment and low-paid work with little security and poor conditions, as well as a deeper division between those with and without decent working conditions (McDowell & Christopherson, 2009).

5 The movement of these sectors is often represented 'as "development prospects" for the south', while corporations in affluent countries maintain strategic, research, design and financial functions (Murray, Gilbert, & Goffey, 2015, p. 193). As capital became more globally mobile and detached from particular localities and polities in the latter decades of the 20th century, the state had less control over it. Labour also became weaker with collective bargaining increasingly being replaced by individual, often short-term contracts (Fisher, 2010). Post-Fordism refers to this new constellation of power and independence of capital from both labour and the state (ibid.).

6 Neilson and Rossiter (2008) argue that employment security applied to male labour based on the family wage under Fordism in the global North is atypical insofar as such conditions of security did not exist before or since. The focus on precarity and precariousness of contemporary work arrangements often forgets this. For example, Munck (2013) argues that precarity captures certain conditions of labour in today's configuration of capitalism (in Europe and the North Atlantic), conditions that have actually been the norm rather than the exception in working-class history – see also Breman and van der Linden (2014) and Neilson and Rossiter (2008). For Judith Butler,

precariousness refers human existence itself as vulnerable based on our interdependent sociality thus making precariousness essentially relational (Millar, 2017).

7 The prevalence of postfeminist ideologies that constitute young women as having 'choice' and 'agency' in achieving their career goals has been severely critiqued by feminist scholars who highlight instead the unequal and unjust terms of this promise (Gill, Kelan, & Scharff, 2017; McRobbie, 2009).

8 In Western liberal democracies in general 'women's very identity as women always already includes within it a discursive link to the realm of encumbrance' (Rottenberg, 2014, p. 166).

9 Many scholars identify a trend towards a deeper saturation of capitalist relations into everyday life worlds, with transformative implications for how gender is done and experienced (Adkins, 2008, 2009; Adkins & Jokinen, 2008; Hardt & Negri, 2000) and indeed, how the boundaries between work and life are dissolved or reconfigured in the process (Adkins & Dever, 2014b; Gill & Pratt, 2008; Morini & Fumagalli, 2010; Weeks, 2007). Of course, these processes are gendered in differentiated and intersectional ways given what many see as an intensified polarisation of skills and dualisation of labour markets and society.

10 See also Gray (1994b, 1994a) and O'Connor et al. (2017) in relation to the gendered norms of academic work.

11 Ó'Riain notes that during the Celtic Tiger years the most successful Irish-owned high-tech firms benefited as much from state support as from private sector interests, and that those companies that received the most state grant aid 'exported more, employed more people and grew faster' (2010, p. 29).

12 Although one of the most open advanced capitalist economies in the world, Ireland is exposed to the volatility of global capitalism, but its close connections with the UK, the US and Europe afford it some strategic flexibility in its approach to economic development (Ó'Riain, 2014). During the Celtic Tiger years and following the economic crash, state policies aimed to engage the diaspora in the US and the UK as well as more widely assumed a mobile workforce, but also capitalised on new connectivity affordances to integrate the Irish economy globally (Gray, 2006, 2013, 2019).

13 Ó'Riain argues that '[t]his logic of financialisation also found its way into the public finances through the structure of taxation and levels of public spending' (2014, p. 287).

14 However, the significant growth in female employment in computer software occupations, at 73 per cent, was far exceeded by a growth in male employment of 167 per cent, so the female share fell from 37 to 27 per cent, confirming its status as a 'male dominated occupation' (Russell, McGinnity, et al., 2009, p. 51). Yet, the growth rate in the number of women researchers in engineering and technology in EU countries was highest in Ireland at 49 per cent between 2002 and 2010 (European Commission, 2012; O'Connor, 2014).

15 Worklife conflict is understood as arising when meeting demands in one domain such as paid work makes it difficult to meet demands in the other – for example, the home (McGinnity & Whelan, 2009, p. 55).

16 Ireland's economic recovery from 2014 is linked to the strong export orientation of the economy, and the buoyancy of its export destinations (Berry & Bergin, 2017; Kinsella, 2017).

17 A series of government reports, including the *Strategy for Science, Technology and Innovation 2006–2013* (Advisory Science Council, 2006), *Building Ireland's Smart Economy* (Government of Ireland, 2008) and the *Report of the Innovation Taskforce* (Government

of Ireland, 2011), continued to emphasise knowledge, creativity and innovation. 'Smart Economic Growth' is described in terms of 'Building the Ideas Economy – Creating the "Innovation Island"' based on an 'interdependence between four forms of capital accumulation (…) human or knowledge capital (…) physical capital; natural or environmental capital (…) [and] social capital' (Government of Ireland, 2008 pp. 13–32).

18 This embedding of academia within the knowledge economy is driven by 'the imperative for greater value and wealth creation by academia' and a perception of this sector as a key element of 'an entrepreneurial system' (Brennan et al., 2008, p. 73).

19 Only two of these 'supra' interviews are drawn on in this book as the main focus is on the work itself, rather than regional and national social and economic polity.

20 In-depth interviews allow participants to explain how they see and understand their world, and the researcher to probe unclear statements. Not imposing a rigid structure to the data collection process affords an organic approach whereby natural conversations may be carried out and the participants may feel more comfortable to provide their opinions on the topics and elaborate their thoughts (Hermanowicz, 2002).

21 The Nomadic Work/Life in the Knowledge Economy (NWL) project was funded by the Government of Ireland with the support of the EU Regional Development Fund, the Irish Social Science Platform (ISSP), the Department of Enterprise, Trade and Innovation and the Higher Education Authority, through the UL Institute for the Study of Knowledge in Society (ISKS).

22 Shadowing consists of 'following selected people in their everyday occupations for a time' (Czarniawska, 2007, p. 17). Put in another way, the researcher moves alongside the participants and, therefore, observes the issues related to the phenomenon as they arise at the different locations where they occur. This method was used in the Academics sub-study to gather information about the situated aspects of using technology for dealing with work activities across locations.

23 Diaries are useful instruments for data collection in different fields of research as they allow researchers to look at actual activities occurring in a 'slice' of people's everyday lives, giving grounds for further investigation (Ciolfi, Bartolucci, & Murphy, 2005; Normark, Bogdan, Adler, Rossitto, & Eklundh, 2005; Perry et al., 2001; Rossitto, 2009).

References

Adkins, L. (2008). From Retroactivation to Futurity: The End of the Sexual Contract? *NORA – Nordic Journal of Feminist and Gender Research, 16*(3), 182–201. https://doi.org/10.1080/08038740802300954

Adkins, L. (2009). Feminism after Measure. *Feminist Theory, 10*(3), 323–339. https://doi.org/10.1177/1464700109343255

Adkins, L. (2013). Creativity, Biography and the Time of Individualization. In M. Banks, R. Gill, & S. Taylor (Eds.), *Theorizing Cultural Work: Labour, Continuity and Change in the Cultural and Creative Industries* (pp. 163–174). London: Routledge. https://doi.org/10.4324/9780203519912-19

Adkins, L. (2017). Speculative Futures in the Time of Debt. *The Sociological Review, 65*(3), 448–462. https://doi.org/10.1111/1467-954X.12442

Adkins, L., & Dever, M. (2014a). Gender and Labour in New Times: An Introduction. *Australian Feminist Studies, 29*(79), 1–11. https://doi.org/10.1080/08164649.2014.913469

Adkins, L., & Dever, M. (2014b). Housework, Wages and Money. *Australian Feminist Studies*, *29*(79), 50–66. https://doi.org/10.1080/08164649.2014.913468

Adkins, L., & Jokinen, E. (2008). Introduction: Gender, Living and Labour in the Fourth Shift. *NORA – Nordic Journal of Feminist and Gender Research*, *16*(3), 138–149. https://doi.org/10.1080/08038740802300947

Advisory Science Council. (2006). *Strategy for Science, Technology and Innovation 2006–2013*. Dublin: Department of Jobs, Enterprise and Innovation.

Aglietta, M. (1979). *A Theory of Capitalist Regulation: The U.S. Experience*. London: New Left Books.

Ahmed, S. (2004). *The Cultural Politics of Emotion*. New York & London: Routledge.

Amin, A. (1994). *Post-Fordism: A Reader*. Oxford: Blackwell.

Balakrishnan, G. (2000). Virgilian Visions. *New Left Review*, *5*(Sep-Oct), 142–148.

Barad, K. M. (2003). Posthumanist Performativity: Toward an Understanding of How Matter Comes to Matter. *Signs: Journal of Women in Culture and Society*, *28*(3), 801–831. https://doi.org/10.1086/345321

Barad, K. M. (2007). *Meeting the Universe: Halfway Quantum Physics and the Entanglement of Matter and Meaning*. Durham, NC: Duke University Press.

Bardzell, S., & Churchill, E. F. (2011). IwC Special Issue “Feminism and HCI: New Perspectives” Special Issue Editors’ Introduction. *Interacting with Computers*, *23*(5), iii–xi. https://doi.org/10.1016/S0953-5438(11)00089-0

Bauder, H. (2015). The International Mobility of Academics: A Labour Market Perspective. *International Migration*, *53*(1), 83–96. https://doi.org/10.1111/j.1468-2435.2012.00783.x

Bellotti, V., & Bly, S. (1996). Walking Away from the Desktop Computer: Distributed Collaboration and Mobility in a Product Design Team. In *Proceedings of the 1996 ACM Conference on Computer Supported Cooperative Work* (pp. 209–218). Boston, MA: ACM. https://doi.org/10.1145/240080.240256

Bennett, T., Grossberg, L., & Morris, M. (2003). *New Keywords: A Revised Vocabulary of Culture and Society*. Malden, MA: Blackwell.

Berland, J. (2003). Mobility. In T. Bennett, L. Grossberg, & M. Morris (Eds.), *New Keywords: A Revised Vocabulary of Culture and Society* (pp. 217–219). Malden, MA: Blackwell.

Berry, F., & Bergin, A. (2017). Business. In W. K. Roche, P. J. O’Connell, & A. Prothero (Eds.), *Austerity and Recovery in Ireland: Europe’s Poster Child and the Great Recession*. Oxford: Oxford University Press.

Bobek, A., & Wickham, J. (2018). The Ownership of Time: Work in the Irish Hospitality Sector. *Irish Journal of Anthropology*, *20*(2), 17–25.

Bogdan, C., Rossitto, C., & Eklundh, K. S. (2007). Towards Considering Nomadicity in Assessing IT Quality. In Å. Walldius & Y. Sundblad (Eds.), *Proceeding of the UITQ Workshop 2007*. Stockholm, Sweden: KTH Computer Science and Communication.

Bogdan, C., Rossitto, C., Normark, M., Adler, P. J., & Eklundh, K. S. (2006). On a Mission without a Home Base: Conceptualizing Nomadicity in Student Group Work. In P. Hassanaly, T. Herrmann, G. Kunau, & M. Zacklad (Eds.), *Cooperative Systems Design: Seamless Integration of Artifacts and Conversations* (pp. 23–38). Amsterdam: IOS Press.

Boltanski, L., & Chiapello, E. (2005). *The New Spirit of Capitalism*. London & New York: Verso.

Boyle, R. (2017). Public Service Reform. In W. K. Roche, P. J. O’Connell, & A. Prothero (Eds.), *Austerity and Recovery in Ireland: Europe’s Poster Child and the Great Recession* (pp. 214–231). Oxford: Oxford University Press.

Brady, W. M. (2016). Territorial Development, Planning Reform and Urban Governance: The Case of Ireland's Second-Tier Cities. *European Planning Studies*, *24*(12), 2217–2240. https://doi.org/10.1080/09654313.2016.1248906

Braun, V., & Clarke, V. (2012). Thematic Analysis. *APA Handbook of Research Methods in Psychology, Vol 2: Research Designs: Quantitative, Qualitative, Neuropsychological, and Biological*, *2*, 57–71. https://doi.org/10.1037/13620-004

Breman, J., & van der Linden, M. (2014). Informalizing the Economy: The Return of the Social Question at a Global Level. *Development and Change*, *45*(5), 920–940. https://doi.org/10.1111/dech.12115

Brennan, J., Enders, J., Valimaa, J., Musselin, C., & Teichler, U. (2008). *Higher Education Looking Forward: An Agenda for Future Research*. European Science Foundation, Strasbourg.

Brenner, N. (1998). Global Cities, Glocal States: Global City Formation and State Territorial Restructuring in Contemporary Europe. *Review of International Political Economy*, *5*(1), 1–37. https://doi.org/10.1080/096922998347633

Brinker, M., & Schwartz, J. (2018). The Untethered Workforce: Empowering the 100 Percent Mobile Worker. *Deloitte Insights, December*. Retrieved from https://www2.deloitte.com/us/en/insights/focus/technology-and-the-future-of-work/untethered-workforce-mobile-workers.html

Brown, B., & O'Hara, K. (2003). Places as Practical Concern for Mobile Workers. *Environment and Planning A*, *35*(9), 1565–1587. https://doi.org/10.1068/a34231

Büscher, M. (2014). Nomadic Work: Romance and Reality. A Response to Barbara Czarniawska's 'Nomadic Work as Life-Story Plot'. *Computer Supported Cooperative Work (CSCW)*, *23*(2), 223–238. https://doi.org/10.1007/s10606-013-9194-6

Chu, J. Y. (2010). *Cosmologies of Credit: Transnational Mobility and the Politics of Destination in China*. Durham, NC: Duke University Press.

Churchill, E. F., & Munro, A. J. (2001). Work/place: Mobile Technologies and Arenas of Activity. *SIGGROUP Bulletin*, *22*(3), 3–9. https://doi.org/10.1145/567352.567353

Ciolfi, L., Bartolucci, I., & Murphy, D. (2005). Meaningful Interactions for Meaningful Places: Investigating the Relationships between Nomadic Work, Tangible Artefacts and the Physical Environment. In *Proceedings of the 2005 Annual Conference on European Association of Cognitive Ergonomics* (Vol. 132, pp. 115–121). Chania, Greece: University of Athens.

Ciolfi, L., & de Carvalho, A. F. P. (2014). Work Practices, Nomadicity and the Mediational Role of Technology. *Journal of Computer Supported Cooperative Work*, *23*(2). https://doi.org/10.1007/s10606-014-9201-6

Conor, B., Gill, R., & Taylor, S. (2015). Gender and Creative Labour. *The Sociological Review*, *63*(1), 1–22. https://doi.org/10.1111/1467-954X.12237

Cooper, M. (2000). Being the "Go-To Guy": Fatherhood, Masculinity, and the Organization of Work in Silicon Valley. *Qualitative Sociology*, *23*(4), 379–405. https://doi.org/10.1023/A:1005522707921

Courtois, A. (2018). The Global Ambitions of Irish Universities: Internationalizing Practices and Emerging Stratification in the Irish Higher Education Sector. In R. Bloch, A. Mitterle, C. Paradeise, & T. Peter (Eds.), *Universities and the Production of Elites* (pp. 127–148). Cham: Springer International Publishing. https://doi.org/10.1007/978-3-319-53970-6_6

Czarniawska, B. (2007). *Shadowing, and Other Techniques for Doing Fieldwork in Modern Societies*. Herndon: Copenhagen Business School Press.

de Carvalho, A. F. P. (2013). *Technologically-mediated Nomadicity in Academic Settings: Tm-N as a Dynamic and Emergent Process. Department of Computer Science and Information Systems*. University of Limerick, Limerick.

de Carvalho, A. F. P. (2014). Collaborative Work and Its Relationship to Technologically-Mediated Nomadicity. In C. Rossitto, L. Ciolfi, D. Martin, & B. Conein (Eds.), *COOP 2014 – Proceedings of the 11th International Conference on the Design of Cooperative Systems* (pp. 209–224). Nice (France): Springer International Publishing. https://doi.org/10.1007/978-3-319-06498-7_13

de Carvalho, A. F. P., Ciolfi, L., & Gray, B. (2011). The Making of Nomadic Work: Understanding the Mediational Role of ICTs. In M. M. Cruz-Cunha & F. Moreira (Eds.), *Handbook of Research on Mobility and Computing: Evolving Technologies and Ubiquitous Impacts* (pp. 381–396). Hershey, PA: IGI Global.

de Carvalho, A. F. P., Ciolfi, L., & Gray, B. (2017). Detailing a Spectrum of Motivational Forces Shaping Nomadic Practices. In *Proceedings of the 2017 ACM Conference on Computer Supported Cooperative Work and Social Computing – CSCW '17* (pp. 962–977). https://doi.org/10.1145/2998181.2998313

Devitt, C. (2016). Mothers or Migrants? Labor Supply Policies in Ireland 1997–2007. *Social Politics: International Studies in Gender, State & Society*, *23*(2), 214–238. https://doi.org/10.1093/sp/jxv034

Dictionary.com. (2019). Definition of Corolla. Retrieved 8 October 2019, from www.dictionary.com/browse/corolla?s=t

Ekinsmyth, C. (2011). Challenging the Boundaries of Entrepreneurship: The Spatialities and Practices of UK 'Mumpreneurs'. *Geoforum*, *42*(1), 104–114. https://doi.org/10.1016/J.GEOFORUM.2010.10.005

Erickson, I., Jarrahi, M. H., Thomson, L., & Sawyer, S. (2014). More than Nomads: Mobility, Knowledge Work, and Infrastructure. *EGOS 2014 Subtheme 52: Mobile Work, Technology, and Issues of Control*, 1–20.

Eurofound. (2010). Telework in the European Union. *European Foundation for the Improvement of Living and Working Conditions (Eurofound)*. Retrieved from www.eurofound.europa.eu/eiro/studies/tn0910050s/tn0910050s.htm

European Commission. (2012). She Figures: Gender in Research and Innovation. Retrieved 9 October 2019, from http://ec.europa.eu/research/science-society/document_library/pdf_06/she-figures-2012_en.pdf

Feldman, M. S., & Orlikowski, W. J. (2011). Theorizing Practice and Practicing Theory. *Organization Science*, *22*(5), 1240–1253. https://doi.org/10.1287/orsc.1100.0612

Felski, R. (1995). *The Gender of Modernity*. Cambridge, MA: Harvard University Press.

Felski, R. (2011). Context Stinks! *New Literary History*, *42*(4), 573–591.

Fisher, E. (2010). Contemporary Technology Discourse and the Legitimation of Capitalism. *European Journal of Social Theory*, *13*(2), 229–252. https://doi.org/10.1177/1368431010362289

Fleming, P. (2014). When 'Life Itself' Goes to Work: Reviewing Shifts in Organizational Life through the Lens of Biopower. *Human Relations*, *67*(7), 875–901. https://doi.org/10.1177/0018726713508142

Fleming, P. (2017). The Human Capital Hoax: Work, Debt and Insecurity in the Era of Uberization. *Organization Studies*, *38*(5), 691–709. https://doi.org/10.1177/0170840616686129

Frenkel, M. (2008). Reprogramming Femininity? The Construction of Gender Identities in the Israeli Hi-tech Industry between Global and Local Gender Orders. *Gender, Work & Organization*, *15*(4), 352–374. https://doi.org/10.1111/j.1468-0432.2008.00398.x

Gallagher, A. (2012). Neoliberal Governmentality and the Respatialisation of Childcare in Ireland. *Geoforum*, *43*(3), 464–471. https://doi.org/10.1016/J.GEOFORUM.2011.10.004
Gerson, E. M., & Star, S. L. (1986). Analyzing Due Process in the Workplace. *ACM Transactions on Information Systems*, *4*(3), 257–270. https://doi.org/10.1145/214427.214431
Gherardi, S. (2016). To Start Practice Theorizing Anew: The Contribution of the Concepts of Agencement and Formativeness. *Organization*, *23*(5), 680–698. https://doi.org/10.1177/1350508415605174
Gill, R., Kelan, E. K., & Scharff, C. M. (2017). A Postfeminist Sensibility at Work. *Gender, Work & Organization*, *24*(3), 226–244. https://doi.org/10.1111/gwao.12132
Gill, R., & Pratt, A. (2008). In the Social Factory? Immaterial Labour, Precariousness and Cultural Work. *Theory, Culture & Society*, *25*(7–8), 1–30. https://doi.org/10.1177/0263276408097794
Gill, R., & Scharff, C. (2011). *New Femininities: Postfeminism, Neoliberalism and Subjectivity*. London: Palgrave Macmillan.
Global Mind Project. (2019). Global Mind Project. Retrieved 8 October 2019, from http://globalmindproject.com/
Government of Ireland. (2008). *Building Ireland's Smart Economy: A Framework for Sustainable Economic Renewal*. Dublin: Stationery Office. Retrieved from http://hdl.handle.net/10147/76919
Government of Ireland. (2011). Innovation Taskforce Report.
Gray, B. (1994a). Women in Higher Education. In S. Davies, C. Lubelska, & J. Quinn (Eds.), *Changing the Subject: Women in Higher Education* (pp. 75–88). London: Taylor & Francis.
Gray, B. (1994b). Women Only Management Training – A Past and Present. In M. Tanton (Ed.), *Women in Management: A Developing Presence* (pp. 202–228). London: Routledge.
Gray, B. (2003). Global Modernities and the Gendered Epic of the Irish Empire. In S. Ahmed, C. Castaneda, A.-M. Fortier, & M. Sheller (Eds.), *Uprootings/Regroundings: Questions of Home and Migration* (pp. 157–178). Oxford: Berg.
Gray, B. (2004). *Women and the Irish Diaspora*. London: Routledge.
Gray, B. (2006). Redefining the Nation through Economic Growth and Migration: Changing Rationalities of Governance in the Republic of Ireland? *Mobilities*, *1*(3), 353–372. https://doi.org/10.1080/17450100600916685
Gray, B. (2013). "Generation Emigration": The Politics of (Trans)National Social Reproduction in Twenty-First Century Ireland. *Irish Studies Review*, *21*(1), 20–36. https://doi.org/10.1080/09670882.2012.759707
Gray, B. (2019). 'Leaving Dublin': Photographic Portrayals of Post-Celtic Tiger Emigration – A Sociological Analysis. *The Sociological Review*, *67*(3), 635–653. https://doi.org/10.1177/0038026118795087
Gregg, M. (2011). *Work's Intimacy*. Cambridge: Polity.
Gregg, M. (2018). *Counterproductive: Time Management in the Knowledge Economy*. Durham, NC & London: Duke University Press.
Grewal, I. (1996). *Home and Harem: Nation, Gender, Empire and the Cultures of Travel*. London: Leicester University Press.
Grewal, I., & Kaplan, C. (1994). *Scattered Hegemonies: Postmodernity and Transnational Feminist Practices*. Minneapolis, MN: University of Minnesota Press.
Grummell, B., Devine, D., & Lynch, K. (2009). The Care-less Manager: Gender, Care and New Managerialism in Higher Education. *Gender and Education*, *21*(2), 191–208. https://doi.org/10.1080/09540250802392273

Hannam, K., Sheller, M., & Urry, J. (2006). Editorial: Mobilities, Immobilities and Moorings. *Mobilities*, *1*(1), 1–22. https://doi.org/10.1080/17450100500489189

Hanson, S. (2010). Gender and Mobility: New Approaches for Informing Sustainability. *Gender, Place and Culture*, *17*(1), 5–23. https://doi.org/10.1080/09663690903498225

Hardt, M., & Negri, A. (2000). *Empire*. Cambridge, MA: Harvard University Press.

Hardt, M., & Negri, A. (2004). *Multitude: War and Democracy in the Age of Empire*. New York: The Penguin Press.

Harvey, D. (1991). Flexibility: Threat or Opportunity? *Socialist Review*, *21*(1), 65–77.

Henry, C., & Johnston, K. (2007). The Creative Industries: Ireland's New Tiger Economy? *Irish Journal of Management*, *28*(2), 211–219.

Hermanowicz, J. C. (2002). The Great Interview: 25 Strategies for Studying People in Bed. *Qualitative Sociology*, *25*(4), 479–499.

Hesmondhalgh, D. (2010). User-Generated Content, Free Labour and the Cultural Industries. *Ephemera*, *10*(3–4), 267–284.

Hultin, L. (2019). On Becoming a Sociomaterial Researcher: Exploring Epistemological Practices Grounded in a Relational, Performative Ontology. *Information and Organization*, *29*(2), 91–104. https://doi.org/10.1016/J.INFOANDORG.2019.04.004

Humphry, J. (2014). Officing: Mediating Time and the Professional Self in the Support of Nomadic Work. *Computer Supported Cooperative Work (CSCW)*, *23*(2), 185–204. https://doi.org/10.1007/s10606-013-9197-3

IBM. (2019). Mobile Workforce: Cutting the Cord to the Physical Office for Greater Productivity, Cost Savings and Efficiency. Retrieved 28 August 2019, from www.ibm.com/topics/mobile-workforce

Ingold, T. (2007). Earth, Sky, Wind, and Weather. *The Journal of the Royal Anthropological Institute*, *13*(2007), S19–S38.

Ingold, T., Introna, L., Kavanagh, D., Kelly, S., Orlikowski, W., & Scott, S. (2016). Thoughts on Movement, Growth and an Anthropologically-Sensitive IS/Organization Studies: An Imagined Correspondence with Tim Ingold (pp. 17–32). Springer, Cham. https://doi.org/10.1007/978-3-319-49733-4_2

Irish Higher Education Strategy Group. (2011). *National Strategy for Higher Education to 2030: Report of the Strategy Group*. Department of Education and Skills.

James, A. (2013). Work–life 'Balance' and Gendered (Im)Mobilities of Knowledge and Learning in High-Tech Regional Economies. *Journal of Economic Geography*, 1–28. https://doi.org/10.1093/jeg/lbt002

Jarrahi, M. H., & Sawyer, S. (2017). More than Nomadicity: The Paradoxical Affordances of Liminality. *International Reports on Socio-Informatics (IRSI)*, *14*(3), 29–32.

Jenson, J. (1990). Representations of Difference: The Varieties of French Feminism. *New Left Review*, *1*(180), 127–160.

Jessop, B. (1992). Fordism and Post-Fordism: A Critical Reformulation. In M. Storper & A. J. Scott (Eds.), *Pathways to Industrialization and Regional Development*. New York: Routledge.

Kalleberg, A. L. (2009). Precarious Work, Insecure Workers: Employment Relations in Transition. *American Sociological Review*, *74*(1), 1–22. https://doi.org/10.1177/000312240907400101

Kaplan, C. (1996). *Questions of Travel: Postmodern Discourses of Displacement*. Durham, NC & London: Duke University Press.

Kaufmann, V., Bergman, M. M., & Joye, D. (2004). Motility: Mobility as Capital. *International Journal of Urban and Regional Research*, *28*(4), 745–756. https://doi.org/10.1111/j.0309-1317.2004.00549.x

Kinsella, S. (2017). Economic and Fiscal Policy. In W. K. Roche, P. J. O'Connell, & A. Prothero (Eds.), *Austerity and Recovery in Ireland: Europe's Poster Child and the Great Recession* (pp. 40–61). Oxford: Oxford University Press.

Kleinrock, L. (1996). Nomadicity: Anytime, Anywhere in a Disconnected World. *Mobile Networks and Applications, 1*(4), 351–357.

Koehne, B., Shih, P. C., & Olson, J. S. (2012). Remote and Alone: Coping with Being the Remote Member on the Team. In *Proceedings of the ACM 2012 Conference on Computer Supported Cooperative Work – CSCW '12* (p. 1257). New York: ACM Press. https://doi.org/10.1145/2145204.2145393

Langfred, C. W., & Rockmann, K. W. (2016). The Push and Pull of Autonomy. *Group & Organization Management, 41*(5), 629–657. https://doi.org/10.1177/1059601116668971

Lash, S. M., & Urry, J. (1994). *Economies of Signs and Space*. London: Sage.

Latour, B. (2007). *Reassembling the Social: An Introduction to Actor-Network-Theory. Clarendon Lectures in Management Studies*. Oxford: Oxford University Press.

Law, J., & Hassard, J. (1999). *Actor Network Theory and After*. Oxford & Malden, MA: Blackwell Publishing.

Lazzarato, M. (1996). Immaterial Labor. In P. Virno & M. Hardt (Eds.), *Radical Thought in Italy* (pp. 133–146). Minneapolis, MN: University of Minnesota Press.

Lazzarato, M. (1997). *Lavoro Immateriale: Forme di Vita e Produzione di Soggettività*. Ombre Corte.

Leborgne, D., & Lipietz, A. (1988). New Technologies, New Modes of Regulation: Some Spatial Implications. *Environment and Planning D: Society and Space, 6*(3), 263–280. https://doi.org/10.1068/d060263

Lipietz, A. (1987). *Mirages and Miracles: The Crisis in Global Fordism*. London: Verso.

Lipietz, A. (1992). *Towards a New Economic Order: Postfordism, Ecology, and Democracy*. Oxford: Oxford University Press.

Luckman, S. (2015). Women's Micro-Entrepreneurial Homeworking. *Australian Feminist Studies, 30*(84), 146–160. https://doi.org/10.1080/08164649.2015.1038117

Ludwig.guru. (2019). I made it to work. Retrieved 7 October 2019, from https://ludwig.guru/s/I+made+it+to+work

Luff, P., & Heath, C. (1998). Mobility in Collaboration. *Proceedings of the 1998 ACM Conference on Computer Supported Cooperative Work*, 305–314. https://doi.org/10.1145/289444.289505

Lynch, K. (2006). Neo-Liberalism and Marketisation: The Implications for Higher Education. *European Educational Research Journal, 5*(1), 1–17. https://doi.org/10.2304/eerj.2006.5.1.1

Makimoto, T., & Manners, D. (1997). *Digital Nomad*. New York: John Wiley & Sons.

Mark, G., & Su, N. M. (2010). Making Infrastructure Visible for Nomadic Work. *Pervasive and Mobile Computing, 6*(3), 312–323. https://doi.org/10.1016/J.PMCJ.2009.12.004

Massey, D. (1995). Masculinity, Dualisms and High Technology. *Transactions of the Institute of British Geographers, 20*(4), 487–499.

McDowell, L. (2008). The New Economy, Class Condescension and Caring Labour: Changing Formations of Class and Gender. *NORA – Nordic Journal of Feminist and Gender Research, 16*(3), 150–165. https://doi.org/10.1080/08038740802302547

McDowell, L. (2012). Post-Crisis, Post-Ford and Post-Gender? Youth Identities in an Era of Austerity. *Journal of Youth Studies, 15*(5), 573–590. https://doi.org/10.1080/13676261.2012.671933

McDowell, L., & Christopherson, S. (2009). Transforming Work: New Forms of Employment and Their Regulation. *Cambridge Journal of Regions, Economy and Society, 2*(3), 335–342. https://doi.org/10.1093/cjres/rsp024

McGinnity, F., & Whelan, C. T. (2009). Comparing Work-Life Conflict in Europe: Evidence from the European Social Survey. *Social Indicators Research, 93*(3), 433–444. https://doi.org/10.1007/s11205-008-9437-y

McRobbie, A. (2007). Top Girls? Young Women and the Post-Feminist Sexual Contract. *Cultural Studies, 21*(4–5), 718–737. https://doi.org/10.1080/09502380701279044

McRobbie, A. (2009). *The Aftermath of Feminism: Gender, Culture and Social Change*. London, Thousand Oaks & New Delhi: SAGE Publications.

McRobbie, A. (2010). *Top Girls: Feminismus und der Aufstieg des neolieberalen Geschlechterregimes*. Heidelberg: VS Verlag.

McRobbie, A. (2011). Beyond Post-Feminism. *Public Policy Research, 18*(3), 179–184. https://doi.org/10.1111/j.1744-540X.2011.00661.x

Menzies, H., & Newson, J. (2008). Time, Stress and Intellectual Engagement in Academic Work: Exploring Gender Difference. *Gender, Work & Organization, 15*(5), 504–522. https://doi.org/10.1111/j.1468-0432.2008.00415.x

Merriam-Webster.com. (2019). Definition of Made-work. Retrieved 8 October 2019, from www.merriam-webster.com/dictionary/made-work

Meyer, M. (2003). Academic Entrepreneurs or Entrepreneurial Academics? Research-Based Ventures and Public Support Mechanisms. *R and D Management, 33*(2), 107–115. https://doi.org/10.1111/1467-9310.00286

Millar, K. M. (2017). Toward a Critical Politics of Precarity. *Sociology Compass, 11*(6), e12483. https://doi.org/10.1111/soc4.12483

Mol, A. (2010). Actor-Network Theory: Sensitive Terms and Enduring Tensions. *Kölner Zeitschrift Für Soziologie Und Sozialpsychologie. Sonderheft, 50*(1), 253–269.

Morini, C., & Fumagalli, A. (2010). Life Put to Work: Towards a Life Theory of Value. *Ephemera, 10*(3/4), 234–252.

Müller, R. (2014). Racing for What? Anticipation and Acceleration in the Work and Career Practices of Academic Life Science Postdocs. *Forum Qualitative Sozialforschung/ Forum: Qualitative Social Research, 15*(3). https://doi.org/10.17169/FQS-15.3.2245

Munck, R. (2013). The Precariat: A View from the South. *Third World Quarterly, 34*(5), 747–762. https://doi.org/10.1080/01436597.2013.800751

Murray, R., Gilbert, J., & Goffey, A. (2015). Post-Post-Fordism in the Era of Platforms: Robin Murray talks to Jeremy Gilbert and Andrew Goffey. *New Formations*, (84/85), 184–208.

Mutch, A. (2013). Sociomateriality — Taking the Wrong Turning? *Information and Organization, 23*(1), 28–40. https://doi.org/10.1016/J.INFOANDORG.2013.02.001

Nash, C., Jarrahi, M. H., Sutherland, W., & Phillips, G. (2018). *Transforming Digital Worlds* (Vol. 10766). Springer International Publishing. https://doi.org/10.1007/978-3-319-78105-1

Negri, A. (1979). *Marx Beyond Marx*. London: Pluto Press.

Neilson, B., & Rossiter, N. (2008). Precarity as a Political Concept, or, Fordism as Exception. *Theory, Culture & Society, 25*(7–8), 51–72. https://doi.org/10.1177/0263276408097796

Nelson, S. B., Jarrahi, M. H., & Thomson, L. (2017). Mobility of Knowledge Work and Affordances of Digital Technologies. *International Journal of Information Management, 37*(2), 54–62. https://doi.org/10.1016/J.IJINFOMGT.2016.11.008

Nielsen, K. (1991). Towards a Flexible Future – Theories and Politics? In B. Jessop, H. Kastendiek, K. Nielsen, & O. K. Pedersen (Eds.), *The Politics of Flexibility: Restructuring State and Industry in Britain, Germany and Scandinavia* (pp. 3–32). Aldershot: Edward Elgar Publishing.

Normark, M., Bogdan, C., Adler, P. J., Rossitto, C., & Eklundh, K. S. (2005). *The UCPD Study – On Nomadic Coordination and Technology Use in Student Projects*. Stockholm, Sweden: Royal Institute of Technology and Stockholm University.

O'Connor, P. (2014). *Management and Gender in Higher Education*. Manchester: Manchester University Press.

O'Connor, P., López, E. M., O' Hagan, C., Wolffram, A., Aye, M., Chizzola, V., … Çağlayan, H. (2017). Micro-Political Practices in Higher Education: A Challenge to Excellence as a Rationalising Myth? *Critical Studies in Education*, 1–17. https://doi.org/10.1080/17508487.2017.1381629

Ó'Riain, S. (2010). Snatching Defeat from the Jaws of Victory: Ireland Rediscovers Crisis. In P. Share & M. P. Corcoran (Eds.), *Ireland of the Illusions. A Sociological Chronicle 2007–2008*. Dublin: Dublin Institute of Public Administration.

Ó'Riain, S. (2014). *The Rise and Fall of Ireland's Celtic Tiger: Liberalism, Boom and Bust*. Cambridge: Cambridge University Press.

Olson, J. S., & Olson, G. M. (2014). How to Make Distance Work Work. *Interactions*, *21*(2), 28–35. https://doi.org/10.1145/2567788

Olubunmi, T., Dey, R., & Sutton, S. (2017). Mobile Minds: An Alternative to Physical Migration in the 4th Industrial Revolution. *Mobile Minds White Paper*. Retrieved from https://remote.co/mobile-minds-project/#whitepaper

Orlikowski, W. J. (2007). Sociomaterial Practices: Exploring Technology at Work. *Organization Studies*, *28*(9), 1435–1448. https://doi.org/10.1177/0170840607081138

Orlikowski, W. J., & Scott, S. V. (2008). Sociomateriality: Challenging the Separation of Technology, Work and Organization. *The Academy of Management Annals*, *2*(1), 433–474. https://doi.org/10.1080/19416520802211644

Paus, E. (2012). The Rise and Fall of the Celtic Tiger: When Deal-Making Trumps Developmentalism. *Studies in Comparative International Development*, *47*(2), 161–184. https://doi.org/10.1007/s12116-012-9111-x

Perry, M., O'Hara, K., Sellen, A., Brown, B., & Harper, R. (2001). Dealing with Mobility: Understanding Access Anytime, Anywhere. *ACM Transactions on Computer-Human Interaction (TOCHI)*, *8*(4), 323–347. https://doi.org/10.1145/504704.504707

Piore, M. J., & Sabel, C. F. (1984). *The Second Industrial Divide: Possibilities for Prosperity*. New York: Basic Books.

Presskorn-Thygesen, T. (2015). The Possibility of Critique under a Financialized Capitalism: The Case of Private Equity in the United Kingdom. *Ephemera*, *725–753*(4), 465–484. https://doi.org/10.1177/1350508414563526

Ringrose, J., & Walkerdine, V. (2008). Regulating The Abject: The TV Make-Over as Site of Neo-Liberal Reinvention toward Bourgeois Femininity. *Feminist Media Studies*, *8*(3), 227–246. https://doi.org/10.1080/14680770802217279

Roche, W. K. (2017). Workplaces. In W. K. Roche, P. J. O'Connell, & A. Prothero (Eds.), *Austerity and Recovery in Ireland: Europe's Poster Child and the Great Recession* (pp. 194–213). Oxford: Oxford University Press.

Ross, A. (2008). The New Geography of Work. *Theory, Culture & Society*, *25*(7–8), 31–49. https://doi.org/10.1177/0263276408097795

Rossitto, C. (2009). *Managing Work at Several Places: Understanding Nomadic Practices in Student Groups. KTH Computer Science and Communication Department*. Stockholm University, Stockholm.

Rossitto, C., Bogdan, C., & Severinson-Eklundh, K. (2014). Understanding Constellations of Technologies in Use in a Collaborative Nomadic Setting. *Computer Supported Cooperative Work (CSCW), 23*(2), 137–161. https://doi.org/10.1007/s10606-013-9196-4

Rottenberg, C. (2014). Happiness and the Liberal Imagination: How Superwoman Became Balanced. *Source: Feminist Studies, 40*(1), 144–168. https://doi.org/10.15767/feministstudies.40.1.144

Russell, H., McGinnity, F., Callan, T., & Keane, C. (2009). *A Woman's Place: Female Participation in the Irish Labour Market*. Dublin: C.ESRI & Equality Authority. Retrieved from www.esri.ie/publications/a-womans-place-female-participation-in-the-irish-labour-market

Russell, H., O'Connell, P. J., & McGinnity, F. (2009). The Impact of Flexible Working Arrangements on Work-life Conflict and Work Pressure in Ireland. *Gender, Work & Organization, 16*(1), 73–97. https://doi.org/10.1111/j.1468-0432.2008.00431.x

Sabel, C. F. (1994). Flexible Specialisation and the Re-emergence of Regional Economies. In A. Amin (Ed.), *Post-Fordism: A Reader* (pp. 101–156). Oxford: Blackwell.

Schmidt, K., & Bannon, L. (2013). Constructing CSCW: The First Quarter Century. *Journal of Computer Supported Cooperative Work, 22*(4–6), 345–372.

Schmidt, K., & Bannon, L. J. (1992). Taking CSCW Seriously. *Computer Supported Cooperative Work (CSCW), 1*(1), 7–40. https://doi.org/10.1007/BF00752449

Schwartz, T., & Porath, C. (2014). Why You Hate Work. *The New York Times, SR1*(June). Retrieved from www.higherambition.org/wp-content/uploads/2014/11/Engagement.pdf

Sheller, M. (2014). The New Mobilities Paradigm for a Live Sociology. *Current Sociology, 62*(6), 789–811. https://doi.org/10.1177/0011392114533211

Shibata, S. (2019). Gig Work and the Discourse of Autonomy: Fictitious Freedom in Japan's Digital Economy. *New Political Economy*, 1–17. https://doi.org/10.1080/13563467.2019.1613351

Skeggs, B. (2004). *Class, Self, Culture*. London: Routledge.

Slaughter, S., & Leslie, L. L. (1997). *Academic Capitalism: Politics, Policies, and the Entrepreneurial University*. Baltimore & London: The Johns Hopkins University Press.

Storme, T., Faulconbridge, J. R., Beaverstock, J. V., Derudder, B., & Witlox, F. (2017). Mobility and Professional Networks in Academia: An Exploration of the Obligations of Presence. *Mobilities, 12*(3), 405–424. https://doi.org/10.1080/17450101.2015.1116884

Su, N. M., & Mark, G. (2008). Designing for Nomadic Work. In *Proceedings of the 7th ACM Conference on Designing Interactive Systems – DIS '08* (pp. 305–314). Cape Town, South Africa: ACM Press. https://doi.org/10.1145/1394445.1394478

Suchman, L. (2002). Located Accountabilities in Technology Production. *Scandinavian Journal of Information Systems, 14*(2), 91–104.

Suchman, L. (2007). *Human-Machine Reconfigurations: Plans and Situated Actions* (2nd ed.). Cambridge: Cambridge University Press. https://doi.org/10.1002/asi.20714

Taylor, S., & Luckman, S. (2018). Collection Introduction: The "New Normal" of Working Lives. In S. Taylor & S. Luckman (Eds.), *The New Normal of Working Lives. Critical Studies in Contemporary Work and Employment* (pp. 1–15). Milton Keynes, UK: Palgrave Macmillan.

Teichler, U. (2017). Internationally Mobile Academics: Concept and Findings in Europe. *European Journal of Higher Education, 7*(1), 15–28. https://doi.org/10.1080/21568235.2017.1254921

Tomaney, J. (1994). A New Paradigm of Work Organization and Technology? In A. Amin (Ed.), *Post-Fordism: A Reader* (pp. 157–194). Oxford: Blackwell.

Urry, J. (2000). *Sociology Beyond Societies*. London: Routledge.

Urry, J. (2004). The Complex Spaces of Scandal. In J. O. Bærenholdt & K. Simonsen (Eds.), *Space Odysseys. Spatiality and Social Relations in the 21st Century* (pp. 16–25). Aldershot: Ashgate.

Virno, P. (2004). *A Grammar of the Multitude*. New York: Semiotext(e).

Virno, P., & Hardt, M. (1996). *Radical Thought in Italy*. Minneapolis, MN: University of Minnesota Press.

Vostal, F. (2015). Academic Life in the Fast Lane: The Experience of Time and Speed In British Academia. *Time & Society, 24*(1), 71–95. https://doi.org/10.1177/0961463X13517537

Walby, S., Gottfried, H., Gottschall, K., & Osawa, M. (2007). *Gendering the Knowledge Economy: Comparative Perspectives*. London: Palgrave Macmillan UK. https://doi.org/10.1057/9780230624870

Weeks, K. (2005). The Refusal of Work as Demand and Perspective. In T. S. Murphy & A.-K. Mustapha (Eds.), *The Philosophy of Antonio Negri* (pp. 109–135). Pluto Press. Retrieved from https://philpapers.org/rec/WEETRO-2

Weeks, K. (2007). Life within and Against Work: Affective Labor, Feminist Critique, and Post-Fordist Politics. *Ephemera, 7*(1), 233–249.

Wiberg, M., & Ljungberg, F. (2001). Exploring the Vision of "Anytime, Anywhere" in the Context of Mobile Work. In M. Wiberg (Ed.), *In Between Mobile Meetings: Exploring Seamless Ongoing Interaction Support for Mobile CSCW* (Vol. RR-01.02, pp. 112–128). Umeå: Umeå University.

Wigfield, A. (2001). *Post-Fordism, Gender and Work*. London: Routledge.

Ylijoki, O.-H. (2003). Entangled in Academic Capitalism? A Case-Study on Changing Ideals and Practices of University Research. *Higher Education, 45*(3), 307–335. https://doi.org/10.1023/A:1022667923715

Chapter 1

Corollary work

The mainstay of mobile knowledge work

> *The last thing we want to do is actually hire people*. We would prefer to have people (…) doing *part-time or bespoke work* (…) the system is actually set up that way; there are so many rights and laws and costs and bureaucracy, it's *cheaper not to hire people*, which is unfortunate. And technology now has conspired with that in that *people can now work quite happily not in a job*. You can actually be a virtual worker for a virtual company (…) it's not that everybody gets more free time, one worker gets loads of free time because they're made redundant and the other lot are working 80 hours a week (…). So, I think the *old model of where you got a job, worked for 50 years, and then got a pension and retired*, isn't quite that anymore (…) *what you're selling is your knowledge, then people will seek out your knowledge* (…) *I can be found if somebody wants me* (…) if you're in the game, that's fine, but *if you're not in the game, tough luck*, you're absolutely out of it. So the gap is sort of widening (…). *The kids* (…) *they're starting to accept that; that's the way life is* (…) *their life is actually online* (…). High-tech people tend to be driven much more by the inherent motivation of what they're doing (…) people are much more open to short-term (…) and *less formal arrangements* (…). In the *high-tech area* particularly (…) *talent gets to be converted into valuable outputs more directly*….
>
> (Jared, ICTM, emphasis added)[1]

Jared (technical director of a scientific software development firm, married, with four adult children) reflects on how work is moving beyond conventional workplaces and formal employment conditions. When the product is knowledge, finding the right worker can be difficult for potential employers like him. Jared emphasises the importance of having a presence in the online labour market. This labour market is mediated by professional self-promotion platforms like LinkedIn, and freelancing platforms, such as upwork.com or freelancer.com. On these platforms, potential workers must present themselves as specific kinds of experts and be easily distinguishable from the competition (Arcidiacono, Gandini, & Pais, 2018; Chiang & Suen, 2015). As growing numbers of workers piece together a livelihood from multiple employment sources, including the 'platform economy', Huws et al. argue that 'work is dynamically reshaped in an interaction between different kinds of employment status and work organisation' (Huws, Spencer, & Syrdal, 2018, p. 113). Jared suggests that these new labour market arrangements are superseding those bureaucratic and formalised employment regulations that his company so eagerly wants to avoid. He notes in passing that should a potential employer seek out his expertise, he can be located online. For younger workers he suggests this is the inescapable 'new normal'.

Yet, Jared is conscious that the 'game' of work is becoming more polarised. As such, the emphasis today is on finding ways of 'staying in the game', even if being in it means endless hours of work. To be out of the game is to be without any form of employment; it is to be invisible – it is 'tough luck'.[2] As Wajcman notes '[b]eing busy is valorized, while having too much time on one's hands signifies failure' (Wajcman, 2015, p. 170). So Jared's opening account alerts us to a contemporary discourse of work that is riddled with contradictions, tensions and inequalities, all of which are explored in detail in the chapters that follow.

If worker identity in the past relied on 'the old model' of a job for 50 years followed by retirement and a pension, then contemporary worklives require personalised and constantly shifting forms of 'identity work', place making, time work and productivity monitoring. The relative security of the employment contract providing for job conditions including salary, working hours, training and development, holiday allowance, workspaces and provision of equipment, is being replaced by worker responsibility for 'securing' employment. The organising, coordinating, equipping, systematising, placing and timing of contemporary MKW falls to MKWrs themselves. Indeed, MKW would not be possible without the ceaseless *corollary work* that generates ambient conditions for generating and sustaining this work.

By way of clearing the ground to address the many forms of 'work' falling into the category of *corollary work*, this chapter begins with an overview of scholarly deliberation on how 'work' is defined, including what we mean by 'knowledge work' and 'mobile knowledge work'. We turn then to recent debates about visible and invisible work and how our analysis is informed by these. In the third section we summarise the various features of the corollary work that makes MKW possible.

Work and mobile knowledge work: elusive concepts

We open our discussion of work in this chapter by differentiating between the terms work and labour, and explaining our decision to frame our discussion in terms of work and worklife practices. In neoclassical economics, work is understood as a commodity based on the individual capacity to work, while labour power is understood as 'an abstract quantity that can be bought and sold' (Budd, 2016, p. 33). The effect is that concrete work is 'reduced to sources of economic value exchanged at price', and the worker becomes a factor of production, subject to the laws of supply and demand (ibid.). Thus capitalist labour and its organisation via the division of labour, private property and class relations are naturalised as eternal (Fuchs & Sevignani, 2013).

In contrast, Marx's approach to work and labour turns on the question of whether work/labour is an essence of human society or an expression of economic domination as under capitalism (ibid.). Broadly, work is understood as those productive activities that transform nature as humans produce their means of subsistence and meet human need; it creates 'use value' and produces material life itself (Fuchs & Sevignani, 2013, p. 239). Labour takes place under the historical conditions of capitalism in which workers do not control the means of production or the product of their labour and exploitative capitalist social relations evacuate work of its dignified and self-fulfilling qualities (ibid.). Because labour power functions as and for capital, it is commodified, and workers are dehumanised as abstract labour (Marx, 1976).[3] Although our discussion is framed primarily by the term work as it captures best the practices discussed, the labour/work distinction re-emerges in those aspects of our analysis that bring work into dialogue with contemporary capitalist restructuring.

Moving beyond accounts of work defined in terms of political economy and capitalist social relations, Budd notes that work is seen and valued 'only when it conforms to our mental models of what work is' (Budd, 2016, p. 28). Similarly, Barley and Kunda suggest that how we talk about it 'indexes our assumptions about how work is organized' (2001, p. 82). But what counts as work is also 'a matter of definition' and depends on who is doing the defining (Star & Strauss, 1999, pp. 14–15). From the unremarkable interweaving of work and life in preindustrial societies to the segregation of work from other spheres of life during the Industrial Revolution, how work is practiced and understood is always changing (Barley & Kunda, 2001). Over time, work has variously been seen as a burden, commodity, source of personal fulfilment, or social relation (Budd, 2016).

The notion of 'knowledge work' is even more slippery and difficult to define than the generic notion of work because all work involves knowledge. Yet, Alvesson concedes that 'knowledge work' is a meaningful category 'with sufficient heuristic value to be useful' (2001, p. 864). The outcomes claimed for knowledge work make it

> impossible to separate knowledge and 'pure' intellectual skills (symbolist–analytical work) from flexibility, organizing capacity, a high level of motivation, social skills, less esoteric technical skills, the ability to follow company methods, standardized ways of operating and other elements in knowledge-intensive companies....
>
> (Alvesson, 2001, p. 865)

The ambiguity of knowledge and the work of knowledge-intensive companies means that ' "knowledge", "expertise" and "solving problems" to a large degree become matters of beliefs, impressions and negotiations of meaning' (Alvesson, 2001, p. 870). For Alvesson, knowledge, because he understands it as socially constructed, 'does not exist on its own, but is dependent on social recognition' (Alvesson, 2001, p. 872). This means that for knowledge work to be recognised as such, a lot of orchestration surrounds its promotion and realisation. At the same time, Alvesson acknowledges that '[t]echnical skills, theoretical knowledge, practical experience, etc. are often vital' and cannot be reduced to images, representations, myth, or discourse (2001, p. 881). His point is that what gets coded as knowledge work involves representational work, especially when what is being sold is 'knowledge'. Think of Jared's assertion – 'what you're selling is your knowledge (...) I can be found if somebody wants me'.

Erickson et al. see knowledge work as including:

> 1) the production and transmission of knowledge, 2) intellectual skill and manipulation of abstractions, 3) problem solving tied to creativity, and 4) theoretical and technical knowledge and/or formal education.
>
> (2014, p. 3)

This definition echoes those definitions of knowledge work that distinguish it from the operational and physical execution of tasks. It is closely linked with cognitive and creative design activities, the generation of information and expert knowledge, relatively autonomous work, a service orientation and high status (Gorman & Sandefur, 2011; Tremblay & Genin, 2010).

As 'knowledge' industries become 'the basis for continuous economic growth, and job mobility (if not social mobility)' (McDowell, 2012, p. 574), business organisational structures shift from contracted employer-employee relations to casual freelance arrangements and project-based working patterns (Bergvall-Kåreborn & Howcroft, 2013). For example, Jared points to how his company bypasses official employment regulation and worker protections because these are considered inflexible and costly. Instead, he suggests that worklife is taking on entrepreneurial qualities, with some lives being absorbed by endless work while others are pushed outside of the game. Of course, this stark polarisation means that even those within the game are subject to the threat of exclusion and associated anxieties. Thus, the shifting work arrangements rehearsed by Jared simultaneously enact autonomy and dependence, motivation and anxiety in the worklives of workers.

From a sociomaterial perspective, knowledge and knowledge work do not inhere in workers, or in the politics of work and sociocultural representations of knowledge work. Rather, work is understood as both a capacity and effect realised in the recursive interweaving of the social and material (Orlikowski, 2007). Human and non-human actions and actors continuously act upon each other to coproduce knowledge both as a resource and worker identity (Fenwick, 2010). For example, the knowledge produced by Google relies on a 'creative sociomaterial assemblage' (Suchman, 2007) of the PageRank algorithm, which dynamically incorporates user searches and use patterns by constantly crawling and indexing the web (Orlikowski, 2007). Similarly, online labour market platforms assemble and reassemble practices that channel and alter employer-employee relations.

One effect of the sociotechnical reconfiguration of work is the rise of MKW (Brown & Palvia, 2015; Pauleen, Campbell, Harmer, & Intezari, 2015). Indeed, 'an increasing range and suite of digital technologies and devices (...) present mobility as a 'norm' and work and technology as inseparable' (Erickson et al., 2014, p. 5). Mobile work takes myriad forms. For example, it is increasingly shaped by cultures of sharing and transaction, such as in telework (associated with remote home or co-working spaces)[4] and 'the use of digital media by networked individuals' to connect and mobilise 'products, services, people and data' via the platform economy (Wessels, 2018, p. 51). As Jared's reflections suggest, many of today's knowledge workers are like 'satellites' defining 'their work not by their presence in a traditional work-related location but by their agile ability to orbit around clients, co-workers, and infrastructures [including crowd employment platforms], integrating inputs and output as they circumnavigate' (Erickson et al., 2014, p. 1).

Diverse configurations and styles of MKW materialise in and through the complex and shifting entanglements of: constantly advancing mobile technologies; the productivity pressures of the knowledge economy; the entry of more women into these sectors; diminishing workplace-based infrastructures and resources; demands for worklife flexibility; expectations of self-fulfilment through work; and the recent political and economic championing of independent workers such as self-employed freelancers and the self-employed (Gregg, 2011, 2018; Langfred & Rockmann, 2016; Tremblay & Genin, 2010). It is in and through this melee of sociomaterial discourses and processes that the practices, norms and infrastructures of mobile work are emerging.

The widespread promotion of entrepreneurial work over the past 20 years has given momentum to the expansion of mobile work (Annink & den Dulk, 2012; Taylor & Luckman, 2018). Indeed, the conditions of self-employment and of knowledge work are analogous to the extent that both are represented in terms of flexibility, mobility, control over work activities, and opportunities for professional development (Tremblay & Genin, 2010, p. 35). Additionally, the rise of self-employment and freelance work as important sources of jobs for women is linked to the promise of mobility and flexibility in combining work and childcare (Annink & den Dulk, 2012; Duffy, 2016).[5] However, the interactive 'working out and carrying through of work[life] related arrangements' (Strauss, 1993, p. 87) tends not to be factored in. Rather, the creation of those conditions necessary for everyday MKW, entrepreneurial or otherwise, are either backgrounded or rendered invisible. In the section that follows, we engage with debates about visible and invisible work, a distinction that is often deployed to differentiate between officially recognised and remunerated work and those forms of work that go unnoticed and unremunerated. Some of the issues raised in these discussions inform our conception of corollary work.

The politics of visible and invisible work

The question of visible and invisible work is a complex one that spans the disciplines of sociology, feminist theory, science and technology studies and CSCW. It relates as much to the politics of how work is represented as to the content of work itself. For example, Suchman (1995) argues that representations of work by various actors and associated assumptions about how work tasks are performed, tend to obscure actual underlying work practices. She goes so far as to argue that secrecy often surrounds the specific knowledge and expertise of workers positioned differently in the same organisation, or work milieu. Moreover, from the perspective of the consumer, service work is often all the more valued the more invisible the work required to deliver the service is (Suchman, 1995).

Received definitions of work normally refer to visible labour that 'is readily identifiable and overt (…). It is typically paid, occurs in the public sphere, is directly profit generating, and has historically been full-time, long-term, and state regulated' (Poster, Crain, & Cherry, 2016a, p. 3). As such, we have come to think of work 'as a commodified, instrumental activity' with all those forms of work that fall outside this narrow frame being 'devalued and rendered invisible' (Budd, 2016, p. 29). Poster et al. address a spectrum of invisible labour from 'disappeared workers' to hypervisible workers engaged in invisibilised aesthetic labour, and all of the un- or under-recognised work in-between. When work is not seen 'it is not valued, either symbolically or materially' (Poster et al., 2016a, p. 5) and the worker becomes a 'nonperson' (Star & Strauss, 1999). The effect is that worker mobilisation and politicisation are undermined and working conditions remain outside legal and policy regulation (Poster et al., 2016a).

In the heyday of Fordist industrial production in the global North, the notion of separate public and private spheres structured divisions between work and life. Yet, questions of unpaid or invisible work were also a matter of concern then. For example, US-based home economists at the turn of the 20th century reframed domestic work as a series of management tasks and refashioned home enterprises in terms of productivity (Gregg, 2018). Their primary concern was with achieving productive efficiency and rationalisation across public and private domains. In contrast, the focus of feminist scholars and activists is on how work in the home intersects with paid labour to reproduce interlocking systems of inequality (Adkins, 2001; Duffy, 2017; Duffy & Schwartz, 2018; Federici, 2004; Jarrett, 2014; Katzman & Kinsella, 2018). For example, socialist feminists argue that the creation of value relies not only on the work of producing commodities, but also the necessary work of (re)producing labour power, i.e. social reproduction (Dalla Costa & Jame, 1972; Fortunati, 1995).

For Fortunati (1995), the social reproduction work undertaken by women is pushed out of view by its indirect input to capital. Surplus value is produced through the exploitation of labour power and involves two phases: first, 'the exchange of the capacities of living labor – labor-power – in the commodified form of labor-time'; and second, those 'activities that reproduce that laboring individual bodily, mentally, and emotionally' (1995, p. 78). While the workers' labour can be exchanged, commodified and exploited in capitalism, the reproductive labour of mainly women in the home is rendered invisible because of its indirect relationship to capital. As the bearers and primary rearers of children, women are prevented from full realisation of their labour power and are thereby systematically discriminated against within capitalism (Duffy & Schwartz, 2018).[6] This gendered division of labour sustains a distinction between exchange and use value as well as between visible and invisible work.

Building on insights from feminist studies of housework (Lopata, 1971; Oakley, 2018), and debates about unpaid work by women, Daniels (1987) highlights the many forms of work that are rendered invisible and devalued. She challenges the modern Western idea that work takes place only 'in the public world, which is dominated by men and separated from those private worlds of family and personal relationships where women predominate' (1987, p. 403). By 'weaving the fabric together in their friendships, families, and work settings', Daniels argues that 'the wheels of social interaction are oiled and women's habitual engagement in these tasks means that women are seen as "naturally" better at this kind of work' (ibid.). The naturalisation of this work as 'women's work' devalues it. However, Daniels calls for its recognition and revalorisation as central to the ongoing social construction of reality (ibid.).

Although the Wages for Housework campaign argued that it is only by receiving a wage that domestic workers become legible in capitalist relations (Schiller & McMahon, 2019), Daniels resists definitions of work solely in relation to 'remuneration for effort' (1987, p. 403). Acknowledging different work motivations, she argues that work should be reconceptualised to include all the work in the private world of the home, the volunteer work in the public sphere, and the emotion work in both public and private worlds (ibid.). She is keen to maintain the use value/exchange value distinction insofar as recognition of these activities as work 'does not imply that all aspects of work should be paid – or that all should have a dollar value assigned' (1987, p. 412). According to Daniels, women's 'nonwork', even if unpaid, should be counted as work so that double exploitation can be exposed; yet as unpaid work, it represents value beyond exchange. Work is invoked as a diverse category by Daniels insofar as she emphasises its different processes, values and ends. Some work is done in and for itself and, even if unpaid, should be recognised. Thus, consideration of 'invisible work', she argues, can tell 'us something about how the fabric of life is woven; it calls attention to what gives life its texture' (1987, p. 413).

Many argue that the organisation and provisioning of domestic and care work is in crisis today as these activities are progressively privatised and their costs are increasingly supported through debt (Adkins & Dever, 2016; Gill & Bakker, 2006). Migrant domestic workers are becoming part of the solution with 'immigration status' giving 'the householder additional means of control over them' (Anderson, 2007, p. 261). But social reproduction and domestic work are not just being reconfigured in the global North by privatisation and the deployment of migrant labour. Domestic labour is increasingly subject to measurement and calculation in terms of its relationship to asset pricing of, for example, the household utilities of water and electricity (Adkins & Dever, 2016). In this way, domestic labour is linked to financial markets via its entanglement 'in the production of speculative financial value' (2016, p. 142).

By recognising domestic work as central to capitalism, these diverse feminist positions prefigure post-Fordist debates about immaterial and affective labour (Schiller & McMahon, 2019). They provide ways of thinking about what happens when affective work associated with 'women's work' extends into all aspects of the contemporary economy (Adkins, 2001, 2009; Alessandrini, 2012; Dalla Costa & Jame, 1972; Federici, 2004). The term 'immaterial labour' refers to the knowledge, creative and communication work that Hardt and Negri see as emblematic of the contemporary global mode of production (Hardt & Negri, 2000, p. 290).[7] Because this work is defined by intangible skills related to the mind, emotions and sentiments (Fortunati, 2018), it demands that the worker put his or her own life experience, communicative competency, and sense of self into the job; 'the very stuff of human subjectivity' is put to work for capital (Neilson & Rossiter, 2005, p. 10).[8] Nonetheless, the evidence suggests that the movement of 'women's work' into the productive domain, while potentially revaluing it, and reworking gender to some extent at least, does not undo or overcome gender unequal relations (Adkins, 2009; Adkins & Jokinen, 2008; Gray, Ciolfi, de Carvalho, D'Andrea, & Wixted, 2017; Morini, 2007; Morini & Fumagalli, 2010; Weeks, 2007).

Many point to how the invisible work associated with women's household and care is now extending into all those activities deemed necessary for generating income, obtaining or retaining jobs, and furthering careers, including unpaid internships and portfolio building (Poster et al., 2016a).[9] Indeed, work for social currency rather than wages is promoted by the idea of loving the work, especially in the ICT and cultural industries (McRobbie, 2010; Tokumitsu, 2014). These shifting trends in the organisation of work 'hide the nature of the labour process itself, including the location of the work; the conditions under which it is done; and the ethnicity, race, and nationality of the workers' (Poster, Crain, & Cherry, 2016b, p. 280). Much of the actual work involved is 'invisible or relegated to a background of expectation' – a form of 'backstage work' (Star & Strauss, 1999, pp. 15–21).

Illich coined the term 'shadow work' to refer to 'that entirely different form of unpaid work which an industrial society demands as a necessary complement to the production of goods and services' (Illich, 1981, pp. 99–100). He compares work to an iceberg, with visible work relying on a much more substantial quantity of invisible work, often undertaken by women. In an essay on telework and the digital delivery of services into the home, Menzies (1997) builds on Illich's notion of shadow work to examine the work generated by digital economy 'microstructures' when 'computer-simplified work' is transferred 'from the paid hands of workers to the unpaid hands of consumers' and migrates into the home and other networked spaces (1997, p. 103). Her argument is that we are witnessing a rise in 'shadow work' associated with the 'personal and technical maintenance around both telework and digital consumption' (1997, p. 118). Menzies echoes Suchman's discussion of how work is defined when she asserts that

> the issues come down to control, control over the definitions of what is recognized as work and what is labelled housework or consumption; and control over the tools, social relations and the context associated with this work.
> (1997, p. 119)

Similarly, DeVault calls for the study of '*all* of the work people are doing' (DeVault, 2014, p. 781, emphasis original). To this end, she invites us to consider: the ways in which work is done 'under the radar (…) beyond and around (…) formal job descriptions' to meet organisational goals; this work 'isn't recognized in the official story of the organization' (DeVault, 2014, p. 785). Yet it is increasingly important, in DeVault's view, because 'we are now living through a major reorganization of work which expands and depends on many kinds of activities that are occurring out of sight' (DeVault, 2014, p. 777).

Hatton takes up this discussion but notes that although the notion of 'invisible work' has received much descriptive attention, it has not been developed as an analytic category (Hatton, 2017, p. 337). She defines invisible work as labour that is concealed and, therefore, economically devalued through intersecting cultural, legal and spatial mechanisms of invisibility. These mechanisms operate in different ways and to different degrees across time and space (ibid.). For example, labour is devalued *socio-culturally* by virtue of hegemonic cultural ideologies (of gender, race, class, ability, sexuality, age and more); *socio-legally* via exclusion from legal definitions of 'employment'; and is *socio-spatially* devalued when 'physically segregated from a culturally defined worksite' (ibid.). 'Invisible labour', therefore, can take place anywhere/anytime and 'may comprise only one aspect of a job or its totality', yet contributes economic value (ibid.). This work may be implicitly, or explicitly required by employers, or by the market. However, and most importantly for Hatton, invisibility operates as 'a structure of disadvantage that encompasses a range of unrecognised, marginalised and/or degraded work (Hatton, 2017, p. 346).

Relatedly, Gregg notes that the workers she interviewed in her study of work's intimacy were grateful for the 'workplace flexibility assisted by mobile devices [which] made them feel lucky to work wherever they could' (Gregg, 2018, p. 20). However, most of these workers were 'unable to "count" as "work" the growing habits of checking email, anticipating contact, and using personal time to catch up on tasks left aside in the service of other, presumably more urgent duties' (ibid.). As such, she suggests that 'the very character of work, and what productive labour actually meant to them, remained largely unexamined' (ibid.).

But how relevant are these debates about visible and invisible work at a time when the organisation of work is undergoing profound transition? For example, the recent turn to what Cherry calls the 'extreme outsourcing' via platforms such as Amazon Mechanical Turk, hides both workers and work from users/consumers (Cherry, 2016, p. 73).[10] Similarly, platforms like TaskRabbit render the client and service provider at least theoretically interchangeable (Richardson, 2018). These forms of 'crowd employment' are increasingly recognised as a 'new form of employment' (Huws et al., 2018). Moreover, surveys in the UK, Germany, Sweden and the Netherlands reveal that 'many of the ICT related practices associated with crowdwork are widespread across the rest of the labour market where a growing number of workers are "logged"' (Huws et al., 2018, p. 114). Availability to check emails, respond to work at short notice via an 'app', and the 'logging' of progress electronically, are all becoming prevalent features of work across the entire labour market (2018, p. 123).

Questions of visible and invisible, recognised and unrecognised work no longer map onto clearly demarcated and gendered domains of public and private, or even different modes of work. As such, differentiating sharply between 'typical' and 'atypical' forms of employment, as in Standing's (2011) distinction between the 'salariat' and 'precariat', or indeed between visible and invisible work are inadequate to the task of capturing the sociomaterial complexities of many contemporary worklives. The picture is even further complicated when much of this reassembling of work and how it is done is spreading internationally 'below the radar of nationally specific regulations' (Huws et al., 2018, p. 125). The question of visibility relates then not only to those sociomaterial practices that make work, but to how these are shaped by larger corporate capitalist shifts that are working at speeds and levels that fall outside national policy and legal regulation frames. Moreover, as spheres of information and symbolic content become detached from physical locales and interwoven with evolving technologies of communication, public/private boundaries become blurred or undone (Thompson, 2011, p. 49).

For Fenwick, conceptions of work resist synthesis because

> [w]ork has been analysed as paid and unpaid, linked to the formal economy or not, visible and invisible, based in organizational action, household chores, care-giving, or individual reflection, distributed across multiple sites and even continents, virtual or continuously mobile.
>
> (2010, p. 106)

Work is becoming even harder to define as the technological entailments of everyday work practices limit our capacity to understand them and our ability to intervene or change them (Orlikowski & Scott, 2008, p. 467).[11]

Debates about the often invisibilised 'second-order' activities of integrating and coordinating work across locations have been taking place within sociology and CSCW for some years. This work focuses mainly on the dovetailing or reconciling of work practices with sociotechnical infrastructures, from digital connectivity to contextual norms, as well as the politics and culture of the work and work contexts (Schmidt & Bannon, 1992). CSCW scholarship does not limit its definition of work to paid labour. Yet some scholars differentiate between primary and secondary work and suggest that 'secondary cases of work' (such as, for example, unpaid care work) should be addressed as 'serious affairs that require effort and concentration, and (…) presume mastery of all sorts technicalities (…). It requires skill and training, stamina and effort, dedication and attention' (Schmidt, 2011, pp. 361–362).

Strauss introduced the term articulation work as 'a kind of supra-type of work in any division of labor', but also as a tool for analysing divisions of labour involving multiple workers. He suggests that it includes:

> First, the meshing of the often numerous tasks, clusters of tasks, and segments of the total arc. Second, the meshing of efforts of various unit-workers (individuals, departments, etc.). Third, the meshing of actors with their various types of work and implicated tasks.
>
> (Strauss, 1985, p. 8)

Articulation work is not just the work of coordination. For example, as Star and Strauss argue, '[j]uggling one's visibility is itself an act of articulation work' (1999, p. 25) and is taking on greater significance in recent years with the rise of social media (Nelson, Jarrahi, & Thomson, 2017). The notion of articulation work facilitates an analysis of the kinds of divisions of labour that enable work to be done involving multiple individuals but also work carried out over a unit of any size (Perry & Brodie, 2006). For Hampson and Junor, these are all 'forms of work that are in danger of remaining invisible' (2005, p. 169). They suggest that work is invisibilised in three ways: first, when it falls outside the rationalist accounts, for example, those of job descriptions; second, when it is externalised from the waged or self-employed relation; and third, when those 'tacit' skills that underpin work processes are deemed 'natural' (2005, p. 170).

While articulation work is concerned mainly with addressing the division of labour in collaborative work or work involving complex tasks, Perry and Brodie (2006) identify a need to address the specific issues affecting mobile workers. They note that technological connectivity is always constrained by the practical issues these workers face by virtue of being mobile (ibid.). Perry proposes the term 'mobilisation work' to refer to the effort involved in becoming (and staying) mobile while at the same time achieving work goals (Perry, 2007, p. 2).

Inspired by the survival strategies of pastoralist nomads, Su and Mark propose the term 'nomadic work' to describe the challenges faced by workers dealing with 'an extreme form of mobile work' involving almost constant, long-distance movement (Su & Mark, 2008, p. 305). These challenges include 'assembling actants, seeking resources, and integrating with others', as well as maintaining visibility and synchronising for meeting (ibid.). In a later article, they emphasise the importance of making local infrastructures visible to those conducting work in new locations (Mark & Su, 2010). The notion of *nomadicity* has subsequently been elaborated to address the implications of the dislocation of work from spatial and temporal constraints, including how environmental and technological discontinuities are addressed (Bogdan, Rossitto, Normark, Adler, & Eklundh, 2006; Rossitto, 2009; Rossitto & Eklundh, 2007), the mobilisation and activation of resources to establish temporary workplaces (de Carvalho, Ciolfi, & Gray, 2011; Perry, O'Hara, Sellen, Brown, & Harper, 2001; Su & Mark, 2008), and human-technology relations in highly mobile spatial, organisational and personal circumstances (de Carvalho, 2013; de Carvalho, Ciolfi, & Gray, 2017; Erickson & Jarrahi, 2016; Jarrahi, Philips, Sutherland, Sawyer, & Erickson, 2018; Nelson et al., 2017). These studies highlight the 'backgrounded' work involved in setting up, maintaining and managing mobile workplaces, as well as improvising solutions such as 'workarounds' to address local limitations, configurations or mixes of technical capacities (Gerson & Star, 1986, p. 267). This work extends to the appropriation and management of digital infrastructure and the organisational, political and economic factors that shape it (Star & Ruhleder, 1994).

Taking a slightly different tack, Mark suggests the term '*metawork*' for the work that 'enables [workers] to get an overview of the state of their fragmented work' (2015, p. 30). This includes configuring the infrastructure (such as the installation, repair and maintenance of digital software and networks) and mobilising tools to monitor work (when there are no shared or agreed forms of scheduling, or project management). Because spatial mobility and a diversity of contextual and temporal shifts give rise to 'context collapse', '*contextual mobilization*' work is proposed by Nelson et al. to describe the mobilisation of technologies that allows workers 'to move between personal and professional contexts on their own terms' (2017, p. 60). Nelson et al. argue that MKWrs are moved 'towards more and more technology usage' by their need for both tangible information and those forms of intangible information that enable productivity (2017, p. 56).

It is the 'very mobility' of MKWrs that creates their need to accomplish work 'in and across several locations' (de Carvalho, 2014, p. 211) and 'yields a corresponding requirement to interact dynamically with infrastructures of all kinds' (Erickson et al., 2014, p. 13). Infrastructures are 'large-scale, technological, political, and institutional entities' and have many components that must interrelate and function as a whole (Erickson et al., 2014, pp. 9–10). Because MKW relies on individualised expertise and creativity, it is less amenable to generic infrastructures but often requires bespoke combinations of infrastructural elements. Additionally, digital infrastructures outside the conventional office are rarely seamless and demand constant improvisation and ingenuity on the part of workers. As such, MKWrs require 'a literacy or a set of capabilities that enables them to construct optimal individual infrastructure strategies' (Erickson et al., 2014, p. 13).

The ICT assemblages identified by the MKWs in Nelson et al.'s study comprised

> desktops, laptops, tablets, mobile phones, printers (or, at least, access to a pay-per-use printer), headphones, and a variety of cables and charging devices, with as many as four backup chargers. Dropbox, One Drive, Google Drive, Facebook, Twitter, LinkedIn, professional listservs, newsletters, Hangouts

and Skype, note-keeping and to-do-listing applications were also central parts of assemblages.

(2017, p. 60)

Such an 'infrastructural assembly, or *bricolage*', as Erickson et al. call it, means that 'the associated boundaries and constraints between and among different infrastructures' exponentially multiplies the need for active coordination, improvisation and creative management of work on the move (Erickson et al., 2014).[12] This process in turn involves a kind of 'gateway' making (Edwards, Jackson, Bowker, & Williams, 2009), or the creation of bridges that connect different infrastructures effectively (Erickson et al., 2014).

It is clear that considerable attention is given within CSCW to the various kinds of backgrounded work involved in achieving work mostly through collaboration but also as work itself becomes more mobile. The focus is primarily on the interface of mobility, technology and infrastructure, which we see as only one part of the sociomaterially entangled process. We take the insights from these analyses and bring them into engagement with concepts and debates within sociology, gender and mobility studies to develop the concept of corollary work as all those shifting entanglements of sociomaterial practices that make MKW possible.

Our analysis of MKWrs' accounts attributes force to both the social and the material in the making of MKWlives. For example, while technology is often attributed a material quality, it is 'a sociotechnical product, patterned by the conditions of its creation and use' (Wajcman, 2015, p. 29). Similarly, shifting social relations of production and social reproduction are impossible to understand separately from those material places, artefacts and devices that shape these arrangements. In keeping with the ways in which these are discussed in the accounts of participants, we extend the focus beyond work to how life is reconfigured as work becomes more mobile. While work is our starting point, we go with the flow of the worker accounts and their renderings of worklife. The most viscerally expressed concerns relate to how optimal conditions for the 'good' MKWlife might be created.

The wide-ranging scholarship on invisible work discussed above alerts us to those systematic ways in which some practices become coded as work and therefore productive and valuable while others are rendered without value partly via their invisibilisation. However, the binary visible/invisible has the unhelpful effect of stabilising practices into one or other side of the binary. Moreover, this binary works in less predictable ways in mobile worklives. We cannot assume, a priori, 'the stability of undervalued, hidden, shadow and invisible work' (Star & Strauss, 1999, p. 26). Rather it is the sociomaterial and political relations that underpin it that require investigation. It is also important to acknowledge that there will always be aspects of work that are 'inevitably left outside (...) representation' (Bannon, 1995, p. 66). Bannon notes that while some seek out 'more powerful representational forms', there is a growing awareness that more adequate representation is not the answer (ibid.). Questions of context, interpretation, distinct semantic communities and representational frameworks are always at play so that 'no representation, or set of representations is [or can be] complete' (Bannon, 1995, p. 67). Instead, as both Suchman and Alvesson argue, it is the politics of representation that is at stake, how these are mobilised, and for what purpose. The question of visibility falls into similar traps. It is impossible, Star and Strauss argue, 'to define anything inherently as visible or invisible; similarly, it is impossible a priori to say that either are absolutely good or bad, desirable or undesirable' (1999, p. 23). For example, invisibility may be interpreted as positive when it affords autonomy, flexibility, personal discretion, mobility and/or creativity. Invisible work may also have the positive connotation of not having to reveal aspects of the work process to others (ibid.).

Because the question of (in)visibility is also a matter of perspective, it is deeply implicated in power relations. The visibilisation of work practices can give them legitimacy or expose exploitation, but it can also reify work, create opportunities for surveillance, or increase administration, procedural, accountability and communication burdens (Star & Strauss, 1999, p. 10). In attempting to account for the corollary work that makes MKW, the question is not a matter of visibility or invisibility because aspects of this work constantly move between visibility and invisibility. Rather our concern is with providing a textured account of the work involved in (re)assembling MKWlives and the specific concerns raised by these workers themselves. This is less a project of making visible than of recognition. It is about rerouting the knowledge/power articulated through these accounts into a grounded analysis that recircuits it in potentially more emancipatory directions for contemporary workers.

Unravelling corollary work

Our notion of *corollary work* emerges from our analysis of the ways in which worklives are formed and transformed in the everyday 'doings' described by our study participants. The texture of MKWlives as recounted cannot be apprehended as an 'existent configuration', but is more helpfully characterised as 'potentializing directionality'; it is always in 'midstream' – moving (Ingold, 2016, p. 17). Corollary work is, therefore, emergent in 'the action of doing undergoing' (ibid). While some aspects are habituated, it also involves constant attentiveness as those sociomaterial practices that make it up move along 'with' shifting places, temporalities, versions of product, productivity and self. It is the practice that is agentic – the doing/undergoing – the becoming MKWlife. Worklife is moving along lines of becoming – it is historical, emergent, contingent. It often requires awareness that is shaped by this going along, which is always awareness *with* before it is ever awareness *of*. We can recognise a movement, and respond to it, before we ever fix it in our sights. The operations of the attentional mind, in short, are not cognitive but ecological (Ingold, 2016).

MKWrs are continually rediscovering themselves through their continual entanglement in and responsiveness to the flow of sociomaterial practices. It is through these sociomaterial practices that the individual, or the I's resonance with movement and its capacity to participate are created (Hultin, 2019). In describing what we mean by *corollary work*, we emphasise its indeterminacy insofar as it is always 'forming and transforming from within the action itself' (Ingold, 2016, p. 17). Nonetheless, we frame it in the chapters that follow through the specific lenses of place making, 'time work', productivity and identity work as articulated in the workers' accounts.

Corollary work as emerging in recursive practices of *place making* is addressed first. This discussion considers place and place making less in terms of how it is inhabited and experienced by human actors (Cresswell, 2004; Tuan, 1977) and more as a coming together, or assemblage of material, social and experiential elements (Pierce, Martin, & Murphy, 2011). The assumption that environments are made into places by human experiences (Tuan, 1977) is upended by the integration of material elements and networked flows of ideas, objects, people and affect in the making of place. Place making and emplaced practices manifest at different degrees of scale, linked by flows of bodies, artefacts, knowledge and relationships (Malpas, 2012). It is because places are interconnected and the result of multiple sociomaterial practices and situated negotiations that they are primarily understood as relational – made by sociomaterial relationships and not simply a backdrop for them (Agnew, 1987; Amin, 2004; Massey, 2005; Nicholls, 2009). It is this more hybridised, synthetic, fluid and relational assembling of diverse elements to make place that underpins our discussion of how MKW is made possible via multiscalar and often contested place making practices in Chapters 2 and 3 of this book.[13]

Some recent theorisations of mobile and nomadic lives, by relying on binary understandings of sedentarism and nomadism, dwelling and moving, assume place to be static, univocally defined, bounded, and having essential qualities (Casey, 1997; Tuan, 1977). However, the move away from 'essentialist' towards 'processual' definitions of place that see it as dynamic, relational and 'progressive' has undermined these positions (Frello, 2008; Kabachnik, 2012; Massey, 1993; Urry, 2007). Many mobility studies scholars redefine place 'in terms of process, meaning, and relations to the surroundings, rather than in terms of essence' (Frello, 2008, p. 26). Indeed, processual and relational understandings of place contribute to the study of how place itself is mobilised, lived and experienced as mobile and/or mobilised (Büscher, Urry, & Witchger, 2011; Sheller & Urry, 2006). In Chapters 2 and 3 we examine the sociomaterial mobilisations of place in the accounts of our study participants and the kinds of *corollary work* that this entails. As the 'cultivation of atmospheres' (Gregg, 2018, pp. 16–17) becomes a prevalent feature of MKW, we ask whether this is a factor in shaping the work of place making for participants? In these chapters we analyse the kinds of place making and unmaking engaged in by MKWrs across locations, scapes and outlooks. Chapter 2 examines the placing of worklives in cities and regions; Chapter 3 is focused on how everyday places are made to work in everyday MKWlives.

Time work is the second feature of *corollary work* and is examined in depth in Chapters 4 and 5. Commentators on the changing nature of work suggest that it is highly educated workers in the knowledge economy who experience the largest increase in working time and associated time pressures (Correll, Kelly, O'Connor, & Williams, 2014, p. 4). Because time economy is at the core of capitalist practices of efficiency and productivity, time saving and time management are central to capital accumulation and technological innovation (Murray, Gilbert, & Goffey, 2015). Under most industrial capitalist arrangements, work time is measured via standardised and abstract units of clock time to enable calculation and the extraction of surplus value. This is further enabled by the organisation of work into specific time periods and places, thus separating it from the rest of life (Moen, Lam, Ammons, & Kelly, 2013; Sennett, 1998). Against this conceptualisation of time, we take up Glennie and Thrift's (1996) invitation to approach time as co-evolving with the interpretation and incorporation of technological time and mobility management devices in everyday life practices.

Time structuring also extends beyond the workplace, or work expectations (Glennie & Thrift, 1996). For example, the post-Fordist extension of profit maximisation into the vital qualities of knowledge, creativity and desires for movement and freedom (Presskorn-Thygesen, 2015), means that it is harder to distinguish any boundaries between what might be called working-time/space and life-time/space (Boltanski & Chiapello, 2005; Morini & Fumagalli, 2010). As such, time itself, previously apprehended and lived through institutionalised 'time cages' and temporal norms, is reworked in post-Fordism (Adkins, 2009; Bauman, 2000; Castells, 2000; Lash & Urry, 1987). It 'unfolds *with* the commodity' (Adkins, 2014, p. 533, original emphasis). And, because commodity value is the outcome of unquantifiable innovations, relationships, communication activities and networks, a crisis of measure is precipitated (Adkins, 2008; Hardt & Negri, 2000). Moreover, with the monetisation of more and more domains of life, 'working time agreements and working time practices' become more divergent (Adkins, 2009, p. 334). And, although mobile and flexible production arrangements do not require Fordist levels of standardisation and regularity, they do demand 'much more intense coordination' (Glennie & Thrift, 1996, p. 287). For example, the rise of the 24-hour globalised work environments requires time-zone adjustment, asynchronous interaction at a distance and more flexible and personalised temporalities (Glennie & Thrift, 1996; Lash & Urry, 1994).[14] We examine the ways in which these temporal shifts shape emergent forms of 'time work' as a significant component of the corollary work described by study participants.

Noting the variety of forms of 'time work' undertaken by individuals in everyday life, Flaherty suggests that actors are proud of their own ingenuity, enthusiasm, wit and irony in the doing of time (2003, p. 30).[15] Taking Flaherty's notion of time work as a starting point, we address the specific temporal orientations that characterise MKW in Chapters 4 and 5. Chapter 4 argues that a temporal orientation of what we are calling *anticipatory availability* emerges through the temporal practices of ICT managers and digital creatives. A qualitatively different temporal orientation is reported in the accounts of academic participants. Chapter 5 addresses the time work described by academics via what we call a temporal orientation of *reflexive rhythmicity*.

The third broad feature of corollary work relates to the *imperative of productivity* and is the topic of Chapter 6. While productivity and the optimising of output have always underpinned capitalist work arrangements, individualisation and the endless potential for mobility of tasks require considerable work on the self to sustain optimum output. Because the thing that is produced is often unclear and emergent in MKW, responsibility is shouldered by workers themselves. This personalisation of the productivity imperative is deepened by the proliferation of new platforms and technologies which render the physical and temporal architectures of work more porous while simultaneously making productivity more visible, measurable and accountable (Gregg, 2018). Additionally, the contemporary imperative of productivity, especially for MKWrs, is not accompanied by guiding principles and criteria. Instead, these workers are characterised and characterise themselves as self-managed, self-motivated, self-organised, and also self-promoting (Arvidsson, Gandini, & Bandinelli, 2016).

The productivity imperative contributes to the attitude that 'there is always something more than one is capable of, a level of self-competence that is not yet achieved and liberated, a degree of excess capacity or potential that can be tapped with the right level of focus' (Gregg, 2018, p. 14). Gregg describes the associated personal anxiety as 'the trauma of productivity' (Gregg, 2018, p. 17). Indeed, for Gregg, the 'work practices enabled by mobile devices call for a new language of labour and limits' (2018, p. 94). Otherwise, she suggests that we are rendered permanently captive to the unrelenting challenge and oppression of finding 'flow' (ibid.). In Chapter 6 we build on these debates about productivity and the productive self to show how the productivity imperative generates the corollary work of constant alertness. We also address the sociomaterial (re)production of productivity as a generalised worklife norm.

Finally, the expectation that work should be a labour of love creates another domain of work on the self and requires incessant *identity work*. As work expands into intangible social processes beyond clearly delimited tasks, the relative autonomy and flexibility that characterises mobile work instils the notion of work as a source of self-fulfilment and happiness. In Chapter 7 we discuss the kinds of work on the self that are generated by the ideas that you should 'do what you love'. This includes the ongoing presentation and promotion of a 'stand out' and passionate worker self to potential employers/customers and, indeed, oneself. MKWrs who work away from their employing organisation must 'find ways to remain visible as professionals and maintain social connections necessary for their work', via social media and other communication technologies (Nelson et al., 2017, p. 57). Similarly, those who are self-employed mobilise their professional selves through communication and collaboration networks and channels in order to sustain the flow of work. These conditions of mobile work destabilise relationships to self and self-identity (Büscher, 2014; D'Mello & Sahay, 2007; Erickson et al., 2014), which is only ever provisionally re-stabilised by constant and agile refashioning of work identities (Coupland & Spedale, 2020, p. 837).

Donzelot (1991) suggests relationships to work across Europe have shifted from 'pleasure through work' to 'pleasure in work'. No longer associated with drudgery, or seen as a necessary evil that funds leisure activities and family security, he argues that work is now seen and experienced as 'a good in itself: a means towards self-realization rather than as an opportunity for self-transcendence' (Donzelot, 1991, p. 251). More recently, terms like 'passion' and 'love' have become so salient to contemporary labour narratives that some social media communities 'have adopted the maxim 'DWYL' (Do What You Love) to describe new employment spaces where pleasure, autonomy and income seemingly coexist' (Duffy, 2016, p. 441). Indeed, Cabanas and Illouz argue that 'investing in one's own happiness has come to be rendered as a *condition sine qua non* for workers to navigate the emerging conditions and requirements of the world of labour' (2019, p. 11). This chapter underscores those sociomaterial practices of identity work that cultivate and sustain a love for work while somehow accommodating its costs. As such, it examines the emotionally mediated identity work through which ambivalence and anxiety are backgrounded so that MKWlives are 'made to work'.

Conclusions

At a time when mobility and flexibility are deemed the vital characteristics of 'good' workers, and are also embraced as cost-cutting strategies for employers as well as 'selling points' in customer service, it is important to gain an understanding of how they feature in the worklives of workers themselves. There is no doubt that MKW is at the forefront of the embedding of these values in the labour market and in work process norms. In this book, therefore, we identify the implications of this valorisation of mobility and flexibility and unpack the essential *corollary work* that makes MKW possible. Shifting work arrangements, including the mobility of work, have led to calls for a reframing of work to incorporate 'diverse contributions of effort, time and emotion (…) [including] the consciousness that necessarily goes along with doing: "planning", "thinking", "deciding", "coordinating", and so on' (Katzman & Kinsella, 2018, p. 1438). As workers 'become their own micro-structures', they increasingly do the work of structures by themselves (McRobbie, 2002; Richardson, 2018). This work undermines and reconfigures Fordist binaries of public/private, visible/invisible work.

The interdisciplinary lens applied in this book brings to light the complex ways in which MKWrs handle the complexities of mobile work and the multifaceted and hidden corollary work that goes into achieving liveable worklives. The testimonies of MKWrs interrupt and confront the normalisation of the 'connectivity imperative' and the ways in which this imperative instantiates a 'default association between technology, flexibility, mobility, and freedom' (Gregg, 2011, pp. 36–37). These first-hand and textured descriptions of the extensive, demanding, exhausting corollary work engaged in by a relatively privileged mobile workforce, give us pause for thought. Although values of business and/or technological mobility and efficiency are shared by many MKWrs, the practices, meanings and relationships they present are not so univocal and open up spaces for reflection and potential collective responses to these shifts.

Corollary work extends well beyond the socially reproductive imperatives of rest and replenishment that underpin work availability and sustainability, it involves fostering and sustaining the conditions for work to take place. Although corollary work comes into existence through the generated effects of intra-related sociomaterial practices and networks, we give priority to workers' accounts of corollary work in the chapters that follow. They describe those ways in which they become 'their own micro-structures' (McRobbie, 2002) and the myriad negotiations necessary to sustaining a worklife that are externalised 'from the employment relation' (Hampson & Junor, 2005, p. 170). But corollary work is more than these. It consists of all those sociomaterial practices that are essential to creating the conditions for MKW and through which worklife itself becomes and is constantly transformed. It involves all those emergent sociomaterial practices of place, time, productivity and self-expression as they are reproduced and transformed in every enactment of MKWlife; it is all that work that potentialises MKW.

The accounts of MKWrs discussed in this book raise questions about how work, when looked to as a site of self-expression and happiness, might also be alienating. We might ask how workers who are constantly engaged with sustaining worklives across locations and time might identify exploitation and challenge it. How can increasing work pressures, surveillance and measurement be resisted by MKWrs when work is itself deemed a site of enjoyment and self-fulfilment? How can the systematic downplaying of corollary work and associated distortions of what MKW involves be addressed in the interests of workers? Like Jared's opening account suggests, there is always the risk of falling out of the game and, given the work-oriented identifications of MKWrs, this would mean becoming 'meaningless, a loss of sense *and* self that is more disempowering than traditional alienation' (Coupland & Spedale, 2020, p. 844, emphasis original). How then do MKWrs 'keep going' and what can we learn about contemporary shifts in how work is organised and the implications for workers' lives? These are just some of the questions addressed in the chapters that follow.

Notes

1 The emphasis in portions of the quotes across the book are those of the authors in order to draw attention to relevant issues.

2 While the employable in this economy are 'mobile, enthusiastic, versatile, having potential to be autonomous, not prescriptive and tolerant', the unemployable individual is designated un-adaptable, immobile, local, rooted and attached (Boltanski & Chiapello, 2005, pp. 112–119).

3 Under capitalism, Marx argues that 'the worker sells his/her labour power as commodity to the capitalist and thereby works during one part of the day (necessary labour time) for creating the 'value of his labour-power, i.e. the value of his means of subsistence' (Marx, 1976, p. 324) and another part of the day not 'for himself', but for the capitalist. During this time, he 'creates surplus-value' (Marx, 1976, p. 325). Marx calls this part of the day 'surplus labour-time, and to the labour expended during that time I give the name of surplus labour' (ibid.).

4 The term telework refers to 'mobile work carried out anywhere outside the office', including at home and is enabled by advanced transportation, information and communication technologies (Tremblay & Genin, 2007, p. 3). Hynes identifies three common elements as 'essential to telework; the temporal and spatial dimensions, and the use of ICTs' (Hynes, 2016, p. 34).

5 Women made up 30.4 per cent of self-employed in Europe in 2009. In 2019, there were 32,581,300 self-employed workers in the EU, from which 10,564,000 were women, i.e. 32.4 per cent. In Ireland, there were 317,700 self-employed workers, from which 74,800 were women, i.e. 23.5 per cent (Eurostat, 2019).

6 While migrant labour is becoming increasingly significant to social reproduction in advanced economies (Adkins & Dever, 2016), global care chains have a long history, and social reproduction has taken on a more transnational form in recent decades (Boris & Parreñas, 2010; Gray, 2006, 2013; Gray et al., 2017).

7 Christian Fuchs critiques autonomist accounts of immaterial labour because for him they imply that 'information work is detached from nature and matter' as if 'there are two substances in the world – matter and spirit – that result in two different kinds of work' (Fuchs, 2014, p. 252). Instead, he argues that information work has to be seen as material work because it is 'based on the activity of the human brain, which is a material system that is part of the human's materiality' (ibid.). He also suggests that informationalisation is actually less important in the post-Fordist economy than finance and oil and gas industries (Fuchs, 2014, pp. 147–148).

8 Feher contrasts the Fordist labourer who entered into an employment labour contract with 'a new form of subjectivity: human capital' that he sees as characteristic of post-Fordism (2009, p. 24). This human capital does not just relate to investments in education and training but to 'all that is produced by the skill set that defines me' (Feher, 2009, p. 26). It arises from 'the things I inherit, the things that happen to me, and the things I do' (ibid.). So, in order to optimise, maintain and interweave personal and professional human capital, the post-Fordist subject must manage 'a portfolio of conducts' pertaining to all aspects of his/her life at once (Feher, 2009, p. 30).

9 For example, Armano and Murgia argue that the difficulties that 'young people with years of investment in training and upskilling (…) [encounter] finding jobs that match their qualifications and aspirations (…) forces them to accept temporary as well as under-skilled works'; 'if they turn down the temporary dead-end job, they may be branded as lazy and a scrounger. If they take it, they may be on a losing track' (Armano & Murgia, 2013, p. 495). Their investment in unpaid labour is driven by the fear of falling out of the game of work before they even gain access to it.

10 Work is also hidden as leisure or volunteerism via 'gamefication' in ways that obscure employer/employee relations (Star & Strauss, 1999).

11 Relatedly, in his study of the often invisible work of photocopier repair technicians, Orr argues that the invisibility of work such as technical service is increased by the lack of understanding of the sociomaterial relationships between worker, customers

and machines, and of the accomplishment of continuous, highly skilled improvisation that managing this relationship requires (Orr, 1996).

12 The notion of 'bricolage', originated by Lévi-Strauss (1966), has been adopted within CSCW and STS in relation to sociotechnical systems by virtue of the work of scholars such as Orr (1996) and Ciborra (1992).

13 As the product of negotiation (Cresswell, 2003; Massey, 2005; Thrift, 1998; Urry, 2000), place making includes conflict, disagreement and cultural and ideological differences (Hochschild, 2010; Malpas, 2009; Pierce et al., 2011). As such, place involves the iterative, evolutionary processes of defining not just boundaries or territories, or 'settings' (Entrikin, 1997), but also the rules and norms against which socio-spatial practices are understood and enacted (Harvey, 1996).

14 Fordist temporal structurings are contested and reconfigured in other ways such as via trade union challenges to the length of the working day and week (Grabham, 2014), and feminist protests against housework and care as beyond value (Federici, 2012; Folbre, 1991; Jaggar, 2013).

15 Taking a human agency approach to time work, Flaherty argues that temporal experience 'does not just happen to us'; rather individuals inhabit and construct situations with the aim of 'bring[ing] about particular types of temporal experience' (2003, p. 29). Flaherty's findings are based on analysis of 398 interview narratives from undergraduate students. For him time work involves efforts 'to modify or manipulate five dimensions of temporal experience': *duration* (making intervals seem shorter or longer), *frequency* (deciding how often something happens in a particular unit of time), *sequence* (ordering events), *timing* (when something happens) and *allocation* (setting time aside for doing things) (Flaherty, 2003, p. 30). Via these strategies, Flaherty argues that 'work' of one kind or another is required such that 'time work typically is marked by purposefulness' (2003, p. 29).

References

Adkins, L. (2001). Cultural Feminization: "Money, Sex and Power" for Women. *Signs: Journal of Women in Culture and Society*, *26*(3), 669–695. https://doi.org/10.1086/495625

Adkins, L. (2008). From Retroactivation to Futurity: The End of the Sexual Contract? *NORA – Nordic Journal of Feminist and Gender Research*, *16*(3), 182–201. https://doi.org/10.1080/08038740802300954

Adkins, L. (2009). Feminism after Measure. *Feminist Theory*, *10*(3), 323–339. https://doi.org/10.1177/1464700109343255

Adkins, L. (2014). Luc Boltanski and the Problem of Time: Notes towards a Pragmatic Sociology of the Future. In S. Susen & B. S. Turner (Eds.), *The Spirit of Luc Boltanski: Essays on the 'Pragmatic Sociology of Critique'* (pp. 517–538). London: Anthem.

Adkins, L., & Dever, M. (2016). *The Post-Fordist Sexual Contract: Working and Living in Contingency*. London: Palgrave Macmillan UK.

Adkins, L., & Jokinen, E. (2008). Introduction: Gender, Living and Labour in the Fourth Shift. *NORA – Nordic Journal of Feminist and Gender Research*, *16*(3), 138–149. https://doi.org/10.1080/08038740802300947

Agnew, J. A. (1987). *Place and Politics: The Geographical Mediation of State and Society*. Boston, MA: Allen & Unwin.

Alessandrini, D. (2012). Immaterial Labour and Alternative Valorisation Processes in Italian Feminist Debates: (Re)Exploring the "Commons" of Re-Production. *Feminists@ Law*, *1*(2), 1–28.

Alvesson, M. (2001). Knowledge Work: Ambiguity, Image and Identity. *Human Relations*, *54*(7), 863–886. https://doi.org/10.1177/0018726701547004

Amin, A. (2004). Regions Unbound: Towards a New Politics of Place. *Geografiska Annaler: Series B, Human Geography*, *86*(1), 33–44. https://doi.org/10.1111/j.0435-3684.2004.00152.x

Anderson, B. (2007). A Very Private Business. *European Journal of Women's Studies*, *14*(3), 247–264. https://doi.org/10.1177/1350506807079013

Annink, A., & den Dulk, L. (2012). Autonomy: The Panacea for Self-Employed Women's Work-Life Balance? *Community, Work & Family*, *15*(4), 383–402. https://doi.org/10.1080/13668803.2012.723901

Arcidiacono, D., Gandini, A., & Pais, I. (2018). Sharing What? The 'Sharing Economy' in the Sociological Debate. *The Sociological Review*, *66*(2), 275–288. https://doi.org/10.1177/0038026118758529

Armano, E., & Murgia, A. (2013). The Precariousnesses of Young Knowledge Workers: A Subject-Oriented Approach. *Global Discourse*, *3*(3), 486–501. https://doi.org/10.1080/23269995.2013.865313

Arvidsson, A., Gandini, A., & Bandinelli, C. (2016). Self-Branding among Freelance Knowledge Workers. In M. Crain, W. R. Poster, & M. A. Cherry (Eds.), *Invisible Labor: Hidden Work in the Contemporary World* (pp. 239–256). Oakland, CA: University of California Press.

Bannon, L. J. (1995). The Politics of Design: Representing Work. *Communications of the ACM*, *38*(9), 66–68. https://doi.org/10.1145/223248.223267

Barley, S. R., & Kunda, G. (2001). Bringing Work Back In. *Organization Science*, *12*(1), 76–95. https://doi.org/10.1287/orsc.12.1.76.10122

Bauman, Z. (2000). Time and Space Reunited. *Time & Society*, *9*(2–3), 171–185. https://doi.org/10.1177/0961463X00009002002

Bergvall-Kåreborn, B., & Howcroft, D. (2013). 'The Future's Bright, the Future's Mobile': A Study of Apple and Google Mobile Application Developers. *Work, Employment and Society*, *27*(6), 964–981. https://doi.org/10.1177/0950017012474709

Bogdan, C., Rossitto, C., Normark, M., Adler, P. J., & Eklundh, K. S. (2006). On a Mission without a Home Base: Conceptualizing Nomadicity in Student Group Work. In P. Hassanaly, T. Herrmann, G. Kunau, & M. Zacklad (Eds.), *Cooperative Systems Design: Seamless Integration of Artifacts and Conversations* (pp. 23–38). Amsterdam: IOS Press.

Boltanski, L., & Chiapello, E. (2005). *The New Spirit of Capitalism*. London & New York: Verso.

Boris, E., & Parreñas, R. S. (2010). *Intimate Labors: Cultures, Technologies, and the Politics of Care*. Stanford, CA: Stanford Social Sciences.

Brown, W. S., & Palvia, P. (2015). Are Mobile Devices Threatening Your Work-Life Balance? *International Journal of Mobile Communications*, *13*(3), 317. https://doi.org/10.1504/IJMC.2015.069128

Budd, J. W. (2016). The Eye Sees What the Mind Knows: The Conceptual Foundations of Invisible Work. In M. G. Crain, W. R. Poster, & M. A. Cherry (Eds.), *Invisible Labor: Hidden Work in the Contemporary World* (pp. 28–47). Oakland, CA: University of California Press.

Büscher, M. (2014). Nomadic Work: Romance and Reality. A Response to Barbara Czarniawska's 'Nomadic Work as Life-Story Plot'. *Computer Supported Cooperative Work (CSCW)*, *23*(2), 223–238. https://doi.org/10.1007/s10606-013-9194-6

Büscher, M., Urry, J., & Witchger, K. (2011). Mobile Methods. New York: Routledge.

Cabanas, E., & Illouz, E. (2019). *Manufacturing Happy Citizens: How the Science and Industry of Happiness Control our Lives*. Cambridge: Polity Press.

Casey, E. M. (1997). *The Fate of Place: A Philosophical History*. Berkeley, CA & London: University of California Press.

Castells, M. (2000). *The Rise of the Network Society*. Oxford: Blackwell Publishers.

Cherry, M. A. (2016). Virtual Work and Invisible Labor. In M. Crain, W. R. Poster, & M. A. Cherry (Eds.), *Invisible Labor: Hidden Work in the Contemporary World* (pp. 71–86). Oakland, CA: University of California Press.

Chiang, J. K.-H., & Suen, H.-Y. (2015). Self-Presentation and Hiring Recommendations in Online Communities: Lessons from LinkedIn. *Computers in Human Behavior*, *48*, 516–524. https://doi.org/10.1016/J.CHB.2015.02.017

Ciborra, C. (1992). From Thinking to Tinkering: The Grassroots of Strategic Information Systems. *The Information Society*, *8*(4), 297–309. https://doi.org/10.1080/01972243.1992.9960124

Correll, S. J., Kelly, E. L., O'Connor, L. T., & Williams, J. C. (2014). Redesigning, Redefining Work. *Work and Occupations*, *41*(1), 3–17. https://doi.org/10.1177/0730888413515250

Coupland, C., & Spedale, S. (2020). Agile Identities: Fragile Humans? In *Oxford Handbook of Identities in Organizations* (pp. 833–846). Oxford: Oxford University Press.

Cresswell, T. (2003). Introduction: Theorizing Place. In G. Verstraete & T. Cresswell (Eds.), *Mobilizing Place, Placing Mobility: The Politics of Representation in a Globalizing World* (pp. 11–32). Amsterdam: Rodopi.

Cresswell, T. (2004). *Place: A Short Introduction*. Malden, MA: Blackwell.

D'Mello, M., & Sahay, S. (2007). "I am kind of a nomad where I have to go places and places".... Understanding Mobility, Place and Identity in Global Software Work from India. *Information and Organization*, *17*(3), 162–192. https://doi.org/10.1016/j.infoandorg.2007.04.001

Dalla Costa, M., & Jame, S. (1972). *The Power of Women and the Subversion of the Community*. Falling Wall Press Ltd.

Daniels, A. K. (1987). Invisible Work. *Social Problems*, *34*(5), 403–415. https://doi.org/10.2307/800538

de Carvalho, A. F. P. (2013). *Technologically-mediated Nomadicity in Academic Settings: Tm-N as a Dynamic and Emergent Process. Department of Computer Science and Information Systems*. University of Limerick, Limerick.

de Carvalho, A. F. P. (2014). Collaborative Work and Its Relationship to Technologically-Mediated Nomadicity. In C. Rossitto, L. Ciolfi, D. Martin, & B. Conein (Eds.), *COOP 2014 – Proceedings of the 11th International Conference on the Design of Cooperative Systems* (pp. 209–224). Nice (France): Springer International Publishing. https://doi.org/10.1007/978-3-319-06498-7_13

de Carvalho, A. F. P., Ciolfi, L., & Gray, B. (2011). The Making of Nomadic Work: Understanding the Mediational Role of ICTs. In M. M. Cruz-Cunha & F. Moreira (Eds.), *Handbook of Research on Mobility and Computing: Evolving Technologies and Ubiquitous Impacts* (pp. 381–396). Hershey, PA: IGI Global.

de Carvalho, A. F. P., Ciolfi, L., & Gray, B. (2017). Detailing a Spectrum of Motivational Forces Shaping Nomadic Practices. In *Proceedings of the 2017 ACM Conference on*

Computer Supported Cooperative Work and Social Computing – CSCW '17 (pp. 962–977). https://doi.org/10.1145/2998181.2998313

DeVault, M. L. (2014). Mapping Invisible Work: Conceptual Tools for Social Justice Projects. *Sociological Forum*, *29*(4), 775–790. https://doi.org/10.1111/socf.12119

Donzelot, J. (1991). Pleasure at Work. In G. Burchell, C. Gordon, & P. Miller (Eds.), *The Foucault Effect: Studies in Governmentality* (pp. 251–280). London: Haverster Wheatsheaf.

Duffy, B. E. (2016). The Romance of Work: Gender and Aspirational Labour in the Digital Culture Industries. *International Journal of Cultural Studies*, *19*(4), 441–457. https://doi.org/10.1177/1367877915572186

Duffy, B. E. (2017). *(Not) Getting Paid to Do What You Love: Gender, Social Media, and Aspirational Work*. New Haven, CT: Yale University Press.

Duffy, B. E., & Schwartz, B. (2018). Digital "Women's Work?": Job Recruitment Ads and the Feminization of Social Media Employment. *New Media & Society*, *20*(8), 2972–2989. https://doi.org/10.1177/1461444817738237

Edwards, P. N., Jackson, S. J., Bowker, G. C., & Williams, R. (2009). Introduction: An Agenda for Infrastructure Studies. *Journal of the Association for Information Systems (JAIS)*, *10*(5), 364–374.

Entrikin, J. N. (1997). Place and Region 3. *Progress in Human Geography*, *21*(2), 263–268. https://doi.org/10.1191/030913297677390879

Erickson, I., & Jarrahi, M. H. (2016). Infrastructuring and the Challenge of Dynamic Seams in Mobile Knowledge Work. In *Proceedings of the 19th ACM Conference on Computer-Supported Cooperative Work & Social Computing – CSCW '16* (pp. 1321–1334). New York: ACM Press. https://doi.org/10.1145/2818048.2820015

Erickson, I., Jarrahi, M. H., Thomson, L., & Sawyer, S. (2014). More than Nomads: Mobility, Knowledge Work, and Infrastructure. *EGOS 2014 Subtheme 52: Mobile Work, Technology, and Issues of Control*, 1–20.

Eurostat. (2019). Self-Employed Persons. Retrieved 9 October 2019, from https://ec.europa.eu/eurostat/web/products-eurostat-news/-/EDN-20190430-1

Federici, S. (2004). *Caliban and the Witch: Women, the Body and Primitive Accumulation*. New York: Autonomedia.

Federici, S. (2012). *Revolution at Point Zero: Housework, Reproduction, and Feminist Struggle*. Oakland, CA: PM Press.

Feher, M. (2009). Self-Appreciation; or, The Aspirations of Human Capital. *Public Culture*, *21*(1), 21–41. https://doi.org/10.1215/08992363-2008-019

Fenwick, T. (2010). Re-thinking the "Thing". *Journal of Workplace Learning*, *22*(1/2), 104–116. https://doi.org/10.1108/13665621011012898

Flaherty, M. G. (2003). Time Work: Customizing Temporal Experience. *Social Psychology Quarterly*, *66*(1), 17–33.

Folbre, N. (1991). The Unproductive Housewife: Her Evolution in Nineteenth-Century Economic Thought. *Signs: Journal of Women in Culture and Society*, *16*(3), 463–484. https://doi.org/10.1086/494679

Fortunati, L. (1995). *Arcane of Reproduction: Housework, Prostitution, Labor and Capital*. New York: Autonomedia.

Fortunati, L. (2018). Immaterial Labor. In G. Ritzer (Ed.), *The Blackwell Encyclopedia of Sociology* (pp. 1–2). Oxford: John Wiley & Sons. https://doi.org/10.1002/9781405165518.wbeos1128

Frello, B. (2008). Towards a Discursive Analytics of Movement: On the Making and Unmaking of Movement as an Object of Knowledge. *Mobilities*, *3*(1), 25–50. https://doi.org/10.1080/17450100701797299

Fuchs, C. (2014). *Digital Labour and Karl Marx*. London: Routledge.

Fuchs, C., & Sevignani, S. (2013). What is Digital Labour? What is Digital Work? What's their Difference? And Why Do These Questions Matter for Understanding Social Media? *TripleC*, *11*(2), 237–293. https://doi.org/10.31269/triplec.v11i2.461

Gerson, E. M., & Star, S. L. (1986). Analyzing Due Process in the Workplace. *ACM Transactions on Information Systems*, *4*(3), 257–270. https://doi.org/10.1145/214427.214431

Gill, S., & Bakker, I. (2006). New Constitutionalism and the Social Reproduction of Caring Institutions. *Theoretical Medicine and Bioethics*, *27*(1), 35–57. https://doi.org/10.1007/s11017-005-5756-z

Glennie, P., & Thrift, N. (1996). Reworking E. P. Thompson's "Time, Work-Discipline and Industrial Capitalism". *Time & Society*, *5*(3), 275–299. https://doi.org/10.1177/0961463X96005003001

Gorman, E. H., & Sandefur, R. L. (2011). "Golden Age", Quiescence, and Revival. *Work and Occupations*, *38*(3), 275–302. https://doi.org/10.1177/0730888411417565

Grabham, E. (2014). Legal Form and Temporal Rationalities in UK Work–Life Balance Law. *Australian Feminist Studies*, *29*(79), 67–84. https://doi.org/10.1080/08164649.2014.901280

Gray, B. (2006). Redefining the Nation through Economic Growth and Migration: Changing Rationalities of Governance in the Republic of Ireland? *Mobilities*, *1*(3), 353–372. https://doi.org/10.1080/17450100600916685

Gray, B. (2013). "Generation Emigration": The Politics of (Trans)National Social Reproduction in Twenty-First Century Ireland. *Irish Studies Review*, *21*(1), 20–36. https://doi.org/10.1080/09670882.2012.759707

Gray, B., Ciolfi, L., de Carvalho, A. F. P., D'Andrea, A., & Wixted, L. (2017). Post-Fordist Reconfigurations of Gender, Work and Life: Theory and Practice. *The British Journal of Sociology*, 1–23. https://doi.org/10.1111/1468-4446.12267

Gregg, M. (2011). *Work's Intimacy*. Cambridge: Polity.

Gregg, M. (2018). *Counterproductive: Time Management in the Knowledge Economy*. Durham, NC & London: Duke University Press.

Hampson, I., & Junor, A. (2005). Invisible Work, Invisible Skills: Interactive Customer Service as Articulation Work. *New Technology, Work and Employment*, *20*(2), 166–181. https://doi.org/10.1111/j.1468-005X.2005.00151.x

Hardt, M., & Negri, A. (2000). *Empire*. Cambridge, MA: Harvard University Press.

Harvey, D. (1996). *Justice, Nature, and the Geography of Difference*. Malden, MA & Oxford: Blackwell Publishers.

Hatton, E. (2017). Mechanisms of Invisibility: Rethinking the Concept of Invisible Work. *Work, Employment and Society*, *31*(2), 336–351. https://doi.org/10.1177/0950017016674894

Hochschild, T. R. (2010). "Our Club": Place-Work and the Negotiation of Collective Belongingness. *Journal of Contemporary Ethnography*, *39*(6), 619–645. https://doi.org/10.1177/0891241610378857

Hultin, L. (2019). On Becoming a Sociomaterial Researcher: Exploring Epistemological Practices Grounded in a Relational, Performative Ontology. *Information and Organization*, *29*(2), 91–104. https://doi.org/10.1016/J.INFOANDORG.2019.04.004

Huws, U., Spencer, N. H., & Syrdal, D. S. (2018). Online, On Call: The Spread of Digitally Organised Just-In-Time Working and Its Implications for Standard Employment Models. *New Technology, Work and Employment*, *33*(2), 113–129. https://doi.org/10.1111/ntwe.12111

Hynes, M. (2016). Developing (Tele)work? A Multi-level Sociotechnical Perspective of Telework in Ireland. *Research in Transportation Economics*, *57*, 21–31. https://doi.org/10.1016/J.RETREC.2016.06.008

Illich, I. (1981). *Shadow Work*. Boston, MA: Marion Boyars.

Ingold, T. (2016). On Human Correspondence. *Journal of the Royal Anthropological Institute*, *23*(1), 9–27. https://doi.org/10.1111/1467-9655.12541

Jaggar, A. M. (2013). We Fight for Roses Too: Time-use and Global Gender Justice. *Journal of Global Ethics*, *9*(2), 115–129. https://doi.org/10.1080/17449626.2013.818415

Jarrahi, M. H., Philips, G., Sutherland, W., Sawyer, S., & Erickson, I. (2018). Personalization of Knowledge, Personal Knowledge Ecology, and Digital Nomadism. *The Journal of the Association for Information Science and Technology*, *70*(4), 314–324. https://doi.org/10.1002/asi.24134

Jarrett, K. (2014). The Relevance of "Women's Work": Social Reproduction and Immaterial Labour in Digital Media. *Television & New Media*, *15*(1), 14–29. https://doi.org/10.1177/1527476413487607

Kabachnik, P. (2012). Nomads and Mobile Places: Disentangling Place, Space and Mobility. *Identities*, *19*(2), 210–228. https://doi.org/10.1080/1070289X.2012.672855

Katzman, E. R., & Kinsella, E. A. (2018). 'It's Like Having Another Job': The Invisible Work of Self-Managing Attendant Services. *Disability & Society*, *33*(9), 1436–1459. https://doi.org/10.1080/09687599.2018.1497949

Langfred, C. W., & Rockmann, K. W. (2016). The Push and Pull of Autonomy. *Group & Organization Management*, *41*(5), 629–657. https://doi.org/10.1177/1059601116668971

Lash, S. M., & Urry, J. (1987). *The End of Organized Capitalism*. Cambridge: Polity.

Lash, S. M., & Urry, J. (1994). *Economies of Signs and Space*. London: Sage.

Lévi-Strauss, C. (1966). *The Savage Mind*. Chicago: University of Chicago Press.

Lopata, H. Z. (1971). *Occupation: Housewife*. New York: Oxford University Press.

Malpas, J. (2009). Place and Human Being. *Environmental & Architectural Phenomenology*, *20*(3), 19–23.

Malpas, J. (2012). Putting Space in Place: Philosophical Topography and Relational Geography. *Environment and Planning D: Society and Space*, *30*(2), 226–242. https://doi.org/10.1068/d20810

Mark, G. (2015). Multitasking in the Digital Age. *Synthesis Lectures on Human-Centered Informatics*, *8*(3), 1–113. https://doi.org/10.2200/S00635ED1V01Y201503HCI029

Mark, G., & Su, N. M. (2010). Making Infrastructure Visible for Nomadic Work. *Pervasive and Mobile Computing*, *6*(3), 312–323. https://doi.org/10.1016/J.PMCJ.2009.12.004

Marx, K. (1976). *Capital Volume 1*. London: Pelican.

Massey, D. (1993). Power-Geometry and a Progressive Sense of Place. In T. Putnam, B. Curtis, J. Bird, & L. Tickner (Eds.), *Mapping the Futures: Local Cultures, Global Change* (pp. 60–70). London: Routledge.

Massey, D. (2005). *For Space*. London: SAGE Publications.

McDowell, L. (2012). Post-Crisis, Post-Ford and Post-Gender? Youth Identities in an Era of Austerity. *Journal of Youth Studies*, *15*(5), 573–590. https://doi.org/10.1080/13676261.2012.671933

McRobbie, A. (2002). Clubs to Companies: Notes on the Decline of Political Culture in Speeded Up Creative Worlds. *Cultural Studies*, *16*(4), 516–531. https://doi.org/10.1080/09502380210139098

McRobbie, A. (2010). *Top Girls: Feminismus und der Aufstieg des neolieberalen Geschlechterregimes*. Heidelberg: VS Verlag.

Menzies, H. (1997). Telework, Shadow Work: The Privatization of Work in the New Digital Economy. *Studies in Political Economy*, *53*(1), 103–123. https://doi.org/10.1080/19187033.1997.11675317

Moen, P., Lam, J., Ammons, S., & Kelly, E. L. (2013). Time Work by Overworked Professionals. *Work and Occupations*, *40*(2), 79–114. https://doi.org/10.1177/0730888413481482

Morini, C. (2007). The Feminization of Labour in Cognitive Capitalism. *Feminist Review*, *87*(1), 40–59. https://doi.org/10.1057/palgrave.fr.9400367

Morini, C., & Fumagalli, A. (2010). Life Put to Work: Towards a Life Theory of Value. *Ephemera*, *10*(3/4), 234–252.

Murray, R., Gilbert, J., & Goffey, A. (2015). Post-Post-Fordism in the Era of Platforms: Robin Murray talks to Jeremy Gilbert and Andrew Goffey. *New Formations*, (84/85), 184–208.

Neilson, B., & Rossiter, N. (2005). From Precarity to Precariousness and Back Again: Labour, Life and Unstable Networks. *The Fibreculture Journal*, (5), 10–13.

Nelson, S. B., Jarrahi, M. H., & Thomson, L. (2017). Mobility of Knowledge Work and Affordances of Digital Technologies. *International Journal of Information Management*, *37*(2), 54–62. https://doi.org/10.1016/J.IJINFOMGT.2016.11.008

Nicholls, W. (2009). Place, Networks, Space: Theorising the Geographies of Social Movements. *Transactions of the Institute of British Geographers*, *34*(1), 78–93. https://doi.org/10.1111/j.1475-5661.2009.00331.x

Oakley, A. (2018). *The Sociology of Housework*. Bristol & Chicago: Policy Press.

Orlikowski, W. J. (2007). Sociomaterial Practices: Exploring Technology at Work. *Organization Studies*, *28*(9), 1435–1448. https://doi.org/10.1177/0170840607081138

Orlikowski, W. J., & Scott, S. V. (2008). Sociomateriality: Challenging the Separation of Technology, Work and Organization. *The Academy of Management Annals*, *2*(1), 433–474. https://doi.org/10.1080/19416520802211644

Orr, J. E. (1996). *Taking about Machines: An Ethnography of a Modern Job*. New York: Cornell University Press.

Pauleen, D., Campbell, J., Harmer, B., & Intezari, A. (2015). Making Sense of Mobile Technology. *SAGE Open*, *5*(2), 215824401558385. https://doi.org/10.1177/2158244015583859

Perry, M. (2007). Enabling Nomadic Work: Developing the Concept of 'Mobilisation Work'. In *ECSCW 2007 Workshop Beyond Mobility: Studying Nomadic Work*. Limerick, Ireland.

Perry, M., & Brodie, J. (2006). Virtually Connected, Practically Mobile. In J. H. E. Andriessen & M. Vartiainen (Eds.), *Mobile Virtual Work: A New Paradigm?* (pp. 95–127). Berlin & Heidelberg: Springer. https://doi.org/10.1007/3-540-28365-X_2

Perry, M., O'Hara, K., Sellen, A., Brown, B., & Harper, R. (2001). Dealing with Mobility: Understanding Access Anytime, Anywhere. *ACM Transactions on Computer-Human Interaction (TOCHI)*, *8*(4), 323–347. https://doi.org/10.1145/504704.504707

Pierce, J., Martin, D. G., & Murphy, J. T. (2011). Relational Place-Making: The Networked Politics of Place. *Transactions of the Institute of British Geographers*, *36*(1), 54–70. https://doi.org/10.1111/j.1475-5661.2010.00411.x

Poster, W. R., Crain, M., & Cherry, M. A. (2016a). Conceptualizing Invisible Labor. In M. Crain, W. R. Poster, & M. A. Cherry (Eds.), *Invisible Labor: Hidden Work in the Contemporary World* (pp. 3–27). Oakland, CA: University of California Press.

Poster, W. R., Crain, M., & Cherry, M. A. (2016b). Conclusion. In M. Crain, W. R. Poster, & M. A. Cherry (Eds.), *Invisible Labor: Hidden Work in the Contemporary World* (pp. 279–292). Oakland, CA: University of California Press.

Presskorn-Thygesen, T. (2015). The Possibility of Critique under a Financialized Capitalism: The Case of Private Equity in the United Kingdom. *Ephemera, 725–753*(4), 465–484. https://doi.org/10.1177/1350508414563526

Richardson, L. (2018). Feminist Geographies of Digital Work. *Progress in Human Geography, 42*(2), 244–263. https://doi.org/10.1177/0309132516677177

Rossitto, C. (2009). *Managing Work at Several Places: Understanding Nomadic Practices in Student Groups. KTH Computer Science and Communication Department.* Stockholm University, Stockholm.

Rossitto, C., & Eklundh, K. S. (2007). Managing Work at Several Places: A Case of Project Work in a Nomadic Group of Students. In *Proceedings of the 14th European Conference on Cognitive Ergonomics* (Vol. 250, pp. 45–51). London: ACM. https://doi.org/10.1145/1362550.1362562

Schiller, A., & McMahon, J. (2019). Alexa, Alert Me When the Revolution Comes: Gender, Affect, and Labor in the Age of Home-Based Artificial Intelligence. *New Political Science, 41*(2), 173–191. https://doi.org/10.1080/07393148.2019.1595288

Schmidt, K. (2011). The Concept of "Work" in CSCW. *Computer Supported Cooperative Work (CSCW), 20*(4–5), 341–401. https://doi.org/10.1007/s10606-011-9146-y

Schmidt, K., & Bannon, L. J. (1992). Taking CSCW Seriously. *Computer Supported Cooperative Work (CSCW), 1*(1), 7–40. https://doi.org/10.1007/BF00752449

Sennett, R. (1998). *The Corrosion of Character: The Personal Consequences of Work in the New Capitalism.* New York: Norton & Company.

Sheller, M., & Urry, J. (2006). The New Mobilities Paradigm. *Environment and Planning A, 38*(2), 207–226. https://doi.org/10.1068/a37268

Standing, G. (2011). *The Precariat: The New Dangerous Class.* London: Bloomsbury Academic.

Star, S. L., & Ruhleder, K. (1994). Steps towards an Ecology of Infrastructure: Complex Problems in Design and Access for Large-Scale Collaborative Systems. In *Proceedings of the 1994 ACM Conference on Computer Supported Cooperative Work – CSCW '94* (pp. 253–264). New York: ACM Press. https://doi.org/10.1145/192844.193021

Star, S. L., & Strauss, A. L. (1999). Layers of Silence, Arenas of Voice: The Ecology of Visible and Invisible Work. *Computer Supported Cooperative Work (CSCW), 8*(1–2), 9–30. https://doi.org/10.1023/A:1008651105359

Strauss, A. L. (1985). Work and the Division of Labor. *Sociological Quarterly, 26*(1), 1–19. https://doi.org/10.1111/j.1533-8525.1985.tb00212.x

Strauss, A. L. (1993). *Continual Permutations of Action.* New York: Aldine de Gruyter.

Su, N. M., & Mark, G. (2008). Designing for Nomadic Work. In *Proceedings of the 7th ACM Conference on Designing Interactive Systems – DIS '08* (pp. 305–314). Cape Town, South Africa: ACM Press. https://doi.org/10.1145/1394445.1394478

Suchman, L. (1995). Making Work Visible. *Communications of the ACM, 38*(9), 56–64. https://doi.org/10.1145/223248.223263

Suchman, L. (2007). *Human-Machine Reconfigurations: Plans and Situated Actions* (2nd ed.). Cambridge: Cambridge University Press. https://doi.org/10.1002/asi.20714

Taylor, S., & Luckman, S. (2018). Collection Introduction: The "New Normal" of Working Lives. In S. Taylor & S. Luckman (Eds.), *The New Normal of Working Lives.*

Critical Studies in Contemporary Work and Employment (pp. 1–15). Milton Keynes, UK: Palgrave Macmillan.

Thompson, J. B. (2011). Shifting Boundaries of Public and Private Life. *Theory, Culture & Society, 28*(4), 49–70. https://doi.org/10.1177/0263276411408446

Thrift, N. (1998). Steps to an Ecology of Place. In D. Massey, J. Allen, & P. Sarre (Eds.), *Human Geography Today* (pp. 295–322). Cambridge: Polity.

Tokumitsu, M. (2014). In the Name of Love. *Jacobin.* Retrieved from www.jacobinmag.com/2014/01/in-the-name-of-love/

Tremblay, D.-G., & Genin, E. (2010). IT Self-Employed Workers between Constraint and Flexibility. *New Technology, Work and Employment, 25*(1), 34–48. https://doi.org/10.1111/j.1468-005X.2009.00237.x

Tremblay, D.-G., & Genin, É. (2007). The Demand for Telework of IT Self-Employed Workers. *The Journal of E-Working*, 1(2), 98–115.

Tuan, Y.-F. (1977). *Space and Place: The Perspective of Experience*. Minneapolis, MN: University of Minnesota Press.

Urry, J. (2000). *Sociology Beyond Societies*. London: Routledge.

Urry, J. (2007). *Mobilities*. Cambridge: Polity.

Wajcman, J. (2015). *Pressed for Time: The Acceleration of Life in Digital Capitalism.* Chicago & London: University of Chicago Press.

Weeks, K. (2007). Life within and Against Work: Affective Labor, Feminist Critique, and Post-Fordist Politics. *Ephemera, 7*(1), 233–249.

Wessels, B. (2018). Virtual Exchange-Based Mobilities: Platform Economy, Exchange and Culture. *Applied Mobilities, 3*(1), 51–65. https://doi.org/10.1080/23800127.2018.1435438

Chapter 2

Cities and regions in the placing of worklives

> In [the city centre] we were on three floors, so sometimes you wouldn't even see people. Whereas here, we're all on the ground floor (...). We have an awful lot more interaction with ourselves since we moved here. And the whole work ethic is a lot better because people can have a cup of coffee, they're talking about what's going on (...). And I think that's a very good thing (...). This would have been our third or fourth move over the last 25 years, and this out here is the last move. (...) The Technology Park was one part of it [reason for moving], but if the name 'Technology Park' and association with the college (...) was one part of it (...) in reality it was just for convenience.
>
> (Jerry, ICTM)

For Jerry (CEO of a software distribution firm, married, with two children of primary school age) workplace spatial and locational arrangements support professional collaboration and social relationships, to 'get things done'. These arrangements also do reputational work by virtue of placing the company in a well-reputed area of the city (the Technology Park) linked to business and innovation, close to the university and other high-tech firms. In this chapter, and in the one that follows, we unpack the ways in which MKWrs engage in and with places (globally, regionally and locally) so that they are made to work, in a constant, evolving process of place making, negotiation and reconfiguration. Characteristics of MKW (as discussed in Chapter 1), including de-institutionalisation, individual responsibility for when/where to work, technologically mediated work and reliance on infrastructural resources such as power and connectivity, all shape how place and emplacement are constituted and experienced. In this chapter, we provide a textured account of the corollary work of placing worklives in relation to cities and regions. We unpack this through two themes: the relational and reputational work of places, and their agentic role in making quality worklives.

The participants in our study are geographically situated in a regional city area in Ireland, and occupy locations such as hubs, offices, homes, as well as many 'third-places' such as cafés (Oldenburg, 1999) and transitional places (trains, hotels, airports, etc.) in their everyday worklives. These places at various scales feature in the participants' accounts not simply as backdrops to, or 'containers' for their activities and social relationships, but as enmeshed in how MKWlives are made. Participants do considerable work both to overcome the limitations and to build on the opportunities of where they are based, and to make good and manageable worklives for themselves in these locations. Through this work, places such as the city and region are made to work by MKWrs not only to 'get things done' in their worklives, but also to place themselves in relation to the culture and rhetoric of MKW as mobile, agile and flexible, and to other places, other cities and other worklives.

The constitution of place and emplacement at any scale relies on practices, concerns and relationships, including managing physical mobility, choosing or avoiding certain places to work and live, place considerations in interaction with clients, competitors and collaborators, as well as with family and friends. The ways in which place is constituted and lived locally and regionally are also shaped by an increasingly globalised worklife outlook (e.g. considerations of international long- and short-term relocations, working with geographically distributed collaborators, etc.). Contra static relationships between spaces and locations and practices and cultural understandings, or static work/home, leisure, divisions, we see place as continuously constructed at different degrees of scale and in relation to flows of artefacts, bodies and knowledge (Malpas, 2012). Therefore, 'context is itself mobilized, or performed, through ongoing sociotechnical and cultural practices' (Sheller, 2014, pp. 793–794). Massey sees places as 'bundles' of space-time trajectories drawn together through cognitive and emotional processes (Massey, 2005, p. 119). It is out of these processual bundles that the ephemeral and impermanent nature of place arises (ibid.). These *placebundles* are socially negotiated, constantly changing and contingent (Kabachnik, 2012): 'temporary constellations' (Massey, 2005, p. 141) that have purpose and meaning, but that may be reconfigured when viewed from other perspectives (Kabachnik, 2012, p. 5). These intra-active sociomaterial negotiations and reconfigurations of physical, cultural, social and emotional landscapes constitute the corollary work that enables place to be inhabited and imagined by MKWrs.

Based on an understanding of place as processual (Frello, 2008; Kabachnik, 2012; Massey, 1993; Urry, 2007) rather than static and bounded, places and place relationships emerge as relational and socially negotiated, constantly changing and contingent, and worked in support of worklife practices (Agnew, 1987). These practices include the headquartering of businesses, the configuration of workplaces, the establishment of long- and short-term relationships, sustaining family and local relationships, dovetailing work with caring activities, all of which give meaning to places at the scale of cities and regions, and therefore constitute these places as meaningful. The quote opening this chapter shows how crucial such considerations of place are for Jerry: company location, workplace design and co-location with others (or lack thereof) are important in terms of the ways in which his organisation operates. Place is also particularly significant in positioning the company and communicating its identity in relation to both regional and global aspirations. As such, place concerns and place making are enmeshed in the planning, management and agency of daily worklife. This happens in interaction and negotiation with other worklife places such as the local community, friendship networks, home, schools and transitional places (Massey, 2005; Thrift, 1998; Urry, 2000). Although place considerations are often backgrounded and the work that goes into addressing them is frequently rendered invisible, they play a central part in the worklives of contemporary MKWrs, with different emphasis and consideration depending on the circumstances (e.g. professional or personal concerns). Understanding place as process is therefore not just about studying how specific places come into being, but rather how they are never-endingly 'becoming' (Frello, 2008, p. 25) in people's worklives. Place, seen as process, does not just denote 'discrete physical territories but as an interlocking bricolage of (always partially) shared place understandings' (Pierce, Martin, & Murphy, 2011 p. 57), therefore assuming the continuous intra-action of various sociomaterial agencies.

Furthermore, the participants' accounts narrate a 'global sense of place' (Massey, 1994) that connects 'the local of a neighbourhood to national territories to an awareness of an interlinked, global environment' (ibid.). Place, understood as processual and relational, emerges in terms of mobility and motility (potential mobility) (Büscher, Urry, & Witchger, 2011; Kaufmann, Bergman, & Joye, 2004; Sheller & Urry, 2006) in relation to the local area and to other cities and regions. Indeed, movement is itself an essential constituent of place, as well as an experiential aspect of it (Thrift, 1996). For Ingold, 'places are formed through movement (…). There could be no places were it not for the comings and goings of human beings (…). Instead of saying that living beings exist in places, I would (…) say that places occur along the life paths of beings' (2008, p. 1799). Rhythms of moving are constantly interwoven into places (Edensor, 2010; Lefebvre, 2004). For example, Edensor argues that 'a human, whether stationary or travelling, is one rhythmic constituent in a seething space pulsing with intersecting trajectories and temporalities' (Edensor, 2010, p. 71). Such intersections of spatialities, temporalities and bodies make for configurations of interactions, or – in David Seamon's words – 'choreographies' producing 'place ballets' (Seamon, 1980).

If we argue that place and its very emergence are bound to movement and to the possibility of movement, then the importance of place in mobile worklives, and particularly in relation to locating one's worklife, becomes paramount. This involves expanding our conception of place both as 'roots' (i.e. places bound to and emerging from individual biographies, experiences and emotions, and local social networks), and as 'routes', i.e. places emerging through connectivity, relationships, motility and mobility (Clifford, 1997; Gustafson, 2001). In any one individual worklife, collections of places differently experienced as rooting, mooring and routing come together in an unstable, ever emerging assemblage. This conception of place enables an analysis of MKWrs' corollary work as it sensitises us to the work involved in how constellations of places emerge, evolve, and how they are managed, understood, shared, negotiated, felt and appropriated via continuous sociomaterial reconfigurations. This corollary 'work to make place work' is processual, relational and embodied.

All three cohorts in our study account for places and place making 'from the armchair to the nation' (Tuan, 1977) as part of their MKW practices: homes, rooms, offices, corporate venues and meeting rooms, neighbourhoods, cities, regions, Ireland and other countries of the globe all feature in their accounts. In the following sections we examine how our participants place their worklives globally, regionally and locally, and illuminate two themes: the continuous relational and reputational work to do with placing worklives, and the work in relation to ensuring worklife quality in place. We compare and draw parallels as appropriate among the three participating cohorts. In the following chapter our discussion of place moves to those local and localised sociomaterial practices of making place in the everyday accomplishment of MKW.

Relational and reputational work in placing worklives

The work of placing one's worklife in the city and region involves a reflexive relationship to self and emplacement. The city and region are made to work through worklife *relational* considerations that are often affective; the *reputational* capital attached to specific places; place relationships in terms of *connectedness* (linked to transport and digital networks as well as specific localised networks) and *imagined alternative* emplacements; as well as *rootedness* (cultural and geographical) via localised family, friendship and leisure activities.

The reputation of the city and region, their branding and how they compare with other cities in Ireland and internationally are main actors and concerns. The participants account for place and placement in relation to business and brand development opportunities locally and elsewhere, for example, by comparing the city (referring to the study city) to other cities, and particularly Dublin (more cosmopolitan, business friendly, proud of itself, etc.).

> When you take other cities such as [City1] (…) you've got a very different (…) branded umbrella, (…) a cohesive mindset in the people up there around successful companies (…) and similar to in [City2]. And I think in Enterprise Ireland's mindset [City1] has taken a direction, [City2] has taken a direction, and I don't think [Enterprise Ireland] have in their mindset that, yes, [our city] is a hub of software development (…). *We're not as inclined as we should be compared to other city regions in Ireland*, we're not as inclined as we should be to exaggerate what we're good at.
>
> (Dean, DC)

Dean (web developer, in his late 30s, married, with one 4-year-old daughter) has a clear view of how being based in another city could mean additional strength in terms of both identity and brand, and related business opportunities. He argues that such self-branding has not been achieved in his city due to a combination of a pre-existing local mindset, and a failure by Enterprise Ireland to support its development. In his account, Dean details the work he is doing to promote his business locally but also nationally, while remaining based in the city. For Dean, developing such place-related brand is important and also something to make the city more competitive and willing to be compared to others.

Earl is a digital creative in his 20s who owns a digital design start-up through which he is supporting himself economically. He is unmarried and has no children. He has never lived anywhere except in the study city, i.e. his home city; he dreams of making his business solid in the next two years, and then maybe relocating elsewhere. When he talks about his future plans, he describes his ideas about potentially growing the business, but also the imagined (and desirable) places he might move to. Earl states that he can do his job as a designer anywhere, 'even on a beach, as long as there is an internet connection'. He suggests that his business may be challenged by his decision to remain in the city by comparison with what a friend in the same line of business is experiencing in Dublin:

> There's a friend of mine (...) working in a marketing company in Dublin, and maybe he's just sugar coating everything but from what I hear (...) it's just an amazingly cool job (...) and he's given loads of opportunities and stuff and it's just something that I've never experienced in [our city] (...) I just think that certain *people have a certain mindset here* (...) 'this is how it's done and this is how it will be done and we can't kind of break away from that'.
>
> (Earl, DC)

Earl's account highlights the relational, emotional and practical aspects of place that come from remaining rooted locally, despite being aware of the obstacles. There is a provincial mindset linked to the place that is difficult to change:

> [Home city] is great, and (...) the art scene has (...) boomed in the past three years really. There's a lot of things going on (...) there's still a major problem about getting just the average punter in the street involved because (...) most of them don't know about it....
>
> (Earl, DC)

Comparing with his Dublin-based friend, he remarks on the difficulties of mobilising people into the arts. Earl, however, is optimistic about his business, and he admits that remaining local is good for him in terms of sustaining hobbies and relationships with friends, who also send work his way. Earl does not have long-term plans (five years plus) for himself or his business but admits that he might move at some point, although he has not thought about where: 'ideally (...) I'd like to have an office base, I don't know where that would be in the world though, but again there's nothing exclusive that says the person who's working for me has to be sitting in the same room as me' (Earl, DC).

Placing oneself and one's worklife involves the work of making decisions about moving or staying, considering the opportunities and challenges that each choice offers, while simultaneously recognising the myriad agencies, connections and mutual relationships that link places. Staying local is as much the result of reflexivity and negotiation as moving is. Reflexivity is a critical stance towards both the self and a whole set of issues to do with one's economic and social context (Adkins, 2004; Popoveniuc, 2014). In Earl's example, while his decision is to remain local for a while, he continuously reflects on the reasons for this, and on the possibilities potentially available elsewhere. Part of this work is also reconsidering one's location in light of emerging opportunities as shaped by national and global trends. Relationships with other places are framed comparatively but equally in terms of connections, business or social relationships. The potential to move, to act on connections and on motility becomes a resource (such as it is for Earl). The ways in which the participants describe their locatedness highlights the 'character of places as always interconnected with other places (such interconnection [is] evident in both the embeddedness of places in other places as well as the implication of places with other places through their mutual locatedness)' (Malpas, 2012, p. 229).

Participants discuss their reasons for being based in the city area. These reasons go from local family support, to professional opportunities, as we will see in further detail later in this chapter. However, several accounts express a view of the city as peripheral and provincial, with respect to both other cities and regions of Ireland (as we saw in both Dean's and Earl's cases), as well as cities abroad that are marketed as quintessential 'hotbeds' for the 'creative class' (Peck, 2005): 'no, *it's not a San Francisco*' (Arthur, DC).

Other participants in both the ICTM and DC cohorts expressed concerns about their city location as not prestigious enough, although they justify why it was chosen (e.g. job availability, spouse's preference, etc.) as well as its qualities or advantages (e.g. good quality of life, presence of a social support network, etc.), which counterbalance its peripheral status to a certain extent. The perceived weight of locations, cities and regions in the global landscape of high-tech work was evident across these two cohorts. For example, Arthur (DC in his early 30s, married without children) goes on to give some practical reasons for his decision to remain in the city. The main one is the presence of the Innovation Hub, currently supporting him as he develops his start-up through the High Potential Start-Ups (HPSUs) innovation programme. His choice of place to live in the area (in a small town close to the city) is also described in comparative terms:

> We're in [nearby town] because I wanted to be on this side of [the city], so if I had to go to work in Dublin or fly (…) from Dublin or whatever (…). So we're living out near [town], it's not like a particularly great spot.
>
> (Arthur, DC)

Arthur's main reason for living where he does is the easier access to Dublin. The town is a better-connected place in the greater city area in terms of Arthur's mobility priorities, and enables him reasonable proximity to likeminded colleagues, networked knowledge and expert resources. The relationality of place is particularly evident in Arthur's account, which emphasises the many implications, connections and possibilities affecting where to place himself as well as how this location enables him to travel and connect. Arthur puts great effort into considering and weighing these. His key concern is being based in a networked, well-connected place, which was not chosen for its cultural attractiveness or its global profile.

Despite the concerns to do with the peripheral status of the city, participants from the digital creative and ICT manager cohorts are also conscious of what the place has to offer, and the high-tech development areas of the city played the most significant role for participants from industry in terms of choosing where to be located. The Technology Park, the Innovation Hub, the university and the Institute of Technology all play important roles in the worklives of our participants, in terms of offering opportunities and in support of their professional goals. High-tech and innovation hubs are developed by public and private investment supporting economic development in the region. Although less advanced than in the capital city Dublin, these resources provide a multi-institutional infrastructure for early stage companies and the self-employed. The Technology Park and Innovation Hub are associated with a drive for entrepreneurship, and the innovation potential of higher education institutions is seen as enabling of certain kinds of career trajectories. For example, the innovative image of the Technology Park is one of the factors for Jerry's company to relocate there (as we saw in the opening quote in this chapter). Organisations increasingly think of themselves in relation to how catchment regions are represented and what they signify for workers' 'ground-level organizational labour required to make the company region happen' (Laurier & Philo, 2003, p. 87). Therefore, locations such as technology parks become places that are 'made to work'; places that organisations and their workers actively shape and contribute to, and that in turn help define and promote their brand. The Innovation Hub, Technology Park, University and Institute of Technology are invested by values of 'entrepreneurial power': they denote prestige and represent a business attitude to innovation, speed, flexibility and creativity. In the participants' accounts these business locations were often sought because they signal these qualities to clients, investors and stakeholders:

> [Moved to the Technology Park] to be associated with technology. I just felt I would like to come in here because *it was having the address of the Technology Park* (...) it would give us a bit of an umph (...). Number two, *it suited.* I live in [nearby town] (...) and it suited a number of people as well (...). If you go to [industrial estate], as an example, it's just very, very closed-in and the companies are on top of each other. Whereas out here (...) it's less density out here, and you look out the windows here and *it's very conducive to work*, and this particular building became available and *it was a lift from our own point as a company*, which got us motivated as well.
>
> (Jared, ICTM)

The considerations behind Jared's decision to locate his company in the Technology Park include: the association with high-tech, convenience for staff, spatial layout of the park, availability of a building that 'lifted' it to the next level, and an environment conducive to work. His account describes the several considerations worked around in placing himself and the company, including: good layout, the right facilities, its relationship to other locations important to workers, its profile and reputation, and its productivity-enhancing and organisation-enhancing environment. Locating one's worklife is a key aspect of making a place work when 'such multiple and intersecting mobilities seem to produce a more 'networked' patterning of economic and social life, even for those who have not moved' (Hannam et al., 2006, p. 3).

Concerns about being in a peripheral location were not voiced as much by the academics. Due to the limited size and increased precariousness of the academic job market, the opportunity to take up an academic job was deemed an attraction enough to motivate people to either stay where they are (i.e. holding on to a university position they obtained after years of short-term contracts), or to move, even internationally (particularly for those who are single and without dependents):

> I am a nomad. I came here to Ireland because I could find the resources for my academic career that I couldn't find in [my home country]. It's because I had set my mind to have this academic career. I couldn't do it there, so I found the resources here. *I planted myself here.*
>
> (Claus, A)

For Claus (full-time lecturer, single, in his mid-30s), the university is not only the place where he found work, but also where he found the resources to realise the kind of career he wanted. His relationship to the university, the region and Ireland is framed in terms of making the most of what is offered – he uses the term 'planting' in relation to himself, as if his professional survival, growth and realisation grew from the place itself.

After working in several European countries, Shannon (full-time lecturer, early 50s, cohabiting with partner, with two adult children from a previous relationship) relocated to the city in order to work with a renowned professor whose reputation was the main reason why Shannon considered moving to Ireland. In the case of Tom (full-time research assistant, mid-40s), the motivating forces behind leaving his native USA were both the prestige of the research group offering the position and the perception of Ireland (a country he had not considered before) as an English-speaking country that might enable easy integration: 'technically a foreign country but (…) more or less they speak my language, so I thought it would be an easier transition to integrate' (Tom, A). In Tom's case, placing himself emerged from a promise of academic reputation and the hope of a manageable worklife in a new country.

The work that MKWrs do to make and operate in places such as the Technology Park, the Innovation Hub, or the conferences and meetings that the academics mentioned as key to their networking, is not just about a good fit in terms of facilities and geographical location, but also in terms of building a community and sharing a certain mindset and working style: 'the great thing with the [Innovation Hub] is that you're *surrounded by people (...) that are all about "living the dream"* kinda thing. So *to be around that actually is very invigorating* as well' (Kathy, DC). For many participants in the DC cohort, such as Kathy (DC in her early 30s, unmarried with no children), location in the Innovation Hub is also a way to counter the limitations of living and working at the periphery of the high-tech world: 'there's not really many people here in [the city], really in the overall scheme of things. You'd find them in buildings like this. *This (...) would be the place to find everybody*' (Arthur, DC). Arthur refers to 'people' meaning colleagues in the same line of business (high-tech start-ups). He and his business being in the Innovation Hub with them is not just about doing the work, but joining and contributing to a community of 'movers and shakers', fully embracing the culture of high-tech entrepreneurship.

Placing in relation to other MKWrs is also about that location (in this case the Innovation Hub) as an enabler of an enterprise-related identity. Place in this sense also 'serves as an aesthetic good for consumption and distinction' (Liegl, 2014, p. 170). While 'being associated with the hip neighborhood in a happening city is indispensable for self-fashioning and self-marketing of creatives and their products' (ibid.), in this case, the association is with sections of a regional city that carry the brand of entrepreneurial drive and innovation.

Innovation hubs support business development and help start-ups to build on the economic strengths of the urban region (in this case, software development). By being in an innovation hub, many of the digital creatives worked with Hub staff to collaboratively engage in place-related strategic planning and branding, with location in the hub itself sending out signals of innovation, dedication and of aiming for success. The relational and processual aspects of place making and emergence are perhaps most evident in this context. This means that corollary work in and around place is continuously occurring as part of the relationship between MKWrs, their locations and the broader political and reputational issues associated with these locations. This relational place making and reputational work helps to counteract the small, peripheral city location through those narratives of innovation that attach to the Technology Park, and broader networks linking innovation hubs across Ireland and beyond. As reputation building is recognised as a central feature of MKW (Arvidsson, Gandini, & Bandinelli, 2016; Gandini, 2016), self-branding and marketing are increasingly integral drivers of the work to make place work. For example, Arthur's resistance to his location in a smaller, regional city is partly countered by his upfront confrontation of its limitations. Yet, Arthur suggests that this does not diminish his personal determination to succeed, to make a mark on the place as a digital entrepreneur, to connect and be visible to others locally and nationally.

However, the productivity-driven and competitive mindset embedded in places such as the Innovation Hub does not accommodate all start-ups equally. Gender emerged as a significant factor in Betty's (DC, married, with two young daughters) account. Although assigned an office, Betty did not use it as much as other members of the Innovation Hub due to her childcare responsibilities. This led to the head of the HPSU innovation programme confronting her on the subject:

> So I had a few shouts with [Head of Programme] and he was giving out to [scolding] me because I wasn't at the office. And I said, 'I explained I wasn't going to be at the office that often'. 'Well, you can't keep it'. 'But – I said – it is part of the programme that you can have it'. 'Oh no, with so many people that want this office and this desk and *it will be perceived that you're not working, not dedicated*', and I said, 'I am, I'm working over 40 hours a week at home but I have to mind my children'. And he says to me, 'Oh you shouldn't mention children'.
>
> (Betty, DC)

Provision of an office is one of the key benefits of the HPSU innovation programme, and the programme head sees presence in the office as an indicator of full dedication to the spirit of business acceleration. It is more than a place to work, it signals commitment and driven entrepreneurship. Betty claimed her right to the office, while the programme head used it as a currency to push her to be there all the time, despite her care responsibilities. While Betty sees it as a resource to use when possible, he sees the office as a 'prize' location that requires embodied presence as a signal of total commitment to the programme and to all it represents. This clash with the programme head negatively affected Betty's experience on the programme. As a woman with young children she felt that her dedication to her start-up was undermined. Betty's place making is highly relational insofar as it involves concomitant commitments to her young children and to her start-up company. She found herself using the office less and less. Her inability to achieve the level of presence required by the Hub manager gave rise to a conflict around where she conducted her work. As a result, her work commitment was questioned and she found herself unable to fulfil the place-related evidence of commitment that was required. In the example of Betty and the programme head we see how the 'affective experience of *locatedness* – of being *here* – is iteratively created and recreated through social and political processes, which work to define and make specific places' (Pierce et al., 2011) in gendered ways. The reputational work to do with placing oneself is also gendered in this case as working from home to facilitate childcare means that Betty is seen by the manager as not in the same league as the other programme members. The place of the home is devalued as a workplace because of its association with the feminised practice of care.

These instances of the corollary work to place their worklives in the city and region show the complexity of relational considerations of place as 'roots' (where to be based, which resources can be drawn on, etc.) and as 'routes' (comparing other places, managing spatial connectivity, developing a place-related reputation perceived externally, etc.) (Gustafson, 2001).

Cities, regions and quality of worklife

Participants also locate themselves in the city and region in relation to a desired and manageable worklife style. Considerations include supporting the career of a partner, taking care of family, enjoying a personalised relationship to the region, the involvement in sporting or other leisure activities locally. Many participants remarked on how they and their businesses could be located anywhere and could be globally mobile, but they also highlighted how rootedness (cultural and geographical) can be key to living good worklives. A reason for choosing to develop one's business locally is the availability of an accessible network of business contacts. Earl, for example, values 'feeling at home' in the city, and word-of-mouth connections means that he is kept very busy professionally, and even had to turn down jobs, although he has not yet officially launched his business and has no other form of promotion (such as a website).

While some (including Earl) imagine other careers in other places, they made a conscious decision to be in the city area because of social, or community ties and opportunities, family relations, or lifestyle – all these contributing to a desired worklife style. For example, ICT manager, Damien (co-owner and managing director of a software development and consulting company, in a relationship but not co-habiting, no children) explained why he set up his own business and settled in the city, after years working for other high-tech companies. He wanted to work for himself, and wanted to be somewhere with a good network of social relationships. He mentions how in the past he has turned down well-paid jobs to remain closer to his family and friends:

> Before I started [software development company], I was offered a job down in [City1] writing software. And another position came up here for less money. And it was less money and (…) close to home and close to my friends (…) I (…) much *prefer to be close to my friends and people that mattered to me than to be in a foreign city earning more money.*
>
> (Damien, ICTM)

Damien is happy with this decision and enthusiastic about the future of his company. However, he is also keenly aware of how being located where he is contrasts with other possibilities, other places, other lifestyles:

> You asked which is more important, *money or location (...). For me it's a case of location (…).* But to be honest, I know one guy now who would actually be back and forth between Ireland and (…) Singapore, but he runs his own business and (…) he'd be travelling (…) around Europe (…) and even over to the States (…). He's the guy who started up the company (…) R&D is done here in Europe, then they've moved now R&D over to Romania where they have the team of highly qualified engineers (…) working on a certain aspect of the software. He then has his facilities over in Singapore whereby

> he would get prototypes done up. He then takes his prototypes (…) to the likes of [multinational] over in Norway, demos them there, then they might have a conference showcasing the stuff in Barcelona, but then they could be over in the States meeting potential investors. *But the guy is always travelling, always on his laptop.*
>
> (Damien, ICTM)

It is clear that Damien deems being close to his friends more important than money and a 'global' lifestyle. Yet, his description of another self-employed MKWr who works across several countries suggests an imagined alternative worklife. Damien paints a rich picture of what this mobile and multi-located lifestyle is like. Damien's work of placing himself consciously forfeited any of the benefits of global mobility by locating himself geographically close to friends and family. This is accompanied by ongoing reflections regarding alternative places and potential other worklives. The alternatives might be exciting and successful ('he's doing that for himself because it's his own business'), but Damien is not willing to take on the costs. His worklife style is lived in relation to what the competition is doing, of the kind of fast-paced and global business activity that might set the pace for his company too. As such, those relationships that fall 'beyond the limits of particular places' shape his life as well (Massey, 2004). Potential is not always worth realising by opening up one's life to long-distance mobility and multi-location when they contrast with a desired, more rooted, worklife style. Other participants mentioned the affordability of the area in relation to suitability for one's work: 'somewhere *where we could work the way we wanted to work and still be able to afford to (…) buy groceries*' (Sara, DC, married, with no children). Frequently mentioned were the networks of family and friends located nearby that enable participants to have a job while also having support, be it childcare, or social opportunities, or hobbies. For Charles (CEO of a software firm, married, with two children under ten), being based in a smaller village is mainly motivated by wanting a family-friendly worklife style:

> Obviously, it doesn't suit everyone, but for me *it is just perfect. Because lifestyle-wise, we live in a fantastic area, and school-wise, there is no traffic, school is around the corner literally, and it is a wonderful community for living.* And for the purposes of work, I find that the advantages outweigh any disadvantages, *our client base is everywhere.* This means we can provide support for them, not practically 24 hours, but I can respond to support an issue at 11 p.m., having the ability to do that.
>
> (Charles, ICTM)

Charles' decision of placing himself outside a city is based on the advantages of working from home as it makes him even more flexible to deal with external demands, especially those of family. Charles does not see his work suffering: he relies on his company being based in the Technology Park, and being connected at home almost 24 hours a day enables him to communicate with his co-workers and to be very responsive to client requests.

For Aoife (part-time lecturer, married, with one baby born during the period of our study), family considerations shape her decision to live in Dublin and commute to the city on her working days at the university. When she was working full-time, Aoife and her husband lived locally in the city, with him teleworking for his company in Dublin. Now that Aoife works part-time, they are based in Dublin so that it is easier for her husband to pursue his business career full-time. For Aoife and her husband, where to live (in this city vs. Dublin) and where to work (commuting vs. telework) were affected by the focus on their careers, rather than by aspiring to be in a certain city. Placing themselves also means considering the manageability of their respective worklives and the working arrangements offered by their employers.

In Maeve's case (full-time lecturer, single mother), working at the university is not as much about wanting to be based in the city, but rather part of her lifelong aspiration to live a worklife that is different to that of the rural and remote place of her birth:

> I am from a tiny island off the coast of Ireland (…) and (…) *you either left the island or you stay with the traditional things, which I had absolutely no interest in doing* (…) I love the place, for me it is still home, and I suppose all the other houses I have lived in since then, they have never really constituted them the same way, the way of place.
>
> (Maeve, A)

While Maeve loves her home village, pursuing her career and living a lifestyle different from the 'traditional things' that come with being in that isolated place, has meant locating herself in a university city. There is a tension in Maeve's account regarding place and quality and desirability of worklife style: she is not living somewhere she loves and considers home; instead, she is somewhere that might not inspire the same feelings but where the worklife that she desires is possible.

Some experienced workers in the three cohorts have moved to the city area from other parts of Ireland and from abroad to work for companies in the Technology Park, or at the university. While we have seen that for some (such as academics like Tom, Shannon and Claus) the main reason was to take up a good job offer, for others moving was about quality of life in Ireland:

> I (…) have Irish roots, and I had been coming over for years, and I'm an amateur horseman in my spare time, and of course, Ireland is just heaven on Earth for people who own and train horses. So (…) I decided that I would pack up myself and my horses and move to Ireland. I had no family (…). Nothing that would have tied me down. I had cash in my pocket and decided *I would go and be a horseman in a country where a horseman is greatly respected* (…)

> I've loved every minute of it in Ireland. About five years ago (...) I became an Irish citizen (...). And really have no intentions of ever leaving Ireland.
>
> (Martin, ICTM)

For Martin (CTO of a manufacture design company, unmarried, originally from the USA), moving to Ireland is about achieving the worklife style he desires. He has many years' experience working successfully for high-tech companies in the United States, however his passion, and the quality of life he would have in Ireland as a horseman, propelled his (now permanent) move. Martin's placing centres on supporting this passion: he is living in a village near the equestrian centre, and he works extensively from home so that he can go riding whenever he has an opportunity. Place is made to work in Martin's worklife chiefly in support of his leisure pursuits.

For others, coming to Ireland might have been opportunistic, but being there has proven to be a positive experience. Betty has lived in several different countries throughout her life. She has never stayed in one place long, and never planned where she would settle long term:

> I never knew what country I was going to be in from one year to another (...) so I don't know; do I have visions [*sic*] for that? I'm kind of easy-going (...) *I want to work and this is lovely (...) I just want a steady comfortable life, that's really it.* (...). Even though I would be more than happy to travel. If my husband said 'I've got a contract in China, Japan, Australia' or whatever, I'd say 'Yes, fine, let's go'.
>
> (Betty, DC)

While she has had some difficult situations to deal with (such as the conflict with the innovation programme head discussed earlier), Betty is happy where she is: she can do her work, and have a comfortable life. She might not feel strongly rooted to the place and would be willing to move again, but for now she is somewhere that suits her both professionally and personally, and lives a manageable worklife.

Making places work is also about imagined futures – for business, productivity or personal and family realisation. For some of our younger respondents, such as Noel (DC, in his late 20s, unmarried, with no children), it is about imagining potential worklives. Noel is establishing himself firmly in the path of a highly mobile, highly digitally engaged knowledge worker, living globally and at speed:

> I would love to be on the road a lot of the time (...) I don't want lots of structure but I'd want to know that maybe one or two days a week I'm in Dublin (...) or I have to fly to London for a training event or something like that. *I'll go anywhere* (...) as far as I'm concerned Ireland has no real attraction to me. I want to be selling something via website or providing a service

> for your website to sell to the UK and America, particularly America. Ireland is so small and anyone who (…) has set up businesses in Ireland, they are all focused on the [local] market you know, it's nuts (…) *I would strive to be as absolutely mobile as possible.*
>
> (Noel, DC)

Noel's aspiration is to live a high-mobility worklife, and he is not just about establishing himself locally, but planning a future global and connected lifestyle with extensive physical mobility within Ireland, and even placing himself in countries that are bigger and offering more opportunity.

For all these participants, worklife horizons are located very much within the place they are in and what it enables or prevents them from doing. They all describe the work they do to both activate the opportunities place offers (i.e. the potential for a friendly, healthy lifestyle) and counterbalance its possible limitations (i.e. need for careful branding in relation to the place, travel to other locations, long-term plans with possible relocations, etc.). This is done in reflexive negotiation with imagined worklives elsewhere or in the future.

Undertaking long-distance travel and working from abroad are also affected by considerations of worklife style (i.e. career stage and family circumstances) that affect openness to long-distance travel. There are also differences among cohorts regarding the need and the willingness to travel away for longer distances. Medium- and long-distance physical mobility is not a pressing requirement for some of the participants. For example, while the digital creatives work mainly locally (due to the early stages of their businesses and the limited resources they have available), the young men imagine a lifestyle of frequent travel (such as in Earl, Noel and Arthur's cases). For academics, medium- and long-distance mobility is varied: a few commute to work (such as Aoife), some travel abroad for projects or conferences, others prefer not to. This is similar to ICT managers, with some important individual differences to discuss.

Jared does substantial and regular long-distance travel. He is engaged in a number of international projects requiring trips abroad. He spends time at his office in the Technology Park, 'but I work just so much at home, or I work in the airports. Like most of my work, last week was down in the hotels in [City Abroad]' (Jared, ICTM). On the other hand, Charles works predominantly from home, although he used to travel a lot in previous jobs he has had. Different decisions in terms of locating oneself in remote workplaces via long-distance mobility are related to career stages, with more experienced people being in high demand for trips and visits, but also able to say no or to delegate when they feel that long-distance travel does not suit. Another example is that of Martin, a very experienced ICTM who is now working for an ICT business with offices in the US, China and Egypt but, having 'logged something over 400,000 miles of travel', Mark notes he only travels to China a couple of times a year now and the US a few times annually. He goes on to reflect that 'it loses its shine (…) the physical act of travel has become tedious but I always like when I'm there and always like getting home again'.

Career stages and life stages seem also to relate to how workplace flexibility is seen by individuals. Some of our more experienced participants expressed some resistance to long-distance or very frequent travel. For example, Charles notes: 'my personal preference [is] not to travel. In my past corporate life, I did lots of travel, and I am kind of allergic to travel. *It takes a lot to make me move*, that applying both in Ireland and outside of Ireland'. Another example is Sara, an experienced digital creative who loves travelling for leisure, but strictly limits the frequency of work-related travel: 'if I need to come to Dublin, I would rather come once a month for two nights and stack up all of the meetings that I need to go to in that 40-hour period (…) I do try to restrict it to just once a month' (Sara, DC).

For many others, particularly when developing new businesses or projects (particularly with new collaborators), it is necessary to success to place themselves where their collaborators are: 'it depends on how old the project is and how and when you know the person you are doing it with. (…) I think that building up a valuable relationship (…) has to happen in (…) more regular meetings (…) face-to-face' (Cathal, A, full-time lecturer in his mid-40s, married with three school-age children).

Finally, frequent mobility may be expected in the workplace, but the choice not to travel to be with customers or colleagues might be down to personal reasons:

> I was a single mother for four years doing creative work and I had to stop because I was being asked at a moment's notice (…) I remember one day I was asked – would I go to Copenhagen the following day for a week? (…) What was I supposed to do? I couldn't, I had to say no.
>
> (Lily, DC)

Lily (married, with two young children and a teenager) is now a self-employed digital creative. Her quote shows that her refusal to travel long-distance at short notice was due to her responsibilities as a mother, and furthermore that it contrasted the expectations of her employer. Lily's current worklife means that she has more agency about where and how to move, travel and base herself. Lily's example shows how worklife style considerations can be gendered, particularly when family and children are involved. Making manageable worklives can be tied to the tension between professional performance in and across places and emplaced family and social support, which particularly affects women.

Conclusions

This chapter highlights relational concerns about the places that they physically occupy, connections to other locations, and the myriad connections and flows that interlink them by means of plans, routines, organisational arrangements and infrastructures. Local and global travel, location arrangements in support of worklives, career changes, family changes, professional and personal relationship maintenance, and new perspectives on the self as worker are all woven into the work of locating oneself. Through these intersecting sociomaterial practices workplace 'bundles' (Massey, 2005) emerge, and are made to work for MKWrs' worklives. In discussing the first theme, we saw that this placing is a relational agency shaped by many factors: the relational and reputational capital attached to specific places; connection to global and localised networks; the constantly negotiated values attached to being somewhere (as in the case of Betty and the Innovation Hub manager); and imagined alternative emplacements and worklives. Corollary work involves both working with the limitations and capitalising on the relational opportunities of particular placings. Secondly, placing one's worklife also involves styling worklives (individual, social and familial); by living and working near family and friends, realising aspirations for an academic career, or making place simultaneously work and family friendly. But placing worklife is also about manageability, for example, by responding to a desire for or achieving rootedness through localised family, friendship and leisure and an ever-evolving awareness of a place's limitations and opportunities in relation to ambitions, affective ties and desired lifestyle.

Digital creatives in the early stages of developing their business particularly and carefully consider their need to relate themselves to locations, hubs and regions branded in terms of innovation. ICT managers are concerned with their company's progress and with their responsibility to develop the business; those who are in charge of well-established companies have greater possibility of choosing where to live and work and how to engage in physical mobility (such as in Charles' case). Academics are more concerned with placing themselves in relation to those sociomaterial assemblages (colleagues, resources, environments, etc.) that enable their chosen career.

These evolving understandings and configurations involve locations, people, organisations and the flows that connect them. They also relate to the broader geography of opportunities, influences, personal boundaries associated with the regional and Irish context, even as these resonate with other advanced economies: association to cities, regional hubs, areas of business investment, etc. (James, 2011; Ó'Riain, 2014). The (often invisible) work of planning, negotiating, constructing and communicating one's placement in the city and region involves complex sociomaterial practices and relationships in the making of 'placebundles' (Massey, 2005).

Even as these workers describe placing themselves, placings are continuously evolving and acquiring values and meanings as they are lived and become characterised by boundaries, opportunities and choices. 'Place-frames' emerge out of the ongoing discursive, political understandings of the process of place production (Martin, 2003) (as in the example of Betty, needing to assert her right to an office space when she was not seen as the expected 'startupper' who is single-mindedly focused on work). MKWrs locate themselves differently in relation to places and their connotations. The city, its different areas, and its surroundings are lived and worked in different ways depending on ever-evolving individual priorities, ambitions and life stages. In other words, there is 'no big picture of the modern city to be had but only a set of constantly evolving sketches' (Thrift, 1996, p. 1485).

The corollary work of placing one's worklife includes making places and making places work. Various capacities (professional, family, personal development, etc.) are embedded through specific locations and are woven into the process of how place is made to work. Choices are continuously (re)made in intra-action with other sociomaterial agencies: these can be everyday decisions in terms of how to reach to a network of peers, but also life choices in terms of residence, family location, and availability for global travel. These decisions are variously affected by the pressure of external expectations, affordances or by individual ambitions. Career stage, age and personal circumstances come into play as particular placings and movements do and do not feature in one's worklife. Cities and regions are made to work by agencies of intersecting moorings, emplacements and mobilities (Hannam et al., 2006), emerging through ever-evolving global, state, regional and local government policy measures as well as multiscale negotiations and imaginings. MKWrs are constantly managing the relationship between their worklife and place, often relocating to achieve an optimum productive and creative work environment, to make a 'mental shift', or facilitate lifestyle choices, domestic or caring demands.

The spatial mobility and multiple work and living possibilities (often afforded by ICTs) occur not only at the urban, regional and national scale, but also in the domestic and professional spaces of everyday worklife (e.g. homes, offices, cafés and travel spaces). The MKWrs' accounts point to how technologies become 'plastic' as they are opportunistically incorporated into practices of everyday life (Büscher, 2014) in combination with decisions about which places specific tasks can best be accomplished, and with work producing these places. We move on to unpack how places at this scale are made to work in the following chapter.

References

Adkins, L. (2004). Reflexivity: Freedom or Habit of Gender? *The Sociological Review, 52*(2_suppl), 191–210. https://doi.org/10.1111/j.1467-954X.2005.00531.x

Agnew, J. A. (1987). *Place and Politics: The Geographical Mediation of State and Society*. Boston, MA: Allen & Unwin.

Arvidsson, A., Gandini, A., & Bandinelli, C. (2016). Self-Branding among Freelance Knowledge Workers. In M. Crain, W. R. Poster, & M. A. Cherry (Eds.), *Invisible Labor: Hidden Work in the Contemporary World* (pp. 239–256). Oakland, CA: University of California Press.

Büscher, M. (2014). Nomadic Work: Romance and Reality. A Response to Barbara Czarniawska's 'Nomadic Work as Life-Story Plot'. *Computer Supported Cooperative Work (CSCW), 23*(2), 223–238. https://doi.org/10.1007/s10606-013-9194-6

Büscher, M., Urry, J., & Witchger, K. (2011). Mobile Methods. New York: Routledge.

Clifford, J. (1997). *Routes: Travel and Translation in the Late Twentieth Century*. Cambridge, MA: Harvard University Press.

Edensor, T. (2010). Walking in Rhythms: Place, Regulation, Style and the Flow of Experience. *Visual Studies*, *25*(1), 69–79. https://doi.org/10.1080/14725861003606902
Frello, B. (2008). Towards a Discursive Analytics of Movement: On the Making and Unmaking of Movement as an Object of Knowledge. *Mobilities*, *3*(1), 25–50. https://doi.org/10.1080/17450100701797299
Gandini, A. (2016). Digital Work: Self-branding and Social Capital in the Freelance Knowledge Economy. *Marketing Theory*, *16*(1), 123–141. https://doi.org/10.1177/1470593115607942
Gustafson, P. (2001). Roots and Routes: Exploring the Relationship between Place Attachment and Mobility. *Environment and Behavior*, *33*(5), 667–686. https://doi.org/10.1177/00139160121973188
Hannam, K., Sheller, M., & Urry, J. (2006). Editorial: Mobilities, Immobilities and Moorings. *Mobilities*, *1*(1), 1–22. https://doi.org/10.1080/17450100500489189
Ingold, T. (2008). Bindings against Boundaries: Entanglements of Life in an Open World. *Environment and Planning A: Economy and Space*, *40*(8), 1796–1810. https://doi.org/10.1068/a40156
James, A. (2011). Work–Life (Im)'Balance' and Its Consequences for Everyday Learning and Innovation in the New Economy: Evidence from the Irish IT Sector. *Gender, Place & Culture*, *18*(5), 655–684. https://doi.org/10.1080/0966369X.2011.601805
Kabachnik, P. (2012). Nomads and Mobile Places: Disentangling Place, Space and Mobility. *Identities*, *19*(2), 210–228. https://doi.org/10.1080/1070289X.2012.672855
Kaufmann, V., Bergman, M. M., & Joye, D. (2004). Motility: Mobility as Capital. *International Journal of Urban and Regional Research*, *28*(4), 745–756. https://doi.org/10.1111/j.0309-1317.2004.00549.x
Laurier, E., & Philo, C. (2003). The Region in the Boot: Mobilising Lone Subjects and Multiple Objects. *Environment and Planning D: Society and Space*, *21*(1), 85–106. https://doi.org/10.1068/d341
Lefebvre, H. (2004). *Rhythmanalysis: Space, Time, and Everyday Life*. London & New York: Continuum.
Liegl, M. (2014). Nomadicity and the Care of Place – On the Aesthetic and Affective Organization of Space in Freelance Creative Work. *Journal of Computer Supported Cooperative Work*, *23*(2), 163–183. https://doi.org/http://dx.doi.org/10.1007/s10606-014-9198-x
Malpas, J. (2012). Putting Space in Place: Philosophical Topography and Relational Geography. *Environment and Planning D: Society and Space*, *30*(2), 226–242. https://doi.org/10.1068/d20810
Martin, D. G. (2003). "Place-Framing" as Place-Making: Constituting a Neighborhood for Organizing and Activism. *Annals of the Association of American Geographers*, *93*(3), 730–750. https://doi.org/10.1111/1467-8306.9303011
Massey, D. (1993). Power-Geometry and a Progressive Sense of Place. In T. Putnam, B. Curtis, J. Bird, & L. Tickner (Eds.), *Mapping the Futures: Local Cultures, Global Change* (pp. 60–70). London: Routledge.
Massey, D. (1994). *Space, Place and Gender*. London & New York: Polity.
Massey, D. (2004). Geographies of Responsibility. *Geografiska Annaler: Series B, Human Geography*, *86*(1), 5–18. https://doi.org/10.1111/j.0435-3684.2004.00150.x
Massey, D. (2005). *For Space*. London: SAGE Publications.
Ó'Riain, S. (2014). *The Rise and Fall of Ireland's Celtic Tiger: Liberalism, Boom and Bust*. Cambridge: Cambridge University Press.

Oldenburg, R. O. (1999). *The Great Good Place: Cafés, Coffee Shops, Bookstores, Bars, Hair Salons, and Other Hangouts at the Heart of a Community*. New York: Marlowe & Company.

Peck, J. (2005). Struggling with the Creative Class. *International Journal of Urban and Regional Research, 29*(4), 740–770. https://doi.org/10.1111/j.1468-2427.2005.00620.x

Pierce, J., Martin, D. G., & Murphy, J. T. (2011). Relational Place-Making: The Networked Politics of Place. *Transactions of the Institute of British Geographers, 36*(1), 54–70. https://doi.org/10.1111/j.1475-5661.2010.00411.x

Popoveniuc, B. (2014). Self Reflexivity: The Ultimate End of Knowledge. *Procedia – Social and Behavioral Sciences, 163*, 204–213. https://doi.org/10.1016/j.sbspro.2014.12.308

Seamon, D. (1980). Body-Subject, Time-Space Routines, and Place-Ballets. In A. Buttimer & D. Seamon (Eds.), *The Human Experience of Space and Place* (pp. 148–165). London: Croom Helm.

Sheller, M. (2014). The New Mobilities Paradigm for a Live Sociology. *Current Sociology, 62*(6), 789–811. https://doi.org/10.1177/0011392114533211

Sheller, M., & Urry, J. (2006). The New Mobilities Paradigm. *Environment and Planning A, 38*(2), 207–226. https://doi.org/http://dx.doi.org/10.1068/a37268

Thrift, N. (1996). *Spatial Formations*. London: Sage.

Thrift, N. (1998). Steps to an Ecology of Place. In D. Massey, J. Allen, & P. Sarre (Eds.), *Human Geography Today* (pp. 295–322). Cambridge: Polity.

Tuan, Y.-F. (1977). *Space and Place: The Perspective of Experience*. Minneapolis, MN: University of Minnesota Press.

Urry, J. (2000). *Sociology Beyond Societies*. London: Routledge.

Urry, J. (2007). *Mobilities*. Cambridge: Polity.

Chapter 3

Everyday worklife placing

> I never worked from home before (...). It's a really hard thing to get used to (...) because *the environment is incredibly important*. I was in the box room and there is a little small bed and a tiny little desk and a really old laptop with keys and stuff missing on it and (...) it really frustrated me (...). Every week I'd move things around in the room, whether I'm facing the window or away from the window *to try and figure out (...) what way am I getting more stuff done*. I've recently moved down into the sitting room which is much better because I used to be at the back of the house, which was always cold because the sun wasn't shining in, so now I'm at the front of the house and it's just a little bit more friendly and [has] more desk space, and the main thing is to get organised and just try and not lose focus during the day.
>
> (Noel, DC)

Having defined place in the previous chapter as relational, processual, and constantly emerging and negotiated 'bundles', in this chapter we extend the discussion to how everyday spaces and places are made to work for MKWrs. These practices of corollary work are part of a recursive process of making places, where places make worklives and where worklives in turn co-construct place. Noel's quote above is about the work undertaken to make a suitable workspace, which is crucial for him as a digital creative working entirely from home. Noting that he has 'never worked from home before', he implies an adjustment from the relative familiarity of a previous institutional workplace to dealing with his home becoming pervaded by work-based concerns and arrangements. Work itself is unsettled and disrupted by the process of finding the right place for work within the home. The resources that Noel seeks in a workspace (that is also his domestic space) are varied: from light and warmth, to desk space. His concern is to achieve work focus. Noel recounts the many 'trial and error' efforts to figure out what works for him: physical and environmental accommodation matter, but he must also find a way of creating spatial arrangements that are conducive to focus, concentration and getting work done.

In this chapter, three central aspects of placing are identified: how *organisational workplaces are made to work* for MKW; how *domestic spaces* are increasingly the territory of *gendered worklife negotiations*; and the work of reflexively negotiating place as conducive to work. These concerns characterise all MKW: when work is mobile, it cannot be contained by, or confined to, a 'traditional' work environment. Even those workers who do have access to an organisational workplace are constantly reconfiguring worklife in relation to mobility and motility, and so, therefore, to other (inhabited and imagined) places. As MKWrs engage in constantly contingent and contested practices of placing, these also become practices of hybridising. Placing worklife in everyday places also requires reflexivity about how placing may or may not be conducive to work. All these nuances of the corollary work (re)produce worklife *scapes* (Appadurai, 1990; Kesselring & Vogl, 2008) by bridging locations, worklife realms, social and technical infrastructures and networks. Key aspects of this work need unpacking: what kinds of relational and processual practices are involved? What are the effects of the constant process of improvisation around the everyday hybridisation of places? What kinds of reflexive relationships are forged between work and place? We begin by reviewing recent relevant debates on place and placing. In the sections that follow we examine how organisational places, third and domestic places are made to work in the everyday placing of MKWlives. In particular, we examine the entanglements of reflexively hybridised worklives and places in the process of placing MKW.

The accomplishment of mobile knowledge work in everyday places

The growing emphasis on global networks rather than localities (Appadurai, 1990; Castells, 2000) and related mobility turn since the 1990s put the question of place under pressure with many seeing it as displaced by mobility and flow. In fact, discourses of mobile knowledge work have long been predicated upon a vision of 'anytime, anywhere' work, which relies on digital tools for communication and productivity and independence from constraints of space, place and location (Chen & Nath, 2005; Davis, 2002; Kleinrock, 1996). As such, many scholars suggest that mobile and flexible work is diminishing the importance and relevance of place and place making (Hislop & Axtell, 2007; Kleinrock, 1996; Sørensen, 2011; Urry, 2000). Some go so far as to suggest their replacement by place-less 'flows' and networks (Castells, 2000). For example, Appadurai's notion of technoscape (Appadurai, 1990) puts flows at the centre of place making even if at the same time it reproduces binary notions of mobility and flow versus static place (Heyman & Campbell, 2009). It also highlights the ways in which 'contemporary landscapes are shot through with technological elements which enrol people, space, and the elements connecting people and spaces, into socio-technical assemblages' (Sheller & Urry, 2006, p. 9). Similarly, research on what is sometimes dubbed the global 'kinetic elite' underscores conventions of corporeal mobility and reproduces an 'up in the air', disembedded relationship to place (Costas, 2013; Presskorn-Thygesen, 2015).

Although critiqued from many perspectives including the sociology of work, mobilities studies, cultural geography, information systems and CSCW, these assumptions are difficult to dislodge (Bogdan, Rossitto, Normark, Adler, & Eklundh, 2006; Brodie & Perry, 2001; Cohen, 2010; Costas, 2013; Cresswell, 2006; D'Andrea & Gray, 2015; de Carvalho, 2014; Gray, 2004; Gregg, 2011; Harrison & Dourish, 1996; Henry & Massey, 1995; Rossitto, Ciolfi, Büscher, Bogdan, & Severinson-Eklundh, 2007). Moreover, empirical investigations (e.g. Ciolfi, Gray, & D'Andrea, 2012; de Carvalho, Ciolfi, & Gray, 2017; Mark & Su, 2010; Perry, O'Hara, Sellen, Brown, & Harper, 2001; Rossitto, Bogdan, & Severinson-Eklundh, 2014) show that MKWrs 'do not work in some sort of decorporalised hyperspace' (Brown & O'Hara, 2003, p. 1566), but are always occupied by place concerns and spatial strategies. The reasons for this extend from the practical need to plan when and where to move, to selecting and preparing appropriate resources (for example, when embarking on a long-distance flight), to configuring and maintaining temporary workplaces. Similarly, Cohen (2010), in her study of mobile hairstylists, shows how 'workscapes' are emergent, inhabited and negotiated in relation to the meanings associated with places (e.g. how private spaces are routinely remade in workplaces).

In this context, digital technologies play an essential role in the contemporary place-related practices of MKW (Gandini, 2016; Sørensen, 2011). Additionally, digital connectivity and digital infrastructure mediate MKWrs' efforts to configure and manage tools and resources across various places (including unfamiliar ones) (Brown & O'Hara, 2003; de Carvalho, Ciolfi, & Gray, 2011; Mark & Su, 2010; Rossitto et al., 2014). They 'convert, adjust and configure the spaces which are available to them so as to be able to do their work in them' (Brown & O'Hara, 2003, p. 1575).

The blurring of professional and personal realms and the rise of flexible work policies increasingly mean that MKWrs occupy a range of workplaces: from conventional offices, to co-working spaces, cafés, and one's own home. Furthermore, this work relies on digital technologies that are 'inherently place contingent' (Fast, Ljungberg, & Braunerhielm, 2019, p. 89), that can detect location, deliver place-specific services, and are powered by spatialised and emplaced material communication infrastructures. These infrastructures and services enable places to carry multiple and hybrid, ever-changing meanings and different potential for configuring and reconfiguring workers' relationships with others (Brown & O'Hara, 2003; Felstead, Jewson, & Walters, 2005). A variety of work and life places are affected by such practices, which often do not map onto the established matching of activities and locations and give rise to new, hybridised places and placing practices.

MKWrs do not just respond to the features or affordances of a physical space. Rather, spaces and their embedded infrastructures shape people's experiences while also providing a 'framework through which our encounters with space take on meaning' (Dourish & Bell, 2007, p. 417). For example, a café can become an infrastructure of shelter, comfort and connectivity that can accommodate some forms of work as the result of a specific set of sociomaterial practices. By making cafés into temporary workplaces, MKWrs and others come to associate to such locations, either temporarily, or more permanently, with particular work practices (Martins, 2015). Furthermore, mobile technologies and networked environments, alongside the movement of people, are implicated in the production of spatiality and spatial experience, shaping individual and collective understandings of how spaces are organised and produced (Brewer & Dourish, 2008, p. 964). With the increasing pervasiveness of digital infrastructures and portable digital technologies, the cultural logics of movement through spaces change as 'information technologies provide sites and occasions for the development of new forms of environmental knowing' (Brewer & Dourish, 2008, p. 969). Through these socially constructed, negotiated and shared practices, spaces and places afford a form of 'collective legibility' (Brewer & Dourish, 2008, p. 970). The interaction between placing practices and place legibility becomes more complex when work colonises and hybridises certain non-organisational environments, such as homes and third places.

The term 'hybrid' has a long history in cultural and postcolonial studies debates around identity and borderlands (Ang, 2001; Bhabha, 1994; Shohat & Stam, 1994; Young, 1995), including historical and contemporary studies of global cultural flows and interdependencies (Frello, 2012). It is most effective in disrupting assumptions of boundedness and fixed identities, emphasising instead those practices and effects of cultural encounters that construct, reproduce and contest difference. Processes of hybridisation involve the interpenetration of diverse logics that manifest themselves in hybrid sites and spaces (Pieterse, 1994), often referred to as 'Third Spaces' (Bhabha, 1994). This includes the blurring and reworking of public and private spaces, as well as the simultaneous combining of multiple organisational forms and practices (Pieterse, 1994). Hybrid spaces emerge out of the interweaving of physical and digital practices as mobile users connect via mobile technology devices. The emergence of portable communication technologies and wireless networks has contributed to the possibility of being always connected to digital spaces, but hybrid places are not constructed by technology. They are materialised by connections between mobile people and artefacts via social networks (de Souza e Silva, 2006). These hybridising practices of digital and physical placing rely on physical and virtual movements and connecting. Spaces become 'splintered' (Frith, 2012) by virtue of both location-based digital services and how they are represented digitally. For example, people can 'read the space through the mapping technologies of their smartphones, and the representations are constructed by their preferences and personal choices' (Frith, 2012, p. 134).

Thus the hybridisation of place occurs in and through the coming together of processes and actants as 'hybrid systems, materialities and mobilities (...) combin[ing] objects, technologies, socialities and affects' to produce and reproduce distinct places (Hannam, Sheller, & Urry, 2006, p. 14). For example, as the modern separation between working-place and life-place dissolves, or becomes blurred (Gregg, 2011; Halford, 2005; James, 2013), 'fluid workplaces' emerge (Kakihara, Sørensen, & Wiberg, 2002). These are temporary work locations that involve particular reconfigurations of place and social relations (ibid.). Relatedly, alternative forms of workplaces unbound from traditional corporate structures (such as co-working spaces) are specifically designed to act as workplaces, meeting points, and locations of recreation and socialising (Moriset, 2014; Spinuzzi, 2012). They are characterised by a '*dynamic multi-functionality* (...) closely related to the emerging phenomenon of multi-local working, since these places are offering formal and informal spaces for work' (Di Marino & Lapintie, 2018, p. 3, emphasis added). This proliferation of worklife places normalises the hybridisation of place and, we argue, hybridises worklife norms too.

Making environments work as workplaces is often referred to as an 'achievement' or 'accomplishment' in literature on mobile work (Brodie & Perry, 2001; Humphry, 2014; Laurier, 2002). This is to emphasise the effort and skill involved in the process of reaching 'the right configuration of people, resources, knowledge and place and can be seen as the spatial aspect of a work trajectory' (Bardram & Bossen, 2005, p. 137). Humphry calls 'the integrated, real time activities and articulations that workers conduct to produce a more or less stable work infrastructure or platform' – 'officing' (2014, p. 190). This involves three interconnected practices: connecting, not only to digital networks and 'preparing interactions with others'; 'it is as much a social process as a material one' (ibid.); configuring, which includes 'assembling resources to make a technology work to some planned action or existing pattern of activity' (2014, p. 192); and synchronising, which refers to the 'temporal adjustments made to bridge time gaps produced by physical dislocation or communication delays' (2014, p. 197). In the case of independent workers, such as contractors or freelancers who perform 'contingent work' (Barley & Kunda, 2004), these efforts also require cultivating relationships to places, routines and people, as these are not arranged or sustained by employer organisations (Petriglieri, Ashford, & Wrzesniewski, 2019). These workers must create 'personal holding environments', which enable them to both 'stay productive and manage the emotions attendant in their work' (Petriglieri et al., 2019, p. 141).

The work of making environments into suitable places is not just functional, but also atmospheric and aesthetic. It includes considering how the (temporary) workplace should look and feel in order to be promotive of work (Gregg, 2018; Hesmondhalgh & Baker, 2010; Vostal, 2015). Atmosphere is crucial in how people experience certain places (e.g. the busy atmosphere of a café vs. the quiet and reflective atmosphere of a library). Thus MKWrs work on identifying and seeking out places that are conducive to work and engage in further practices to enhance the work ambiance of particular places (de Carvalho, 2013). These practices range from bringing one's favourite cup to a café, and choosing a café on the basis of the 'little performances of "the social drama"' that generate the right ambiance, to identifying the right co-working spaces, which are often 'glamourised' through artworks and humorous content (Gregg, 2018, p. 35). This 'aesthetic consumption of place' includes identifying 'happening places' that animate work and often involves the strangely work-enabling practice of letting 'the social scenery comprised of human and non-human elements pass by' (Liegl, 2014, p. 174).[1]

The everyday placing of worklives also requires specific efforts on the part of MKWrs to make these emplaced worklife arrangements work for them. For example, the 'relocation of work into domestic space on the one hand, and the dislocation of work into cyberspace on the other' (Halford, 2005, p. 19), requires ongoing worker adaptability, translation and agility. These daily practices of placing mediate 'processes of identity formation' (Humphry, 2014) because 'practices of self-interrogation and self-fashioning' (Liegl, 2014, p. 169) are central to finding and making the right place. Moreover, workers develop affective bonds with those workplaces through which a sense of 'working self' is developed and nurtured (Petriglieri et al., 2019, p. 143). We turn now to how study participants articulate their everyday practices of placing; first, via the placing of MKWlives in *organisational workplaces*; second, by reconstituting *homes as worklife places*; and third, through the development of *reflexive relationships to worklife places*.

Reconfiguring worklife around organisational workplaces (and vice versa)

Organisational workplaces, for the purposes of our discussion, are those that are owned, managed and monitored by an organisational entity that is not the individual worker. These might include: corporate premises, university spaces, but also co-working spaces, publicly funded working spaces such as the Innovation Hub, and those 'third places' where work may be done but that are places of business belonging to an external institution/organisation (from libraries, to cafés, hotel lobbies, etc.). MKWrs do not have to maintain these environments which provide an infrastructure for work (e.g. the basics of seating, light, sockets, connectivity, etc.). On some occasions, MKWrs might take advantage of the unexpected availability of an infrastructural resource (e.g. connectivity, power, etc.) in an unfamiliar third place. For example, Seán (marketing director of a software platform development company in his second marriage, with two grown-up children and two stepsons) stated: 'the most valuable thing you could do is a long-haul flight, because you've got nothing else to do. I get tremendous amounts of work done' (Seán, ICTM). Despite lack of connectivity, Seán knows that he can get a lot of work done while flying so he makes sure to bring work with him – thus deploying 'planful opportunism' (Perry et al., 2001) in a setting that is not explicitly geared for work.

While participants across all three cohorts use these spaces to different extents, corporate and institutional premises are particularly important for ICT managers and academics, who not only have access to conventional workplaces (such as offices) through their employment, but also are expected to spend at least some work time there. Because the infrastructures underlying operations are visibly available and maintained by dedicated professionals (e.g. wireless networks, power supply, networked services such as printing, etc.) in conventional workplaces, less infrastructural work is needed. Yet, such places may still require the organisation of tangible artefacts, from specialised equipment, to printed documentation and coffee cups as well as the management of spatial configurations, social relationships and ambiance:

> The lab is just out here, my postgrads are just down in the open plan area down below so the reality is we will meet in the lab or we'll meet in our office, because of the fact that we're all on the one floor. So most of my conversations in relation to research take place here on this floor because *that's where our lab is and that's where the people are. It doesn't really make much sense to work anywhere else really* (...) the equipment present in that place (...) this is where the lab is.
>
> (Philip, A)

Philip's university environment gets its vitality as a workplace from the presence of a lab, equipment, people (students, colleagues), office spaces and ways of coming together (such as meetings). In his account, Philip mentions the environmental, infrastructural and social aspects of how the workplace works for him. It is also a relational networked place that easily affords if not stimulates work. All these things make it work. In the previous chapter, Jerry (CEO of a software distribution firm) rationalised his company's latest office move in terms of bringing employees onto the same floor thus creating space for informal encounters: 'and the whole work ethic is a lot better because people can have a cup of coffee, they're talking about what's going on' (Jerry, ICTM). The company premises are therefore highly valued in terms of organisational relationality. Apart from providing a more advanced infrastructure, and professional support for work (which is greatly valued by the ICT manager cohort), the conventional workplace is made to work through relational interactions and trajectories.

ICT managers see the traditional, office-based arrangement as enabling easier management, and relationship building especially in younger, small and medium-sized companies:

> Everybody comes to the office (...). And I think it's a good way of developing relationships (...). In a young company, we want to foster communication and *get the culture right*. In the future there may be a situation whereby people can go out and work on the road (...). In a larger organisation you can certainly do hotdesking, or have a couple of guys working remotely, and in the office you might have a couple of stations where they can plug in if they need to come into the office for meetings or whatever else....
>
> (Damien, ICTM)

Making the workplace work for his team involves Damien in a continuous process of 'developing' and 'fostering' such fruitful relationships, anticipating future situations and planning alternative spatial configurations and their potential implications as the company grows.

The work of managing the relationality of workplaces is a concern for all three cohorts in our study: for academics working with students and colleagues (such as in Philip's case); for digital creatives, whose livelihood depends on personal recommendations and individual rapport with customers; and for ICT managers for the purpose of maintaining team interaction and because encouraged worker flexibility creates the need to arrange opportunities and locations to meet and collaborate (Hislop & Axtell, 2007, p. 36). However, this relationality plays out differently in different circumstances. For example, we saw in the conflict between Betty and the Innovation Hub manager (in Chapter 2) how, for solo entrepreneurs, who are not in the position to set up an independent workplace, an office in the Innovation Hub can be central to the success of their business. The Innovation Hub provides digital creatives in start-up companies with possibilities for networking and relationship building (i.e. 'the place to find everybody', as described by Arthur, a digital creative), as well as infrastructural resources. Working alone and/or remotely can be isolating and perceived as inefficient by many participants.

Arthur, a digital creative who has a business partner, particularly values co-location, even if (by virtue of his company's business model) this is less frequent than for established ICT businesses as his partner is remote:

> My technical partner (…) actually lives in Belgium. So he's by default (…) remote. But when I start formalising those kinds of relationships [I] still want him in the office (…) for a few days a month anyways. I think the remote working is okay up to a point, (…) *in a start-up environment you need the team aspect to it (…). Which is not to say that (…) you can't have a remote team, but I think it'll just add to a layer of complexity* on top of something that's already fairly complex, *you would need everybody on the same page.*
>
> (Arthur, DC)

Arthur operates his business on a common model for start-ups, with a small workforce of two, located in two different countries and relying on technology for collaboration at a distance. Yet, he suggests that being physically co-located with his technical partner on a regular basis is important for the success of the company. Because he needs everybody 'to be on the same page', he suggests they need to physically share the same workplace, at least some of the time, so that teamwork is facilitated. For Arthur, emplaced co-presence is both an operational concern and a company strategy.

Shared place understandings are important factors for collaboration and communication with colleagues, customers and other stakeholders. The work done to make places work in support of emplaced collaboration (Bogdan et al., 2006; de Carvalho, 2014; Rossitto et al., 2014, 2007) and relationship management

(Ciolfi et al., 2012) is continuous and is shaped by the evolution of teams and organisations in those places. The ICT managers are responsible for teams and this means that the relational aspects of corollary work around place are central. For example, Angela (the managing director of a small programming firm, who is married, with a son and a daughter, and also studying part-time for a PhD) is an experienced professional and is also co-owner of the company. She works at her company office during the day and at her home office in the evenings and on specific days. She travels a lot (also internationally, at least once a month) to meet customers. Her worklife placescape consists of several locations, places and of the many trajectories through which they interconnect. Angela also sees herself as having to take care of people and of relationships in all these places. This work includes making sure the infrastructure is suitable, connections are maintained, customers are happy and that her children are cared for. She is constantly making workplaces suit her many responsibilities and the needs of those she is relating with.

While 'traditional' organisational workplaces are still valued and used by many MKWrs, these environments are changing, and increasingly accommodating less formal ways of working including the expansion of shared spaces for socialising and relaxation. Flexible work policies also facilitate the moving of work away from institutional workplaces. This movement is often to third places[2], which take on particular importance as useful workplaces for the academics. Josh mentions going to cafés, Shannon goes to a hotel and Tom works extensively in cafés and hotel lobbies:

> I choose to go *somewhere where there is no internet access so I don't have that option* [using the internet] (…). Mobile phones are great tools most of the time, but there is this assumption that one is always available.
>
> (Tom, A)

Tom seeks out temporary workplaces with limited connectivity to be free of interruptions. His place making concerns are relational, although by working at these locations he seeks to filter and screen social and digital connectivity rather than boosting it. Working at such locations also means managing their hybrid nature. Third places are inherently 'hybrid', as they are generally intended for congregation rather than for the execution of particular tasks. Yet, they commonly become temporary workplaces for MKWrs. The characteristics of these environments (shared, social, with a relaxed ambiance) are often seen as conducive to creativity and 'thought work' (Noonan, 2015). Many participants describe the practicalities of creating temporary workplaces at these locations, including choosing which equipment to bring, configuring temporary infrastructures in place and managing which tasks to pursue at which location. Cafés resemble co-working spaces[3] insofar as they provide a potentially relaxed atmosphere that is conducive to serendipitous encounters and discoveries.[4]

While third spaces epitomise processes of hybridisation in placing work, Philip's university office regularly serves as a place for childcare:

> My wife is going to call in here [the office]. My kids call up fairly regularly because (…) of the proximity of the national school where my children are. In general, they're collected by their mother but if there's after school or whatever *they can come to me here and they can do their homework on the table here.*
>
> (Philip, A)

Where there is enough flexibility in terms of work arrangements, which is often the case in academia, institutional offices can also become places for family care.

Corporate workplaces are also increasingly 'domestic' and informal, in terms of physical design, arrangement, and encouraged practices, often embodying the idea that certain environmental configurations can stimulate productive creativity as well as social interaction. Kathy, a digital creative worker, experienced such hybridity in her previous job with a creative design company:

> We were *encouraged (...) we would spend ages watching TV on a couch* (…) there was a TV room where you'd just go in and watch cartoons and *that's actually work* because it's important that you're exposed to what the best are doing (…). And *that would obviously trigger ideas*, so (…) *an environment where you're encouraged to seek out inspiration* is important as well (…). It is part of your work to actually go out there and actually explore and to find inspiration which is important as well.
>
> (Kathy, DC)

As organisational workplaces hybridise to incorporate faux third places, workers have to move between these places (within the workplace) in nuanced ways, constantly negotiating diverse framings of mood, relationships, work and persona. The placing of worklives in everyday place scapes requires considerable effort, therefore, as work moves across workplace and life realms through emerging sociomaterial configurations of (intra-acting) infrastructures, resources, opportunities and relationships. This corollary work is not about setting boundaries between worklife 'realms of experience' (Nippert-Eng, 1996, p. 25), rather it requires dissolving, reconfiguring, relaxing, or sculpting these boundaries as worklife requires (Ciolfi & Lockley, 2018; de Carvalho, 2013; Gray, Ciolfi, de Carvalho, D'Andrea, & Wixted, 2017; Nippert-Eng, 1996). Even designated formal workplaces no longer signal a straightforward set of norms, rules or structures through which work practices, ambiance or relationships are shaped and rendered legible.

Reconstituting homes as worklife places

Homes feature centrally in the worklives of participants across all three cohorts. Many describe the setting up of home offices or arranging corners as temporary workplaces when working from home, or at home in the evening. Homes are further hybridised by the entanglements of domestic technologies and relationships with professional infrastructures, tools and networks.

Gone is the modern notion of home as a private, personal space of respite from work. Home is now an increasingly significant site of work extending recently to 'hofficing'[5] and network hospitality which have become legitimised means of income generation (Lampinen, 2016; Rossitto & Lampinen, 2018). Homes are remade as worklife spaces via the moving and mobilising of people, objects, information and ideas in ever-evolving ways (Büscher & Urry, 2009, p. 112). These trends have generated some benefits (particularly for women and those with care responsibilities), but also intensify the imperative of increased productivity (Halford, 2005). The productivity imperative generates pressure to demonstrate visibility and professional performance and weighs more heavily on women whose work from home is frequently combined with caring work (Halford, 2005, p. 21). Homes are also sites of other unpaid activities such as personal finance management, healthcare appointments, supervising children's homework, etc. (Steward, 2000; Verne & Bratteteig, 2016). As such, they are sites of mobile arrangements of paid and unpaid work, professional or quasi-professional practices, care and leisure. Home can no longer be associated with rest. Even if this version of home was never the case for women, home is a place of work, tight scheduling and busyness across these accounts (see Chapters 4 and 5).

For MKWrs, practices of work at home vary according to job demands (i.e. the need to work in the evenings and weekends and preferring to do so from home). Sometimes, homes are specifically sought out as enabling quiet and uninterrupted work. Home as workplace (exclusively or partially) is in some cases unavoidable. For example, digital creatives even beyond start-up phase often cannot afford an independent workplace and, for those with caring responsibilities, home is often a more convenient workplace. For others home is just one site in a wide repertoire of work locations and personally customised worklife practices (see Chapters 4 and 5).

Betty (a digital creative) was assigned a place for one year in the Innovation Hub but did not use it every day due to childcare demands at home and her remote rural location (as discussed in Chapter 2). She worked from home much of the time during the HPSU innovation programme, and afterwards ran her business (a web portal supporting parents) entirely from home:

> I have a home office (…) which is kind of in the centre of the house (…). It's not a closed-off room, *it's actually an open room on the second floor so I have full access to everything that is happening around the house* (…) I actually don't have any problem with disturbances and maybe it's a female multitasking as well but it just doesn't bother me. I mean I can switch off and switch on very easily from one thing to another.
>
> (Betty, DC)

The home is invested with multiple pressing demands and conflicting associations require need workarounds. As a solo digital creative, having made a career change from journalism following her move from Sweden to Ireland, Betty chose self-employment as a means of saving on childcare costs and being present for her children while sustaining a personal career. As her husband works full-time for an external company, Betty notes: 'I pretty much do everything around here' (Betty, DC).[6]

Working from home requires the conversion of rooms for office use either permanently or occasionally as well as maintaining and repairing technical and technological infrastructures (e.g. fast internet connection, networked devices, etc.). While some participants embrace work from home as a worklife style, others resent the work/life blurring that this brings about (Hardill & Green, 2003). For example, Lily (a digital creative) has office space at the Innovation Hub, but has also converted a room in her home into an office. However, her children have 'invaded' this space:

> The den (…) is *a fantastic office* but I'm kind of pushed out of there now because *[the children] do their stuff in there* and *I tend to actually sit on a high table in the kitchen* (…) is where all my work stuff is now, but yes that office [the den] is there.
>
> (Lily, DC)

The hybridised den/office, kitchen/office are shaped as places by who gets priority in occupying them and defining them at any one time. Here hybridisation is not a smooth blending because its shifting and combined use is shaped by who is in a position to claim the place and define it at any one time. These shifting place appropriations are central to the process of hybridisation. Although often presented as a fluid mixing, the process of hybridisation is more the result of conventions and hierarchical social relationships – for example, across gender and between adults and children within the home. As a mother, Lily feels impelled to concede the den to the children and move her work to the kitchen table.

In another case, Aoife (an academic) describes the daily work of removing all her work stuff from the kitchen table every evening before dinner, piling up books, papers, disconnecting her laptop and moving everything to the floor: 'this was very *disruptive to my work* and made it hard to separate relaxation from work space' (Aoife, A). Placing work at home can involve conflictual relational practices as workers assemble and arrange their interactions with specific parts to the home, devices and other family members. Making a space a place of work, if only temporarily (as in the kitchen table examples) also involves negotiating the use of 'the kitchen table' which is variously seen as a desk, a social space, or for dining. Place, family and work are co-constructed relationally via the placing of worklife activities.

For Dean, working at home facilitates negotiating care responsibilities for his daughter with his wife. His account contrasts with Betty's early account of her open office space and constant distraction by her children's demands. He describes how he interprets and responds to possible interruptions:

> I'd be having office time while my wife has our daughter and *the odd time* (…) *she might pop into the office with my daughter*. And I sometimes could well do with just taking my head out and screaming before I get square eyes, and just chat with [wife] for five or ten minutes, *that suits me fine too*.
>
> (Dean, DC)

Dean describes the relational creation of the office at home where he separates himself from his family and dedicates himself to work. When this placing of work gets undone by his wife and daughter popping in, this family interruption is interpreted as enforcing a much-needed break and diversion. Thus the work of everyday placing involves a flux of shifting priorities, emotional registers and unanticipated(able) demands. Boundaries are not fixed but are constantly negotiated through the relational making and remaking of home workplaces.

But managing home as workplace is not only to do with others. It also requires a reflexive relationship to identifying the right place for work (as in Noel's case), when to make it or unmake it (as with Aoife getting the table ready for dinner), and how and when to draw a line, take a break, or end the working day:

> Even if you're working for yourself and you have your own office space, there is a sense of when you physically close the door, you will still have things on your mind but there's a better sense of separation (…). Just *walking from one room to another room doesn't really give you enough closure on the day* to some extent (…) so yes (…) it is hard but the flexibility is fantastic.
>
> (Sharon, DC)

Sharon is a digital creative on her second start-up, working predominantly from home; she is married, with two daughters of primary school age and a baby son. She describes the challenge of working around the short physical distances within her home in order to achieve a mental distance from work. Sharon's self-employment promises flexibility and autonomy, yet her home-based workplace makes it difficult to pause and distance herself from work.[7] Boundaries are always provisional, and continuously 'sculpted' in relation to sociomaterial configurations of myriad work demands, family demands, temporal frames and spatial arrangements.

As work procedures, schedules and tasks are mobilised, the places where these occur are increasingly the province of individual planning and management, and of individual responsibility (for example, when to rest, to sleep, etc.). These accounts describe the work of identifying and managing work locations, environments and their interconnections, as well as connecting and/or separating them. Like Sharon, Angela emphasises that crossing the threshold of her home office into the rest of the house is too slim a physical boundary to enable work to stop:

> At home (…) there's one particular room that's work only (…). And when I close that door, *it has to be a bit like closing the door [of the office]* because the danger is (…) you might be doing (…) something [with] family, and you say OK, I'll just go in for ten minutes and I'll check email. Now ten minutes becomes an hour and (…) *you can get dragged into it.*
>
> (Angela, ICTM)

Angela describes the burden of upholding the boundary against the odds. By its presence in the home office, work is too close to turn off completely; it also becomes even more seductive, something that Angela has to constantly guard against.

Both women and men optimise opportunities for working while mobile, but women rationalised this more in relation to freeing time for care or home-based activities. Like Betty and Lily's accounts, Sharon's account below describes the ways in which her home office is suffused by the presence of her three young children and the family's convivial spaces nearby. The transformation of her family space into a workplace is convenient, but it is not straightforward:

> I've *got my printer, fax machine, computer, all set up in there.* So I would go down there, make myself a cup of coffee, head in and I'd usually start with checking the emails and then I might just check Twitter (…). The kids get up and the rule is *'Mammy is working' so quite often I'll come in [the kitchen] and have a quick breakfast with them (...) and then (...) head back in. At least they've seen Mammy* (...). My office is quite often used as a den in the evening because it's a smaller room and it's cosy and the chairs are closer to each other, so quite often [husband] might put a film on, animation or something (…) and there's a piano inside, [daughter] is learning the piano, so he might be doing the piano with her.
>
> (Sharon, DC)

As for the others, childcare and work become hybridised practices as they both move in and between hybridised rooms and spaces of the home. For Sharon, work takes priority: although she is physically present in the house and her children can see her (for example at breakfast), she is working, and should not be disturbed. Work and life spaces are both hybridised. The space of parenting is occupied by work and work by family relations and activities, but there is a sense in which work is sacrosanct in both domains for most of the participants. In the section that follows we examine the ways in which MKWrs reflexively work at creating the sense of feeling 'at home in the work' (Petriglieri et al., 2019, p. 144). When work comes 'home' then the very notion of home is itself upturned; the task is to make work feel homely.

Reflexive worklife placing

It is clear at this point that worklife places are made, experienced and lived as flexible sociomaterial configurations of physical and intangible resources, people, connections and understandings. As knowledge work is largely mobile and can be done in most places, MKWrs must reflexively consider where they can best engage in work. Reflexivity as a situated, critical process and stance (Adkins, 2004; Popoveniuc, 2014), includes constant evaluation of worklife and how these workers come to know and inhabit it. For example, Angela, an experienced owner and manager of a software development company, reflexively resists the hybridisation of her home and how it affects her worklife. When she spent one month in Spain so that her son could learn Spanish, much of her time was taken up with reflexively managing her work to look like she was located locally and how she might have organised her work arrangements differently:

> It was a village outside Malaga, so a lot of the *apartments (...) didn't have wireless*. So my day tended to be when *I was in the school, I was working on (...) Skype or whatever*, but in the afternoon, if I was relying on a mobile call, it just didn't tend to happen (…) *I tended to miss that customer interface* and that tended to slip over that while (…). And maybe *if I'd set it up better before I went*, and if I was going again, it's something I would think of.
>
> (Angela, ICTM)

In the mornings, Angela skyped colleagues and customers from the Spanish school her son was attending (which had wireless internet). While she could be reached via her mobile phone at any time, this did not maintain the right level of relationality with her customers. Lack of network connectivity was not the core of the issue, rather her concern related to the lack of easy connection to remote people so that she could work with them as she would at home, or travelling on business. Thus she reflects on and re-envisions alternative spatial arrangements and ties across locations and how she might anticipate better the work that arises from her network of customers and colleagues.

The placing of worklife is a reflexive process of responding to emergent configurations of place and how they relate to anticipated worklife relational considerations. While it requires skills in making the distributed agencies of technologies, artefacts and infrastructures work together, it is also shaped by a reflexive relationship to self and worklife. This reflexive self emerges as these configurations are personalised. For example, Shannon describes her reasons for moving but which in turn prompts the reflexive question: 'So *what makes me choose a place over another?*'. She continues:

> Let's think about the internet connection first of all. So, if I prepare a lesson, would I do it from home or would I come here [the office]? The internet connection at home sucks (…) I don't have a proper internet connection to allow

> me to watch videos [for teaching purposes] at home. So I would come [to the office]. Sometimes I cross the road from home to [nearby hotel] because they have good Wi-Fi, and if I need to do work and my internet connection is down, I go to the hotel.
>
> (Shannon, A)

Shannon's work is by necessity anticipatory as she must constantly consider what resources are required, for example, will she need to include videos in her lecture material? And where can she get the necessary preparatory work done?

When working to produce a workplace somewhere unfamiliar, this binding together of 'heterogeneous distributed agencies' (Orlikowski, 2007, p. 1445) relies on personal strategies for managing these situations:

> When I was travelling I went to see my uncle who is very ill, and something work-related did come up and I needed to get a file. [My uncle] didn't have wireless, he only had a modem (…). My hotel had wireless but they had locked it up badly so I couldn't send email because their firewall was poorly done. So I went to my uncle's who I knew (…) had a modem, so what I ended up having to do was hack my way through, because I couldn't get the modem to work on my computer, it was so old (…) so I (…) had to hack my way through to the UNIX level to be able to send an email through web technology (…) it was one of the rare times I remember thinking, 'why don't you have wireless?', or thinking at the hotel, 'why doesn't your wireless work?' [laughs] I wanted to shake somebody.
>
> (Jenny, A)

Jenny is a full-time lecturer, single, in her late 30s, originally from the US. The unevenness of connectivity and infrastructural facilities necessitates the cultivation of a flexible and reflexive self, that is open to learning and improvising as an inevitable consequence of mobile work.

Earlier in this chapter, Noel and Seán describe how they made their workplaces work for them as individuals as Noel suggested that he can best keep focus more in a sunnier, warmer room and Seán welcomed the lack of interruptions or distractions on a long-haul plane journey. It is clear that defining and knowing oneself as a worker (Liegl, 2014) are central to worklife placing.

Given the mobile nature of MKW a heightened sensitivity to place and place configurations and how these shape worklife is evident across the three cohorts. For example, Noel's opening quote details his efforts to (re)configure his working space at home, and the self-knowledge he developed in terms of what suits him and helps him maintain his focus. Dean remarked on how pausing his work and talking to his wife and daughter might not be a waste of his worktime, but a helpful way for him to pause when he needs to. The emotional, physical, social and cultural placing of worklife relies on a highly reflexive orientation towards workplace and work practice, as well as the relationship between these. MKWrs have to work on themselves in identifying what and where works for them and how to make the 'where' of work, in relation to the potential and actualisation of real and imagined places:

> I suppose if I need to be in an environment where I am not going to be distracted, I will come to my office (…) because it's easy to be distracted, you know, someone comes up, a colleague or wherever when you are working away and wants to have a coffee with you, and so on, or a student sees you (…) and I am also a sociable person so, if I am in an environment where there is a possibility of having a social interaction my work will sometimes suffer as a result. So, *I have to discipline myself by going to a space where it is going to be minimal social interaction.*
>
> (Josh, A)

Josh (full-time lecturer, married, in his early 50s) mentions needing to be in a place where something he enjoys (social interaction) will be 'minimal', in order for his work not to suffer. As for others, his work practices are developed in response to the questions: 'how do I work best? And where?'. It is the mobility of work and workers that makes reflexivity so central to placing worklife.

For academics, meeting with students and colleagues is part of their job, however much of their work requires solitary concentration and the kinds of conditions that support this. Tom, for example, relies on third places such as cafés to get work done. He lives in a city centre apartment and dislikes his university-based office: 'I don't really like working in the office, it's ok now, but especially in the summer we don't get good ventilation (…) so it can become really stuffy' (Tom, A).

The office does not suit him, while he can concentrate in different environments:

> To be able to go to a place, you know, *a café in work, is a nice change of pace* and (…) it can be more comfortable. But (…) *curiously I think there are fewer distractions in a way*, because I'm away from all my resources (…) if you are in an environment like that where there is a lot of background activity it all turns to kind of merged together and form *more of a backdrop than a distraction.*
>
> (Tom, A)

The café evokes the right mood for creative work (such as writing research papers). The significance of atmosphere is linked to mood and inclination: '… working from the hotel, from the hotel lobby, from the hotel bar, from the café down the street, it's a choice of which environment suits my mood at the time, more than the resources I need at the time' (Tom, A). Tom, Josh and Noel's accounts suggest a reflexive relationship to how they mobilise and place themselves for work.

Reflexive self-knowledge is also about which places will be conducive to relational practices, such as collaboration. We saw, for example, that ICT managers such as Jerry and Angela, and academics such as Philip tend to place themselves in order to work closely with their teams and to access specialised resources. In Angela's case, due to her frequent travel, she is concerned about maintaining connection with colleagues and customers. For these workers who have management responsibilities and are therefore often sought by others, finding a suitable place for reflection and planning is less about personalised ambiance and more about a place that enables concentration:

> During the daytime I can be subjected to anybody in the office walking up to me and saying 'Damien, can I talk to you for a minute?' 'Damien, how are we going to do this?' (…) The phone could ring (…). So you don't get to do any planning (…). *If you want to really plan, be strategic and think things through, you need to do that outside of the work, so you might go for a walk.*
>
> (Damien, ICTM)

Later, Damien notes that he might also do some planning work in the quiet of the evening at home: 'I sit down, I've had my dinner, I'll have the laptop out, the television will be on in the corner' (Damien, ICTM).

Thinking about and around worklife places is not just about managing and/or reconfiguring resources or environments for Tom and Damien, but about placing themselves in the right conditions for the kind of work that they need to do. Thus a reflexive relationship to placing oneself and work in particular environments is developed. Kathy also describes a reflexive approach to managing work placing:

> Deliberately (…) I've just moved into an apartment in town, I haven't got the internet [at home] purely so that (…) *I'm forced to actually come into the office (...). There's things I do to push myself.* I will try and get work done here if it means stay late rather than take it home.
>
> (Kathy, DC)

An internet connection at home means that Kathy will work. Rather than work on her difficulty with resisting work, she relocates to an apartment without internet connection and far away from her work office at the Innovation Hub. This requires a strong managerial relationship to the self as she is 'forcing' and 'pushing' herself to develop separate work and life patterns in relation to these places.

Reflexivity is also evident in how workers make the most of emplaced sociomaterial resources. For example, Seán states:

> I worked for a long time in Dublin, and I'd go from here early in the morning, but I had the train ride up and the train ride down. And what that meant was that if I was going up to meet you (…). And *I had three hours on the*

> *train to do absolutely nothing except think about [you], and to focus on the meeting....*
>
> (Seán, ICTM)

In Chapter 2, we saw how Aoife (part-time lecturer) works both at home in Dublin and in her office at the university. She finds places such as cafés and trains distracting and difficult to work in. However, having recently had a baby, she now works on her train commute to the university in order to make the most of her time and describes the work she has to do on herself to re-think her relationship to working on the train and to change her work patterns:

> I find it hard to write on the train because of the noise, *but I would do reading on the train, maybe work that doesn't involve a lot of thought, making lists and going through non-complex tasks*, but they would really be the only two places that I would work, at home, on the train and here in the office.
>
> (Aoife, A)

Placing work is central to the making of a worklife in more ways than the practical 'art and craft' of place making (Büscher, 2014; Watts, 2008). It also prompts reflexivity regarding personal sensibilities and inclinations, worklife patterns and relationships to place and mobility.

Conclusion

The corollary work of placing worklives and making everyday places work has been the focus of this chapter. This work consists of all those sociomaterial practices that connect myriad locations, trajectories, mobilities and movements with people, artefacts, physical/digital infrastructures, and personal inclinations or moods. This placing of worklives for MKWrs is variously relational, processual and reflexive. Worklife place scapes are constantly worked and re-thought in relation to concerns of time and productivity (Lyons & Urry, 2005) and with regard to the inescapable hybridity of worker, place, artefacts and practices. The practical accomplishment of worklives occurs not only through 'mobilisation work' or 'officing', but through sociomaterial practices across myriad places, knowledge, resources and persons (Bardram & Bossen, 2005).

Worklife placing is also about reflexively accessing and incorporating knowledge about one's own inclinations and patterns. All participants moved their work between places, mobilising technologies to make diverse spaces into productive places. Across cohorts, the home, far from a place of respite, is where the world of work is perhaps evident in all its intensity. This intensity plays out in gendered ways as the accounts discussed testify to how the home affords different work possibilities to women and men. Meanwhile, there is some evidence that professional and corporate spaces are becoming differently codified and increasingly fluid in terms of their structures, configurations and boundaries. The effect is that even in conventional workplaces workers have to negotiate movement between places which demands different forms of sensibility, relationality and work orientations. These MKWrs' accounts of placing worklife also incorporate other dimensions of the corollary work including the anticipatory aspects of placing worklife (see Chapter 4) and the rhythmicity of movement and (re)location as these intersect with the spatial trajectories of worklives (see Chapter 5). We continue to develop our analysis of the corollary work that underpins MKW by addressing these temporal orientations and the kinds of 'time work' involved in the two chapters that follow.

Notes

1 Of course, the 19th century urban figure of the flâneur is assumed to be masculine and is associated with leisure, privilege and anonymity (Wolff, 1993). Women, especially middle-class women, assumed to respectably remain within the domestic sphere, were not able to walk the city in the same way and were thus written out of public space and agency. The legacies of these gendered public/private dualisms continue to unequally impact the worklives of women and men in today's digital economy.

2 The term 'third place' (Oldenburg, 1989) was originally coined to refer to those mainly urban places 'out of the home and the office where people use to convene and socialize in a free, informal manner'. These include cafés, hotels and airport lounges, the hairdresser or barbershop, but were originally linked to the creative classes (Moriset, 2014).

3 Co-working spaces are managed by organisations, but used mainly by independent workers, and accommodate a mix of socialisation, business networking and individual work (Moriset, 2014). These spaces are closely associated with the idea of 'accelerating serendipity', or unexpected chance discoveries, as stated by co-working pioneer Chris Messina, cofounder of Citizen Space in 2006 (Moriset, 2014, p. 8). Co-working spaces are often designed as 'living-room-office-hybrids' (Liegl, 2014) to encourage creativity, social interaction and a relaxed professional environment.

4 However, they are also sites of growing individual and corporate entrepreneurship that while enabling collaboration and sharing of knowledge and resources simultaneously produce 'competition' (Bouncken, Laudien, Fredrich, & Görmar, 2018).

5 'Hoffice' (a portmanteau of 'home' and 'office') is a self-organising network (founded in Sweden in 2014) to facilitate the collective use of private homes as shared co-working spaces according to an agreed code of practice (Rossitto & Lampinen, 2018).

6 In *Work's Intimacy*, Gregg (2011) notes that the women participating in her study of Australian ICT workers had home offices that were located more centrally in their houses, enabling them to monitor other ongoing activities (such as children). While Betty describes her home office in such a way, there were no other such accounts in our data. Therefore, no gender-related distinction in the positioning of home working spaces can be made for the participants in our project.

7 Research on people who work exclusively at home has shown that time becomes 'task-based, rather than clock-based' (Halford, 2005, p. 27), to end the working day (Steward, 2000).

References

Adkins, L. (2004). Reflexivity: Freedom or Habit of Gender? *The Sociological Review*, *52*(2_suppl), 191–210. https://doi.org/10.1111/j.1467-954X.2005.00531.x

Ang, I. (2001). *On Not Speaking Chinese: Living between Asia and the West*. New York: Routledge.

Appadurai, A. (1990). Disjuncture and Difference in the Global Cultural Economy. *Theory, Culture & Society*, *7*(2–3), 295–310. https://doi.org/10.1177/026327690007002017

Bardram, J. E., & Bossen, C. (2005). Mobility Work: The Spatial Dimension of Collaboration at a Hospital. *Computer Supported Cooperative Work (CSCW)*, *14*(2), 131–160. https://doi.org/10.1007/s10606-005-0989-y

Barley, S. R., & Kunda, G. (2004). *Gurus, Hired Guns, and Warm Bodies: Itinerant Experts in the Knowledge Economy*. Princeton, NJ: Princeton University Press. Retrieved from www.jstor.org/stable/j.ctt7s7rt

Bhabha, H. K. (Ed.). (1994). *The Location of Culture*. London & New York: Routledge.

Bogdan, C., Rossitto, C., Normark, M., Adler, P. J., & Eklundh, K. S. (2006). On a Mission without a Home Base: Conceptualizing Nomadicity in Student Group Work. In P. Hassanaly, T. Herrmann, G. Kunau, & M. Zacklad (Eds.), *Cooperative Systems Design: Seamless Integration of Artifacts and Conversations* (pp. 23–38). Amsterdam: IOS Press.

Bouncken, R. B., Laudien, S. M., Fredrich, V., & Görmar, L. (2018). Coopetition in Coworking-Spaces: Value Creation and Appropriation Tensions in an Entrepreneurial Space. *Review of Managerial Science*, *12*(2), 385–410. https://doi.org/10.1007/s11846-017-0267-7

Brewer, J., & Dourish, P. (2008). Storied Spaces: Cultural Accounts of Mobility, Technology, and Environmental Knowing. *International Journal of Human-Computer Studies*, *66*(12), 963–976. https://doi.org/10.1016/J.IJHCS.2008.03.003

Brodie, J., & Perry, M. (2001). Designing for Mobility, Collaboration and Information Use by Blue-collar Workers. *ACM SIGGROUP Bulletin*, *22*(3), 22–27. https://doi.org/10.1145/567352.567356

Brown, B., & O'Hara, K. (2003). Places as Practical Concern for Mobile Workers. *Environment and Planning A*, *35*(9), 1565–1587. https://doi.org/10.1068/a34231

Büscher, M. (2014). Nomadic Work: Romance and Reality. A Response to Barbara Czarniawska's 'Nomadic Work as Life-Story Plot'. *Computer Supported Cooperative Work (CSCW)*, *23*(2), 223–238. https://doi.org/10.1007/s10606-013-9194-6

Büscher, M., & Urry, J. (2009). Mobile Methods and the Empirical. *European Journal of Social Theory*, *12*(1), 99–116. https://doi.org/10.1177/1368431008099642

Castells, M. (2000). *The Rise of the Network Society*. Oxford: Blackwell Publishers.

Chen, L., & Nath, R. (2005). Nomadic Culture: Cultural Support for Working Anytime, Anywhere. *Information Systems Management*, *22*(4), 56–64. https://doi.org/10.1201/1078.10580530/45520.22.4.20050901/90030.6

Ciolfi, L., Gray, B., & D'Andrea, A. (2012). Social Aspects of Place Experience in Nomadic Work/Life Practices. In J. Dugdale, C. Masclet, A. Grasso, & J.-F. Boujut (Eds.), *Proceedings of the 10th International Conference on the Design of Cooperative Systems*. Marseille: Springer.

Ciolfi, L., & Lockley, E. (2018). From Work to Life and Back Again: Examining the Digitally-Mediated Work/Life Practices of a Group of Knowledge Workers. *Computer Supported Cooperative Work (CSCW)*, *27*(3–6), 803–839. https://doi.org/10.1007/s10606-018-9315-3

Cohen, R. L. (2010). Rethinking 'Mobile Work': Boundaries of Space, Time and Social Relation in the Working Lives of Mobile Hairstylists. *Work, Employment and Society, 24*(1), 65–84. https://doi.org/10.1177/0950017009353658

Costas, J. (2013). Problematizing Mobility: A Metaphor of Stickiness, Non-Places and the Kinetic Elite. *Organization Studies, 34*(10), 1467–1485. https://doi.org/10.1177/0170840613495324

Cresswell, T. (2006). *On the Move: Mobility in the Modern Western World*. New York: Routledge.

D'Andrea, A., & Gray, B. (2015). The Work and Life of Corporate Expatriates: New Patterns and Regimes of Mobility in the Knowledge Economy. *International Review of Social Research, 3*(1), 87–107. https://doi.org/10.1515/irsr-2013-0006

Davis, G. B. (2002). Anytime/anyplace Computing and the Future of Knowledge Work. *Communications of the ACM, 45*(12), 67–73. https://doi.org/10.1145/585597.585617

de Carvalho, A. F. P. (2013). *Technologically-mediated Nomadicity in Academic Settings: Tm-N as a Dynamic and Emergent Process. Department of Computer Science and Information Systems*. University of Limerick, Limerick.

de Carvalho, A. F. P. (2014). Collaborative Work and Its Relationship to Technologically-Mediated Nomadicity. In C. Rossitto, L. Ciolfi, D. Martin, & B. Conein (Eds.), *COOP 2014 – Proceedings of the 11th International Conference on the Design of Cooperative Systems* (pp. 209–224). Nice (France): Springer International Publishing. https://doi.org/10.1007/978-3-319-06498-7_13

de Carvalho, A. F. P., Ciolfi, L., & Gray, B. (2011). The Making of Nomadic Work: Understanding the Mediational Role of ICTs. In M. M. Cruz-Cunha & F. Moreira (Eds.), *Handbook of Research on Mobility and Computing: Evolving Technologies and Ubiquitous Impacts* (pp. 381–396). Hershey, PA: IGI Global.

de Carvalho, A. F. P., Ciolfi, L., & Gray, B. (2017). Detailing a Spectrum of Motivational Forces Shaping Nomadic Practices. In *Proceedings of the 2017 ACM Conference on Computer Supported Cooperative Work and Social Computing – CSCW '17* (pp. 962–977). https://doi.org/10.1145/2998181.2998313

de Souza e Silva, A. (2006). From Cyber to Hybrid: Mobile Technologies as Interfaces of Hybrid Spaces. *Space and Culture, 9*(3), 261–278. https://doi.org/10.1177/1206331206289022

Di Marino, M., & Lapintie, K. (2018). Exploring Multi-Local Working: Challenges and Opportunities for Contemporary Cities. *International Planning Studies*, 1–21. https://doi.org/10.1080/13563475.2018.1528865

Dourish, P., & Bell, G. (2007). The Infrastructure of Experience and the Experience of Infrastructure: Meaning and Structure in Everyday Encounters with Space. *Environment and Planning B: Planning and Design, 34*(3), 414–430. https://doi.org/10.1068/b32035t

Fast, K., Ljungberg, E., & Braunerhielm, L. (2019). On the Social Construction of Geomedia Technologies. *Communication and the Public, 4*(2), 89–99. https://doi.org/10.1177/2057047319853049

Felstead, A., Jewson, N., & Walters, S. (2005). *Changing Places of Work*. New York: Palgrave Macmillan.

Frello, B. (2012). Cultural Hybridity. In *The Encyclopedia of Applied Linguistics*. Oxford: Blackwell Publishing Ltd. https://doi.org/10.1002/9781405198431.wbeal0297

Frith, J. (2012). Splintered Space: Hybrid Spaces and Differential Mobility. *Mobilities, 7*(1), 131–149. https://doi.org/10.1080/17450101.2012.631815

Gandini, A. (2016). Digital Work: Self-branding and Social Capital in the Freelance Knowledge Economy. *Marketing Theory*, *16*(1), 123–141. https://doi.org/10.1177/1470593115607942

Gray, B. (2004). *Women and the Irish Diaspora*. London: Routledge.

Gray, B., Ciolfi, L., de Carvalho, A. F. P., D'Andrea, A., & Wixted, L. (2017). Post-Fordist Reconfigurations of Gender, Work and Life: Theory and Practice. *The British Journal of Sociology*, 1–23. https://doi.org/10.1111/1468-4446.12267

Gregg, M. (2011). *Work's Intimacy*. Cambridge: Polity.

Gregg, M. (2018). *Counterproductive: Time Management in the Knowledge Economy*. Durham, NC & London: Duke University Press.

Halford, S. (2005). Hybrid Workspace: Re-Spatialisations of Work, Organisation and Management. *New Technology, Work and Employment*, *20*(1), 19–33. https://doi.org/10.1111/j.1468-005X.2005.00141.x

Hannam, K., Sheller, M., & Urry, J. (2006). Editorial: Mobilities, Immobilities and Moorings. *Mobilities*, *1*(1), 1–22. https://doi.org/10.1080/17450100500489189

Hardill, I., & Green, A. (2003). Remote Working – Altering the Spatial Contours of Work and Home in the New Economy. *New Technology, Work and Employment*, *18*(3), 212–222. https://doi.org/10.1111/1468-005X.00122

Harrison, S., & Dourish, P. (1996). Re-place-ing Space: The Roles of Place and Space in Collaborative Systems. *Proceedings of the 1996 ACM Conference on Computer Supported Cooperative Work*. Boston, MA: ACM. https://doi.org/10.1145/240080.240193

Henry, N., & Massey, D. (1995). Competitive Time-Space in High Technology. *Geoforum*, *26*(1), 49–64. https://doi.org/10.1016/0016-7185(94)00022-Y

Hesmondhalgh, D., & Baker, S. (2010). 'A Very Complicated Version of Freedom': Conditions and Experiences of Creative Labour in Three Cultural Industries. *Poetics*, *38*(1), 4–20. https://doi.org/10.1016/J.POETIC.2009.10.001

Heyman, J. M., & Campbell, H. (2009). The Anthropology of Global Flows: A Critical Reading of Appadurai's "Disjuncture and Difference in the Global Cultural Economy". *Anthropological Theory*, *9*(2), 131–148. https://doi.org/10.1177/1463499609105474

Hislop, D., & Axtell, C. (2007). The Neglect of Spatial Mobility in Contemporary Studies of Work: The Case of Telework. *New Technology, Work and Employment*, *22*(1), 34–51. https://doi.org/10.1111/j.1468-005X.2007.00182.x

Humphry, J. (2014). Officing: Mediating Time and the Professional Self in the Support of Nomadic Work. *Computer Supported Cooperative Work (CSCW)*, *23*(2), 185–204. https://doi.org/10.1007/s10606-013-9197-3

James, A. (2013). Work–life 'Balance' and Gendered (Im)Mobilities of Knowledge and Learning in High-Tech Regional Economies. *Journal of Economic Geography*, 1–28. https://doi.org/10.1093/jeg/lbt002

Kakihara, M., Sørensen, C., & Wiberg, M. (2002). Fluid Interaction in Mobile Work Practices. *Proceedings of the First Global Mobile Roundtable*. Tokyo, Japan: Institute of Innovation Research.

Kesselring, S., & Vogl, G. (2008). Networks, Scapes and Flows – Mobility Pioneers between First and Second Modernity. In W. Canzler, V. Kaufmann, & S. Kesselring (Eds.), *Tracing Mobilities. Towards a Cosmopolitan Perspective* (pp. 163–180). London & New York: Routledge.

Kleinrock, L. (1996). Nomadicity: Anytime, Anywhere in a Disconnected World. *Mobile Networks and Applications*, *1*(4), 351–357.

Lampinen, A. (2016). Hosting Together via Couchsurfing: Privacy Management in the Context of Network Hospitality. *International Journal of Communication, 10*, 1581–1600.

Laurier, E. (2002). The Region as a Socio-technical Accomplishment of Mobile Workers. In B. Brown, N. Green, & R. Harper (Eds.), *Wireless World: Social and Interactional Aspects of the Mobile Age* (pp. 46–61). London: Springer-Verlag. https://doi.org/10.1007/978-1-4471-0665-4_4

Liegl, M. (2014). Nomadicity and the Care of Place – On the Aesthetic and Affective Organization of Space in Freelance Creative Work. *Journal of Computer Supported Cooperative Work, 23*(2), 163–183. https://doi.org/10.1007/s10606-014-9198-x

Lyons, G., & Urry, J. (2005). Travel Time Use in the Information Age. *Transportation Research Part A: Policy and Practice, 39*(2–3), 257–276. https://doi.org/10.1016/J.TRA.2004.09.004

Mark, G., & Su, N. M. (2010). Making Infrastructure Visible for Nomadic Work. *Pervasive and Mobile Computing, 6*(3), 312–323. https://doi.org/10.1016/J.PMCJ.2009.12.004

Martins, J. (2015). The Extended Workplace in a Creative Cluster: Exploring Space(s) of Digital Work in Silicon Roundabout. *Journal of Urban Design, 20*(1), 125–145. https://doi.org/10.1080/13574809.2014.972349

Moriset, B. (2014). Building New Places of the Creative Economy: The Rise of Coworking Spaces. In *Proceedings of the 2nd Geography of Innovation International Conference*. Retrieved from https://halshs.archives-ouvertes.fr/halshs-00914075/

Nippert-Eng, C. E. (1996). *Home and Work: Negotiating Boundaries through Everyday Life*. Chicago & London: University of Chicago Press.

Noonan, J. (2015). Thought-Time, Money-Time, and the Temporal Conditions of Academic Freedom. *Time & Society, 24*(1), 109–128. https://doi.org/10.1177/0961463X14539579

Oldenburg, R. (1989). *The Great Good Place: Cafés, Coffee Shops, Community Centers, Beauty Parlors, General Stores, Bars, Hangouts, and How They Get You through the Day*. New York: Paragon House.

Orlikowski, W. J. (2007). Sociomaterial Practices: Exploring Technology at Work. *Organization Studies, 28*(9), 1435–1448. https://doi.org/10.1177/0170840607081138

Perry, M., O'Hara, K., Sellen, A., Brown, B., & Harper, R. (2001). Dealing with Mobility: Understanding Access Anytime, Anywhere. *ACM Transactions on Computer-Human Interaction (TOCHI), 8*(4), 323–347. https://doi.org/10.1145/504704.504707

Petriglieri, G., Ashford, S. J., & Wrzesniewski, A. (2019). Agony and Ecstasy in the Gig Economy: Cultivating Holding Environments for Precarious and Personalized Work Identities. *Administrative Science Quarterly, 64*(1), 124–170. https://doi.org/10.1177/0001839218759646

Pieterse, J. N. (1994). Globalisation as Hybridisation. *International Sociology, 9*(2), 161–184. https://doi.org/10.1177/026858094009002003

Popoveniuc, B. (2014). Self Reflexivity: The Ultimate End of Knowledge. *Procedia – Social and Behavioral Sciences, 163*, 204–213. https://doi.org/10.1016/j.sbspro.2014.12.308

Presskorn-Thygesen, T. (2015). The Possibility of Critique under a Financialized Capitalism: The Case of Private Equity in the United Kingdom. *Ephemera, 725–753*(4), 465–484. https://doi.org/10.1177/1350508414563526

Rossitto, C., Bogdan, C., & Severinson-Eklundh, K. (2014). Understanding Constellations of Technologies in Use in a Collaborative Nomadic Setting. *Computer Supported Cooperative Work (CSCW), 23*(2), 137–161. https://doi.org/10.1007/s10606-013-9196-4

Rossitto, C., Ciolfi, L., Büscher, M., Bogdan, C., & Severinson-Eklundh, K. (2007). Situating Mobility, Understanding Nomadic Work. In *Workshop held at the European Conference on Computer-Supported Cooperative Work.*

Rossitto, C., & Lampinen, A. (2018). Co-Creating the Workplace: Participatory Efforts to Enable Individual Work at the Hoffice. *Computer Supported Cooperative Work (CSCW)*, *27*(3–6), 947–982. https://doi.org/10.1007/s10606-018-9319-z

Sheller, M., & Urry, J. (2006). The New Mobilities Paradigm. *Environment and Planning A*, *38*(2), 207–226. https://doi.org/10.1068/a37268

Shohat, E., & Stam, R. (1994). *Unthinking Eurocentrism: Multiculturalism and the Media*. New York: Routledge.

Sørensen, C. (2011). *Enterprise Mobility: Tine Technology with Global Impact on Work*. New York: Palgrave Macmillan.

Spinuzzi, C. (2012). Working Alone Together: Coworking as Emergent Collaborative Activity. *Journal of Business and Technical Communication*, *26*(4), 399–441. https://doi.org/10.1177/1050651912444070

Steward, B. (2000). Living Space: The Changing Meaning of Home. *British Journal of Occupational Therapy*, *63*(3), 105–110. https://doi.org/10.1177/030802260006300303

Urry, J. (2000). *Sociology Beyond Societies*. London: Routledge.

Verne, G., & Bratteteig, T. (2016). Do-It-Yourself Services and Work-Like Chores: On Civic Duties and Digital Public Services. *Personal and Ubiquitous Computing*, *20*(4), 517–532. https://doi.org/10.1007/s00779-016-0936-6

Vostal, F. (2015). Academic Life in the Fast Lane: The Experience of Time and Speed in British Academia. *Time & Society*, *24*(1), 71–95. https://doi.org/10.1177/0961463X13517537

Watts, L. (2008). The Art and Craft of Train Travel. *Social & Cultural Geography*, *9*(6), 711–726. https://doi.org/10.1080/14649360802292520

Wolff, J. (1993). On the Road Again: Metaphors of Travel in Cultural Criticism. *Cultural Studies*, *7*(2), 224–239. https://doi.org/10.1080/09502389300490151

Young, R. J. C. (1995). *Colonial Desire: Hybridity in Theory, Culture and Race*. London: Routledge.

Chapter 4

Anticipatory availability

'Time work' in the worklives of ICT managers and digital creatives

George, an Enterprise Ireland official with responsibility for High Potential Start-Ups (HPSUs), frames the environment of contemporary business development and entrepreneurship as follows:

> We live in times now where *things have to move a little bit quicker* (...) I just want businesses that will *expand and grow and create employment fast* (...) we are looking for people who will *grow and expand rapidly* because we want to get the job numbers up (...) I see companies that come on the programme and they will put in 35, 40 hours a week, and they don't get anywhere, and some of those businesses have not survived (...). We've won eight major awards in the last four and a half years and if you look at the guys that have won those awards, all of them, even now (...) will put in 80, 90 hours a week (...) nine to five extends perhaps *from six till midnight* (...) there are three things: *ambition, passion and potential* (...). It's all very well to have passion, but if you haven't got ambition....
>
> (George, DC)

Most of the digital creatives and a few of the ICT managers taking part in our study benefited from the regionally available infrastructures of the state-supported Enterprise Ireland, including the HPSU innovation programme. George suggests that if new entrepreneurs are to excel and the state is to meet its job creation targets, individuals and start-up companies must combine passion and ambition with speedy growth and extremely long hours. As Wajcman observes: 'when you are in start-up mode, you have to innovate very very quickly: "time is everything"' (Saxenian, 1994, p. XI, citated in Wajcman, 2018, p. 6). But this constructs time as an individual resource rather than a relational accomplishment (Wajcman, 2019). George continues:

> The average age of an entrepreneur in America is 18 or 19 years of age (...) in Ireland [it] is (...) between 34 and 45 (...) if entrepreneurs are coming through at that age (...) *the females of that age will have families; either having families, or looking after kids* that are going to school (...) the man is out working,

> the typical two and a half family (…) it's just pure demographics (…) on the HPSU stage, the women are few and far between (…). *They don't have the time, they don't have the mental time, not the physical time.* They don't have the mental time to concentrate on what it is to bring a business to commercialisation (…). The ones that have access to it are equally as successful as the men (…) and some of them were just purely *single minded* that they were going to do this regardless.…[1]

The materiality of care work and '[w]omen's attitudes and behaviours clearly fall outside the boundaries of proper entrepreneurialism' (Joseph, 2014, p. 105), defined by George as the domain of the middle-aged, unencumbered male. Motherhood is 'the identity that dares not speak its name in the business world' (Ekinsmyth, 2014, p. 1243),[2] while fatherhood is located outside entrepreneurial temporalities altogether.

Notwithstanding optimistic portrayals of entrepreneurship as an attractive career option for women in recent years, and the increase in numbers of women becoming entrepreneurs (de Bruin, Brush, & Welter, 2006), international evidence indicates that almost twice as many men as women become entrepreneurs (Acs, Arenius, Hay, & Minniti, 2005; Gupta, Turban, Wasti, & Sikdar, 2009; Wheadon & Duval-Couetil, 2017). And, despite claims that labour market participation, rather than selfless, home-based caring is the marker of the 'good mother' (Bianchi, 2011; Ekinsmyth, 2011; Luckman, 2015), George's account reproduces a naturalised connection between women, family and home (except for the single-minded, single and child-free). Through this connection, mothers are deemed as lacking the 'mental' and 'physical' time necessary for a business start-up. The gendered temporalisation of entrepreneurial subjectivity as speeded-up and time-devouring is echoed in the account of George's colleague, Leo, who is also an Enterprise Ireland official:

> You need people to *move at speed* (…) the focus for getting onto the next phase is really about the promoter or the entrepreneur and their business idea (…) we call them promoters at the early stage and they become entrepreneurs at the end (…) so we are looking at *somebody who can be developed into the type of person* that's going to create a company that's going to employ people (…) it's going to be of benefit to the economy (…). The individual is going to *give up whatever else they are doing* and they are going to *spend 100 per cent of their time* over the next six months dedicated to setting up the business … the characteristics you are looking at there is somebody who is *flexible* and somebody who is *resilient* (…) it's the desire they have; a *burning desire* to create something and to build it (…) and then yes, it may go on, but in a lot of cases they do tend to *sell it on and they do start to build again.*
>
> (Leo, DC)

In these accounts, start-up enterprises and entrepreneurship are defined by the multiple capacities of economic and state infrastructures, business ideas and a 'type of person' who combines passion, burning desire, ambition, flexibility, resilience, speed and 100 per cent commitment. A speculative attitude and short-term business horizons intensify the anticipatory orientation of the start-up. For example, even before the business is up and running, there is the expectation that entrepreneurs anticipate readiness for selling off in a few years and beginning the cycle again. In this chapter, we propose the structuring temporal orientation of *anticipatory availability* to capture those sociomaterial practices that emerge in the accounts of the ICT managers and digital creatives. Building on the worklife placing and place making discussed in Chapters 2 and 3, we examine the 'time work' through which this worklife temporality is reproduced. The temporal orientation reported by our academic cohort departed so much from that of *anticipatory availability* that we devote a separate chapter to their *reflexive rhythmic* worklife orientation (see Chapter 5).

In the sections that follow we unravel the kinds of time work undertaken to reproduce a temporal orientation of *anticipatory availability* and how it is represented in the accounts of both the digital creative and ICT manager cohorts. In doing so, we investigate the mobile sociomaterial practices that shape anticipatory availability. Which sociomaterial practices sustain or subvert this temporal orientation? Are these different for ICT managers and digital creatives and within these sectors? How is worklife conjoined or not via these practices? Following a brief review of scholarship on contemporary reconfigurations of time and temporal dispositions, we address those practices that reproduce the temporality of anticipatory availability before moving on in the third section to examine the kinds of time work involved in sustaining this work-devoted temporal orientation and its worklife effects.

Time work as corollary work

The acceleration of technological and social change has implications for the pace of worklife and intensifies the time work engaged in by MKWrs. Because things can change in seconds, MKWrs have to be practiced in living with change, unpredictability and contingency (Rosa, 2013). Time acceleration is multifactorial and includes: 'machine speed', a hypervaluation of work productivity, intensified consumption patterns, speculation and capital accumulation, as well as social and cultural changes, including dual career families, heightened expectations about parenting and the promise of rewarding lifestyles (Wajcman, 2015).[3] Although there is some evidence of time acceleration in the accounts of ICT managers and digital creatives, the dominant temporal orientation is one of anticipatory availability. This temporal orientation underpins the corollary time work that makes their MKW possible.

Flaherty defines 'time work' as 'individual or interpersonal efforts to create or suppress particular kinds of temporal experience' (2003, p. 17). It is shaped by how individuals interpret the situations they find themselves in and how they customise temporal experience in relation to future possibilities in current or anticipated circumstances (2003, p. 29). Despite this emphasis on individual interpretation and co-construction, Flaherty concedes that most time work 'operates within cultures, organizations, and relationships without challenging the status quo (…) [it] is largely a product of existing arrangements and contributes to their reproduction' (2003, p. 32). Insofar as a central focus and effect of most time work is the reduction of 'the friction between self and society', he suggests that this work tends to reproduce the status quo (ibid.). Yet, the above remarks by George and Leo suggest that those setting up businesses must work on bringing their selves into line with work demands. There is a sense in which the self must be extended and mined in pursuit of an agile and ever-ready openness to opportunity and change.

For Moen et al. (2013), time work involves more *constrained agency* than that suggested by Flaherty. It is constrained insofar as the options open to the 'knowledge workers' they studied 'are limited by compliance with those temporal work norms and associated cultural and structural arrangements' that shape everyday interaction (2013, p. 84).[4] These workers have to 'decide when they are *not* working' and experience almost constant 'pressure to engage in or at least be available for job-related tasks' (2013, p. 83, emphasis original). They identify a proliferation of time work demands as a kind of 'master structure' that shapes 'the duration, sequencing and rhythms of roles, relationships, and behavior in and out of formal paid work obligations' (Moen et al., 2013, p. 103). Because of the 'boundaryless' nature of the work, they see time work as 'doing boundary work' (2013, p. 98). This work is concerned with a desire to work more effectively, mental health considerations and rest. It is represented as a private, individualised problem requiring personalised solutions (2013). It is only by moving work to more convenient times and places, i.e. 'time shifting' and undertaking other life tasks in 'work time' that resistance to work temporalities takes place.

In Moen et al.'s study, non-work demands are only occasionally placed above work demands and the prioritising of family tends to be more cognitive than behavioural. The dominant pattern across gender is alignment of lives with job time demands to achieve better fit with varying degrees of success. Key time work strategies include a partner/spouse in part-time work and the 'hiring out' of home duties. Overall, however, they conclude that time work consists of those strategies adopted '*to lessen the negative effects of the stress of higher status on their lives*' (2013, p. 81, emphasis original).

Moving beyond definitions of time work that assume an intentional subject that pre-exists the doing, we are interested in how time work emerges as a capacity that is realised via the association of human and non-human actors in relational and emergent ways. By studying the varying forms that worklife assumes, we gain insight into 'the capacity to act' as an agency that is the result of particular configurations of actors (Barad, 2003; Orlikowski, 2007; Suchman, 2007). This is not a static relationality, as Barad argues, but 'a doing' that incorporates the material as active in the *becoming* of worklife. These doings in the present bear the imprint of past doings, but are also future oriented. Because worklife temporal practices and norms work through diverse 'institutions, discourses, environments, including technologies and life processes' (Butler, 2015, p. 7), they are multiple and contradictory. Thus, workers come into being as particular kinds of worker subjects through a matrix of relations and through intersecting and sometimes conflictual temporal norms and practices. Our focus is on those sociomaterial practices that (re)produce the temporal orientation of *anticipatory availability* and how these practices are implicated with ideas of the entrepreneur, ICT management and self-employed digital creative work. We see time work therefore as a heterogeneous practice involving multiple interacting performances.

Time itself, the worker, worklife and product are all performatively constituted through the time work enacted by workers in entanglement with their emplaced environments, digital infrastructures, mobile devices and social relations. In this chapter, we unravel the textures of *anticipatory availability* by examining how this temporal orientation emerges in the workers' accounts. We also highlight how time work is done and redone in the intra-action of myriad material and non-material actors. We propose that anticipatory availability is concerned with the 'scope of optimisation' and relies on constant availability in order to avail of potential opportunities (Adams, Murphy, & Clarke, 2009, p. 256). It (re)produces a radically uncertain future marked by ever-receding horizons of uncertainty. It is a mode of becoming that is reproduced in the constant time work of anticipating speedy changes in technology and knowledge domains, expanding customer expectations and constantly changing life circumstances. In the following section, we consider the ways in which temporal norms of anticipatory availability are enacted and reproduced in the accounts of ICT managers and digital creatives.

Anticipatory availability and the entrepreneurial imperative

Anticipatory practices are underpinned by two conditions: first, the meaning attributed to futures that 'are far enough to be uncertain, and on which a variety of actors have to agree and ultimately act'; and second, those emergent expectations about the future that are embedded in practice and which trigger other future-oriented activities, for example, via processes of problem-solving for customers (Alvial-Palavicino, 2015, p. 154). Contemporary norms of anticipation are reproduced by speedy technological change, mobile connectivity, intensified competition, shifting customer demand, which in turn summon expectations of *availability* and constant alertness to indicators of change. For example, Charles (ICTM) notes 'we are much more connected, and the speed of things is much faster …'; Dan (ICT manager in his late 20s, unmarried) asserts that 'being in a technology company means you need to be connected as much as possible'; and Nancy (ICT manager in her 30s, unmarried and with no children), notes: 'I do some of the research (…) to help our sales guys build the case for long-term future energy price increases (…) there is that kind of continuous thing'. Damien, the owner and director of a small software development and consulting start-up, acts in the present based on perceptions of future competition:

> In a situation where you're providing somebody with a service, *you always need to be available to deal with that customer* (…). So there's no stopping(…) every single customer is potentially your boss (…) unless you have a competitive advantage (…) to guarantee the business you have to (…) give them the best service (…) you've got to work harder (…). And in the evenings then, I tend to catch up on emails at home, and my brain goes into default mode where I'm always thinking of 'how can I improve things?'… So literally, I eat, I sleep and I wake up and drink work (…) *I always try to think ahead and try to find better ways to do things, better ways to use time.*
>
> (Damien, ICTM)

The future is constructed in the present, not via prediction, but in constant adjustment to an anticipated future that is uncertain and highly dynamic (Alvial-Palavicino, 2015).

Customer demands and perpetual striving for competitive advantage create constant pressure to 'keep up', but upskilling is mostly done outside of 'office hours' in what is often described as 'down time' (Ross, 2004). Damien characterises the masculine embodiment of the always-connected ICT worker as follows:

> You know the stereotype of the big guy with the beard and the sandals in 'The Simpsons' (…) with his computer everywhere he goes (…) he has to be connected to the internet? And a certain amount of being in a technology company means you need to be connected as much as possible (…).
>
> (Damien, ICTM)

Being connected means remaining available to capitalise on unanticipated opportunities. Staying informed about possible futures is mandatory. For example, Damien notes that because '[we] are building our name, building our credibility as a *viable partner for somebody who might have a great idea in the future* (…) it buys us time to (…) do our own market research'. He compares this with the work of academics: 'if your paper is delayed by a month, and the funding money is there, well it doesn't matter. You're still going to get paid at the end of the month'. In business there is 'a different level of urgency (…) it comes down to the time frames'. Martin comments:

> I might find a link to a very good article on integrating ERP [enterprise resource planning] data, and rather than read it here [at the office], I'll just email that link to my home mail address, and when I get home and have some dinner (…) then I'll (…) read it at home, study it there (…) *this is not a job you leave at the desk.*
>
> (Martin, ICTM)

Flows of new information and research are always and instantly available via digital technologies (Lindley, 2015). Martin describes those sociomaterial practices by which he ensures that he can keep up, including the designating of office-based and home-based tasks and moving them via email.

The imperative of keeping up to date shapes both the long-term temporality of worker employability and the shorter-term working day. For example, Derek (a small ICT company owner/manager, cohabiting with his fiancé) observes:

> The logic behind people starting work at nine o'clock in the morning and finishing at half five (…) it just has to be one of the most stupid ideas on the planet (…) if you hired a guy ten years ago who's very clever, *if he hasn't kept up to date, he's no good. It's a constantly changing industry….*
>
> (Derek, ICTM)

Derek cultivates an 'ethos of preparedness' (Adams et al., 2009, p. 254) by remaining at the office until six or seven and then working from home checking 'what's happening in technology in America (…)? (…) [and] some customers (…) will ring me after eight o'clock at night'. This temporal orientation becomes more urgent during recession: 'in recessions (…) the upward swing tends to be technology driven'. Derek goes on to pose questions about what might follow the post-2008 recession:

> So *what technology would bring us out of this*? Will it be thermonuclear power (…) will it be replicating the way the sun works to generate energy, will it be a change in the environment, will it be recycling? *I don't know. I can't tell you.*
>
> (Derek, ICTM)

Annabel (in charge of software quality assurance for a small international telecom company, cohabiting with partner, with no children), echoes this theme of material uncertainty linked to the recession:

> What I see that's going to happen in the future (…) I don't really know. This recession, *none of us might have jobs soon. We might all be at home having families (...) to get a bit of money from the dole.* (…) *it's very hard to predict now the future.* Whereas *before, people would have predicted the future* (…) like if you keep developing software etcetera and keep your software product at a higher level and *keep getting the features out before your competitors do* and new aspects to the software out before your competitors do, you'll always be on top, so you'll always have that competitive edge over the rest of them.
>
> (Annabel, ICTM)

Although capitalist anticipatory regimes 'tend to work through logics of expansion in which new territories for speculation must be continually found to keep the anticipatory logic moving' (Adams et al., 2009, pp. 250–251), Annabel perceives the contemporary tech sector as particularly precarious. Stressing that prediction is no longer possible, she speculates on a future in which she loses her job and starts a family as a means of improving her chances of a livelihood via welfare support. The state rather than the market, and social reproduction rather than production, are looked to as potential sites of material survival. As more and more actions in the present are shaped by ever-receding and short-term horizons of the future, 'anticipation has become a dominant new virtue' (Bear, 2016, p. 493). However, because the future can no longer be predicated on the basis of the present, this anticipatory disposition is marked by a sense of disorientation.

Unlike the logic of risk, which suggests some level of calculability and processes that are known to some extent at least, a temporal regime of anticipatory availability emanates from an absence of 'ways of knowing the future' (Alvial-Palavicino, 2015, p. 157). Anticipatory availability, as it emerges in the accounts above, suggests a pre-emptive logic in which practices are shaped by uncertainty about future events in a 'world of strong interdependencies' (Alvial-Palavicino, 2015, p. 156). The intra-action of customer organisation schedules, shifting customer needs and constant technological change requires mobilising resources to sustain availability and to anticipate demands. This anticipatory orientation is also built into many of the tools that enable this work. Nonstop anticipation, and availability to respond to a constantly changing worklife environment are conjoined in these accounts of ICT managers which describe practices of agility, mobility and vitality as both pragmatic and virtuous. It is only in relation to the effects of recession that an existential uncertainty emerges.

In contrast, nearly all of the digital creative participants express an ambivalent, even anxious relationship to this temporal orientation. While it looms as the ideal, it requires a lot of work in the organising of worklife to achieve it. This is particularly the case for mothers or those who wish to be. Only one woman in this cohort described anticipatory availability in ways that suggest pleasure and even excitement. Sara, who is self-employed, working from home and living with her partner and without children, states:

> If you look at a *big company* like [big Pharma company] and (…) how they do their product development, what they do compared to what I do (…) it *moves at the speed of a glacier*. It could take two years to get a new product onto a supermarket shelf, and that would be considered a *very rapid product deployment. But I get to do that 18 times a year (…) it's a huge buzz.*
>
> (Sara, DC)

The sustainability of Sara's online service relies on speediness of service delivery, with deadlines energising the work but also requiring long days:

> I'm at my computer about *20 minutes after I wake up with a cup of coffee and I sit there for the next 18 hours*. And then I go to bed (…) there's a break for

> dinner at about 9 p.m. and that's it (...) the thing about being self-employed and a freelancer is (...) *I work, under the kind of pressure on the projects I enjoy working on....*
>
> (Sara, DC)

Sara's attachment to her computer and her cup of coffee signal her work presence and fast subjectivity. Anticipatory availability requires long hours and is inhabited all the more alertly when time pressure delivers the 'buzz' of tight deadlines and working with small businesses. However, Sara's is a lone voice in our digital creative cohort.

Most of the other digital creative workers describe anticipatory availability as an unrealisable or tyrannical imperative. For example, Earl established his online company to indulge his interest in problem-solving, but finds the temporal demands of this kind of creative work difficult to manage personally: 'I guess I kind of wanted to put myself more in an environment that allows a little bit more creativity (...) I'm a nerd like; I'm a nerd pretty much' (Earl, DC). Despite his keen interest in the work, Earl notes that 'it's a constant thing that I have to drive myself, or else I'll end up reading a book or playing guitar or doing something'. In contrast, Kathy craves routine as a buffer against anticipatory availability:

> I *struggle to have a routine* but I've had to *really force myself* (...) [I'm] not an early riser, work late throughout the night and that's when I'm actually most creative (...) I do to push myself, to make sure that I am in here early (...) I'll do that till all hours of the night (...) just cos the demand (...) I work probably, its averaged out around 60 hours but your mind is actually on it 24/7 (...) I don't expect to get full weekends, but if I get six hours done on the Saturday, and actually I don't like working the Saturdays, I don't mind working the Sundays, so I'll actually do a full day on the Sunday. But I will try and like take a Saturday evening off (...) at the very least ... *that stereotype of working every hour God sends.*
>
> (Kathy, DC)

The all-consuming quality of anticipatory availability makes it difficult to put limits on work. Like Earl, Kathy struggles with how she can personally manage this temporal imperative and finds herself caught between the moral imperatives of constant work availability and temporal overwhelm.

Kathy is also caught by the dilemma of how to sequence career and maternity. Having invested in her career as middle-class women are invited to do, she has postponed maternity based on the promise of fulfilment through work (Rottenberg, 2017). This promise circulates in popular culture and (neo)liberal feminist manifestos that put work first for upwardly mobile women and suggest that with the right management of their lives they can have it all (Sandberg, 2013; Slaughter, 2012). However, material bodies are less 'programmable' than work practices, and Kathy, who is 33, struggles with the conflict between the temporal demands of work and making worklife:

> *I'd love to have children* (…) I had a conversation with my doctor … he gave me the biggest scare ever (…) 'if you want children … it could be a year trying'. (…) he was adding up the years for me and it was pretty scary stuff (…) he said, *if I want to postpone it till later (…) then I would have to look after myself health-wise.* So, in your 30s you start to really notice that energy, being deprived of energy, you just start to age and if you don't maintain yourself healthily then, then it will suffer (…) it's a priority that is rising (…) it would be a good thing if I could get more time for that.
>
> (Kathy, DC)

Relatedly, Damien, quoted earlier as sleeping, eating and drinking work, later states that:

> Maybe we [he and his partner] should step back a little bit from the business, accept a lower level of service for our customers, and go onto the next step (…) in life, which is creating a family, buying a (…) family home and (…) settling down really….
>
> (Damien, ICTM)

Both Kathy and Damien's accounts point to how work-based anticipatory availability 'binds' them into socially meaningful embodiment by prioritising work and postponing family. Yet, the social and material effects of this postponing of family are gendered and are articulated in terms of embodied distress in Kathy's account.

Their provisionally anticipated heteronormative life trajectories are further predicated on a 'right' time for particular life stages, such as intensive career focus and establishing a family. Freeman (2010) calls these temporalising practices 'chrononormativity' due to their normative power in reproducing capitalist ideologies that discipline bodies to be both socially and economically 'productive'. However, in Kathy and Damien's accounts, the present becomes anxious based on the uncertainties of how their future work and family lives might emerge. Their availability for work makes availability for other aspects of life impossible in the present. Indeed, the future is made all the more unpredictable by a continuous anxious present that seems impossible to escape. This is a present mired in work so that family is put on hold indefinitely. There is no 'until'; it is 'like a car with its wheels stuck in the mud' (Bryant, 2016, p. 21). Neither 'the biological clock' in Kathy's case, nor Damien's desire to buy a house and 'settle down', seem capable of jerking them out of this work-mired pothole. The temporal orientation of anticipatory availability saturates their present and bogs it down. It leaves their futures stranded. Their time work is focused on keeping work going while they anxiously background other life desires and temporalities.

Anticipatory availability for work becomes burdensome and anxiety provoking in other ways too. For example, Betty (an early stage digital creative with two children) resists anticipatory availability as a profit-driven temporal norm:

> It's not like you're going to work 20 hours a day, or whatever it is some people might be doing, and know for sure you're going to make the profit (…) *sure it's flexible, you can come in at 10 a.m. (…) but it's expected that you stay until (…) that you give up weekends and you give up time.*
>
> (Betty, DC)

She continues:

> It's not that I don't feel entrepreneurial it's that *I'm not driven by profit in that way* (…) because I like working with people and I don't like the stress of money – *I'm not a natural (…) people expect you to say 'I'm the most driven, I eat and breathe this'.*
>
> (Betty, DC)

In Betty's account this hegemonic temporal orientation conflicts with an inclination towards the more organic time of human interaction and 'working with people'.

Rita (a digital creative who owns a start-up, married with three children) incorporates her children's school timetables in her anticipatory availability so that she can be physically present for them:

> *I felt self-employed was the best route for me to go that would afford me the flexibility with the kids* (…) I get up at (…) sixish, six-thirty and I try and get an hour done on stuff, (…) I could get work done from two to four (…) I generally get (…) about an hour of work if they are doing homework four to five (…) I do stuff in the weekends as well (…) every single day, every week there are deadlines of some sort that have to be met (…) the hardest thing is (…) carrying it with you all the time (…) *I think it works for me with the family at the moment, they don't notice too much that I'm working all the time.*
>
> (Rita, DC)

Although physically present for her children, Rita is attentionally absent. Her account resonates with Moen et al.'s (2013) finding that the prioritising of family can be more cognitive than behavioural. She embraces the potential for time flexibility via self-employment, but her account suggests a central tension between time flexibility and having a 'never-ending job' (Raval & Dourish, 2016, p. 100). She strives to meet the normative expectation that middle-class women can 'pursue a fulfilling career without having to forfeit family life or raising children' (Rottenberg, 2017, p. 330). One of the ways in which Rita approximates this ideal is by being present with her children at specific times in the day while 'working all the time'. This resonates with Sharon's account of working from home discussed in Chapter 3. Although Sharon joins her children in the kitchen for breakfast, she is simultaneously preoccupied by the work that is awaiting her attention and pulling her back to her home office.

Dean, who has one child and engages in demanding leisure activities, set up his company specifically to counter a work temporality of anticipatory availability:

> In all of *my 20s I was extremely career-focused* (…) now, as somebody who's self-employed (…) the usual KPIs [key performance indicators] (…) aren't my KPIs (…). Rather than say that I'm trying to achieve a turn-over or a margin of X or Y or Z, (…) I say, okay, this week I worked 30 hours (…) it's a case that it gave me time, sufficient time *to apply to my family situation and to my own (…) personal or selfish pursuits which are cycling [and] triathlon (…)* it's been a shift I suppose in the early to mid-30s in my life, it's been a shift in mindset as to what's important.
>
> (Dean, DC)

The temporal orientation of anticipatory availability is avoided by working only with clients who are relatively undemanding and are not working to tight deadlines.

> The clients I'm dealing with, *they're not really fussed whether the content changes in the next four hours or 14 hours or 24 hours* (…) so (…) I have that scope to do whatever it is I want to do, if it's 'me time' or 'family time'.
>
> (Dean, DC)

In the accounts of many of the digital creatives, and Damien who is an ICT manager, anticipatory availability paradoxically enacts stuckness in a continuous and never-ending worklife present. So, while many of the ICT managers suggest pragmatic sociomaterial practices of anticipatory availability in sustaining worklife, for the digital creatives this temporal orientation emerges as a tyrannical ideal that in practice has the ironic effect of miring them in a continuous and anxious present. In the section that follows we examine the ways in which worklife is conjoined in the materialisation of anticipatory availability for work.

The routinisation of worklife

Like the doing of MKW, the doing of family relationships of care and intimacy involve constant anticipation of unpredictable time demands (Altomonte, 2016; Gerstel & Clawson, 2018). Yet, most accounts describe personal life practices of temporal ordering that potentially reduce any negative effects on work. In this section, we show that anticipatory availability materialises MKW by either reducing or rigidly routinising intimate non-work relationships and other life activities. For example, Damien notes:

> *Tuesday night (...) is sports at seven o'clock.* I go *play soccer for an hour* (...). *My fiancé, she lives in Dublin, so I always put a few minutes aside every evening, maybe 20 minutes, we have a conversation, just catch up every day* (...) get to bed maybe half 11, 12 o'clock, and it starts again....
>
> (Damien, ICTM)

Via a routinisation of non-work practices, Damien sustains contact with his fiancé and continues to play soccer, while sustaining anticipatory availability for work. Similar temporal ordering practices of minimising work interference arise in Kathy's account:

> I am seeing someone, but *both of us are entrepreneurs so we both understand the dynamic of, we don't have all this time (...) my personal life has accommodated the drive and my whole-time input into the business.*
>
> (Kathy, DC)

Sara also actively schedules non-work time. By ensuring that most life needs are otherwise met, she protects anticipatory availability for work:

> So if *I want to do something other than work, I have to actually put it down in my schedule and (...) find two or three days to do that,* whatever it is (...) we hired a housekeeper (...). We get our *groceries delivered and everybody does their own laundry.*
>
> (Sara, DC)

Potential temporal conflicts are also avoided in Derek's life via a gendered division of labour and complementary lifestyles:

> *I don't do any house chores,* so that's really easy, but (...) I like to cook (...) that's my hobby at home. I like to cook so, and she [his fiancé] doesn't. So it's just, *we're lucky we found each other. She's very good at sleeping, I'm not. I don't sleep very well. So when we're on holiday, she likes to sleep late in the morning, I work.*
>
> (Derek, ICTM)

At the very least, complementary lifestyles mean that the temporality of coupledom does not interfere with temporal investment in work. It is the absence of family that emerges in Seamus' account as ensuring constant work availability:

> People like myself (...) *we work 24/7, a lot of the time, 365 days a year (...) I'm still unmarried like, I don't have a family.* So I (...) don't have

> responsibility to that degree. If I did, I'm sure I would decide (…) I'm clocking out of here at eight o'clock and I'm going to have dinner with the family and I'm going to spend time with the kids.
>
> (Seamus, DC, single entrepreneur in his late 30s without children)

While family time holds the potential to counter work availability for Seamus, the accounts of mothers enact family less in terms of work boundarying and more in relation to challenging practices of conjoining work and family. In some accounts, the temporalities of work and life/family actively collide. Having recently set up her own online business, Betty reflects on the time required to care for her children. Like her business, childcare involves constant availability and anticipation of future care demands:

> The *business is moving along too slow* (…) it should be moving along faster (…) it's just that it gets so interrupted the whole time (…) and the fact that I'm working on my own, it gets stagnant (…) *I might be there with a really important thing I need to get done and then your child (…) hurts herself so you can't say no (…) I need to answer these ten emails now (…) I'd say my business is second-hand, my family is first.*
>
> (Betty, DC)

Anticipatory availability for her children trumps the similar temporal demands of the business: '[it] is a question of money, regardless, a question of time (…) *the business is just there to fund my life and my family*' (Betty, DC). Yet the business represents her self-identity 'I *want my own life*' but '*my girls, I gave them a lot of time (…) and then (…) your guilt* about it …'. We are returned to George's opening account and to Betty's own experience with the HPSU innovation programme manager (Chapter 2), which pitted entrepreneurial work time (and space) and the temporality of motherhood as incompatible.

In a different way, Sharon's passionate preoccupation with work conflicts with the presence and availability that constitute good mothering in her account:

> In five *years' time (…) I think I'll probably still be working, still doing it until three o'clock or two o'clock, maybe doing a four-day week* because I'm just very conscious of time passing, I just *don't want the kids to be latchkey kids, I don't want them to think back on their childhood 'Mammy was always working. Mammy was always on Twitter*. Mammy was always just trying to get this email done before'.
>
> (Sharon, DC)

Echoing Rita's earlier quote, which describes the work of hiding the fact that she is always working from her children, Sharon judges her worklife practice in the present based on anticipated evaluations by her children in the future. Yet, there is a sense that despite her wish to shift her work-oriented temporal practices, she is not hopeful about achieving this. There is an obligatory yet fatalistic tone to the temporal practices of motherhood articulated in both Betty and Sharon's accounts.

Rita's account highlights the personal responsibility she assumes for the domination of her worklife by anticipatory availability to the extent that all other temporal practices fall by the wayside. She describes this as a failure of the planning and managing necessary to make life outside of work happen.

> It is *planning and managing and we don't do enough* of that definitely (...) you do *sacrifice seeing friends* and (...) for too long now (...) I've been saying (...) we will catch up and I've *missed out a lot of social things recently* because (...) I'm really kind of committed to getting [work] done (...) I'll go to the market on Saturday morning, I love that but (...) *I'm just not doing enough social stuff.* I suppose but I don't feel like I miss it, but I probably am missing it (...) I probably should be doing it (...). As a couple, I would say that and I would be a *believer in making time to go and do stuff maybe once a week and that is a problem we are not doing that* (...) the exercise I should be doing more (...) I'm a believer in healthy body, healthy mind and I don't do it.
>
> (Rita, DC)

The notion of 'quality time' is defined by Lynch as time in which 'the (positive) presence of the other (...) allows for the trust and understanding to develop' (2007, p. 566). Although primarily associated with intimate, family and friendship relationships, in these accounts it emerges as much (if not more) in relationships to customers, fellow workers, information/knowledge, work practices and devices as it does to partners, children, friends and neighbours. In Rita's account discourses of health and sociality compete with work dedication, but by default social and personal time is not made. Non-work life time is difficult to schedule when work time prevails. The time work required for non-work activities to take place is privatised and individualised (Moen et al., 2013).

As in Moen et al.'s (2013) study, only one male participant, Charles, a company owner who had considerable international experience, reported a complementary anticipatory availability for work and family. Like their participant, Charles' sense of autonomy over and contentment with both work and family life temporalities would not have been possible for him ten years previously, when his work status and income were lower.

> You spend *more real time with your children*, and also do the household chore aspect, which is shared better (...). *Certainly I work more hours by being at home (...) I embed [work] in my lifestyle, so I don't necessarily have a defined divide between the two things, it doesn't bother me to get up and answer some work at 11 p.m., if I need* to. It is different than I used to do things in the past, when I had a divide. *But that's because I am a company owner now....*
>
> (Charles, ICTM)

Charles' account includes a detailed account of family and community practices that flow along with his work practices. This confluence of sociality, family and work is enabled by a networked home, financial stability and an established business.

In contrast, Dean, whose priority now is availability for his child and his leisure pursuits, avoids anticipatory availability for work by taking on less-demanding customers and by gathering systems and tools around him for closely scheduling other aspects of life. His account paradoxically emphasises temporal flexibility while at the same time describing the considerable work that goes into mobilising systems, devices and his relationships with his partner and clients to structure worklife temporalities:

> We'd sit down on a *Sunday evening, laptops open [laughing] on the couch (...) calendar open on the Microsoft Outlook* and we actually plan how the week is going to shape up and what each of us can do, where, when and what (…) *we sync our diaries* – that way everything really works (…) we're *careful that we have individual time, collective time, together as couple, as a family with our friends* (…) it just needs a little bit of planning and a little bit of give and take and *a little bit of flexibility.*
>
> (Dean, DC)

The sociomaterial assembling of personal time slots contrasts starkly with the agile and flexible practices that underpin anticipatory availability for work. Time takes on the qualities of individual 'me time', or 'collective', 'family' and 'friends' time. It is non-work temporalities that are tightly scheduled. Family life, relationships and leisure are organised by tight daily and weekly timetables so that family life is more 'taylorised' than working life (Hochschild, 1997; Ylijoki, 2013, p. 247). For example, as Dean continues:

> We were swimming with her [daughter] on Friday and then we *have her pizza and DVD night on Friday.* So that's how we start the weekend (…) if we're taking a bit of time gap out like, Saturday (…) we were more kind of focused on ourselves. So, we pre-empt that with her thing on the Friday (…). So even at the *weekend everyone is getting this together time, there's individual time.*
>
> (Dean, DC)

Wind-down time before sleep is also scheduled for:

> We'll cut off at ten *o'clock (...) laptops or whatever away at ten o'clock and that's our time then to have (...) a pot of tea and watch whatever our favourite thing is on telly….*
>
> (Dean, DC)

Anticipatory availability is the dominant work-based temporal orientation for ICT managers and digital creatives. However, Dean's time work prioritises allocating and designating time slots to non-work relationships and activities. This gives rise to the further time work of scaling back on work commitments and assessing the temporal expectations of the customers he takes on. He is able to counter the digital creative work norm of anticipatory availability because his partner is in full-time employment by a state agency. However, it seems that whether anticipatory availability for work is embraced, ambivalently enacted or resisted, when it comes to non-work practices, these must be tightly planned and managed, if they are to happen at all.

Conclusions

As in Leo and George's opening accounts, anticipation is in part about optimising the conditions of possibility for availing of economic opportunities and ensuring competitive advantage. Proliferating technologies sociomaterially designed to incorporate anticipation further normalise this temporal orientation. Yet, this temporality and the time work that sustains it manifest in diverse ways in the everyday worklife practices described above. The ICT managers describe optimising their companies' success by presencing work across their worklives and sustaining an orientation of anticipation and preparedness for unpredictable work demands. They report constant alertness to leveraging new opportunities and reconfiguring their sense of 'the possible' (Adams et al., 2009 p. 258). The work of achieving anticipatory availability is only ever 'good enough for the already fading moment of the now, as the conditions, opportunities, exposures and perils it needs to exploit and master are already changing again' (Müller, 2014). While a similar temporal rationality of anticipatory availability is evident in the accounts of the digital creatives, exhaustion and anxiety about how their future worklives might pan out emerged as a strong theme.

Worklife anticipatory availability 'is less of a state of being than of becoming'; always attempting to become 'what it is supposed to already be' (Müller, 2014, p. 7). Contra Marx's predictive narrative of capitalism, in which the future is the outcome of present relations, these accounts suggest a sense that future developments and events are beyond a 'development of what we presently know' (Berardi, 2011, p. 127). The temporality of anticipatory availability is underpinned by systematic uncertainty. For the digital creatives in particular this uncertainty produces a sense of 'stuckness' in the present. This is particularly the case for some of the younger women and men participants.

This uncertainty legitimises imperatives of constant connectivity and availability to customers. Expectations of availability are further heightened by the unpredictable conditions of networked 'interconnectivity' including expectations of 24-hour temporal business generation, management and customer service. In addition, ideas- and solution-driven products and services involve constant updating on technological and other knowledge advances. The 'prevailing economic value [placed] on total availability' (Mazmanian & Erickson, 2014, p. 768) requires that these MKWrs are reachable, connected, on hand, always prepared and perpetually anticipating potential customer support and service needs. Anticipatory availability is part of what is being sold; it is product. It figures centrally in the narratives of productivity discussed in Chapter 6.

Additionally, the hypervaluation of work time is built into the technological devices that facilitate connectivity and availability (Sutherland & Jarrahi, 2017). Various algorithmically controlled systems, prompt functionalities and automated emails promise flexibility, but these productivity-oriented features cajole workers into working across all times and spaces (ibid.).[5] However, these accounts point to the emergence of often obsessively scheduled non-work and family activities. For mothers this means making themselves present with children and in the home while simultaneously working. This can produce an unsatisfactory smoothing over of colliding temporal orientations (Freeman, 2010). Relatedly, time invested in constant upskilling or establishing a start-up company means that the fertility window is narrowed, causing some to worry about the biological clock if they were going to 'have it all' (Rottenberg, 2017). Some of the younger men participants also expressed concerns about how anticipatory availability for work seemed to be diminishing their chances of achieving a family life in the future.

For Flaherty (2003), a central focus and effect of most time work is the reduction of 'the friction between self and society', while for Moen et al. time work consists of those strategies adopted '*to lessen the negative effects of the stress of higher status on their lives*' (Moen et al., 2013, p. 81, emphasis original). These accounts of time work confirm the privileging of work temporalities but also highlight deeper anxieties at the heart of this time work. These relate to a sense of being captured by a present mired in anticipatory availability, the precarity and unpredictability of the future, and a gendered clash of temporal orientations between work and mothering in particular. By way of compensation, the accounts of ICT managers in particular suggest that anticipatory availability takes on the status of a virtuous temporal practice (Adams et al., 2009, p. 247). The corollary work of cultivating this temporal orientation is supported by these workers' high achieving middle-class dispositions but is differentiated by gender, professional status, and stage in the lifecycle. It also differs between these economic sectors. The ICT managers practice anticipatory availability for work as a way of life. However, as the opening quotes from George and Leo indicate, these temporal demands are even more intense for start-ups and digital creatives, who, for the most part, characterise anticipatory availability as either an out-of-control temporal tyranny, or overwhelming of worklife aspirations. This is even more acutely the case for mothers.

Workers, places, artefacts and multiple notions of time enact anticipatory availability in a constantly shifting relational process. Temporal practices are always sociomaterial, and the time work involved in making these worklives is calibrated with and by machines (Wajcman, 2015), but also in and through the mobilities of people, work and devices. If anticipatory availability takes on the quality of ever-readiness for uncertain proximate and far futures, it also relies on a tight scheduling of non-work activities and family for some and the anxious backgrounding of family aspirations for others.

Notes

1 The Global Entrepreneurship Monitor found that as in 2011 and 2012, about 8 per cent of the adult population in Ireland intended to set up their own business. While the OECD average was 14.4 per cent, the EU-27 average was 14.8 per cent and 16.5 per cent in the US (Fitzsimons & O'Gorman, 2013, p. 28). Entrepreneurial activity by men in 2012 stood at 8.3 per cent (a drop from 14.2 per cent in 2005), while for women the rate dropped to 4 per cent from an average of 4.7 per cent from 2003 to 2008 (2013, p. 37). Early stage entrepreneurial activity is relatively low among the 18 to 24 age group (4.5 per cent) consisting of 12 per cent of all entrepreneurs in Ireland. The greatest proportion of early stage entrepreneurs is between 25–44, with those 45 and over accounting for almost equal numbers (34 per cent) but are in latter stage entrepreneurial activities (Fitzsimons & O'Gorman, 2013, p. 33). The GEM report for 2016 reports that one in every 23 people in Ireland (aged 18–64 years) is a new business owner, figures which are similar to the US and high compared to European countries. Men accounted for 63 per cent and women 37 per cent of entrepreneurs, and Enterprise Ireland has now established a dedicated female entrepreneurship unit to help reduce the gender gap. This report also found that although 40 per cent of entrepreneurs were focused exclusively on the Irish market in 2007, this figure had dropped to 20 per cent in 2016, indicating that EI's internationalization strategy is successful (Hart, Bonner, Levie, & Heery, 2017).

2 This resonates with Betty's account of her clash with the HPSU innovation programme manager that we discussed in Chapter 2.

3 Macnaghten and Urry (1998) argue that as our responses are contracted into nanoseconds, to even times of a billionth of a second by advanced technologies, 'instantaneous-time' is created (p. 49). This temporality is marked by 'speeds beyond the feasible realm of human consciousness' and is separated 'from social experience and the rhythms of the social world' (ibid).

4 Moen et al.'s (2013) findings are based on a study with 53 professional 'knowledge workers'.

5 As a temporal divide between faster and slower time deepens, the latter is often romanticised and the former is either valorised as productive, or turned into a form of tyranny. Such time binaries also do considerable work in marking out geopolitical differences as well as boundaries of class, race and gender by dividing citizens into 'fast classes and slow classes' (Sharma, 2013, p. 313). The notion of evolutionary time is also invoked as a temporal response to the damaging effects of social acceleration on the environment leading to a remaking of spaces and times of lingered experiences rather than of speeding through (Lash & Urry, 1994). At the same time, new forms of deceleration (Dercon & Miller, 2001; Virilio, 2010) are emerging, including: the proliferation of workplace-based mindfulness programmes and sleep workshops (Huffington, 2016); turns to 'slow travel' (Dickinson & Lumsdon, 2010); 'slow food' (Andrews, 2008); 'slow science' (Lutz, 2012); 'slow scholarship' (Mountz et al., 2015); and 'unhasty time' (O'Neill, Martell, Mendick, & Müller, 2014). There has also been a turn to sleep as a strategic resource (Barnes & Spreitzer, 2015). Programmes like Sleepio, an online

sleep coach, the LinkedIn sleep fair, and Huffington's company Thrive Global educate employees on the importance of sleep (see Huffington, 2016). These deceleration practices are increasingly mediated by digital technology design, which increasingly incorporates 'quiet modes', screen time cut-off mechanisms, etc. Time, it would seem, in all its permutations, is a central contemporary concern in relation to the workplace in particular.

References

Acs, Z. J., Arenius, P., Hay, M., & Minniti, M. (2005). *Global Entrepreneurship Monitor: 2004 Executive Report*. London: GEM United Kingdom.

Adams, V., Murphy, M., & Clarke, A. E. (2009). Anticipation: Technoscience, Life, Affect, Temporality. *Subjectivity*, *28*(1), 246–265. https://doi.org/10.1057/sub.2009.18

Altomonte, G. (2016). Beyond Being on Call: Time, Contingency, and Unpredictability Among Family Caregivers for the Elderly. *Sociological Forum*, *31*(3), 642–662. https://doi.org/10.1111/socf.12267

Alvial-Palavicino, C. (2015). The Future as Practice: A Framework to Understand Anticipation in Science and Technology. *Italian Journal of Science & Technology Studies (Tecnoscienza)*, *6*(2), 135–172. Retrieved from www.tecnoscienza.net/index.php/tsj/article/view/239

Andrews, G. (2008). *The Slow Food Story: Politics and Pleasure*. London: Pluto Press.

Barad, K. M. (2003). Posthumanist Performativity: Toward an Understanding of How Matter Comes to Matter. *Signs: Journal of Women in Culture and Society*, *28*(3), 801–831. https://doi.org/10.1086/345321

Barnes, C. M., & Spreitzer, G. (2015). Why Sleep Is a Strategic Resource. *MIT Sloan Management Review*, *56*(2), 19–21. Retrieved from http://mitsmr.com/1uOVn7K

Bear, L. (2016). Time as Technique. *Annual Review of Anthropology*, *45*(1), 487–502. https://doi.org/10.1146/annurev-anthro-102313-030159

Berardi, F. B. (2011). *After the Future*. Edinburgh & Oakland, CA: AK Press.

Bianchi, S. M. (2011). Family Change and Time Allocation in American Families. *The ANNALS of the American Academy of Political and Social Science*, *638*(1), 21–44. https://doi.org/10.1177/0002716211413731

Bryant, R. (2016). On Critical Times: Return, Repetition, and the Uncanny Present. *History and Anthropology*, *27*(1), 19–31. https://doi.org/10.1080/02757206.2015.1114481

Butler, J. (2015). *Senses of the Subject*. New York: Fordham University Press.

de Bruin, A., Brush, C. G., & Welter, F. (2006). Introduction to the Special Issue: Towards Building Cumulative Knowledge on Women's Entrepreneurship. *Entrepreneurship Theory and Practice*, *30*(5), 585–593. https://doi.org/10.1111/j.1540-6520.2006.00137.x

Dercon, C., & Miller, D. (2001). Speed-Space: Interview with Chris Dercon. In J. Armitage (Ed.), *Virilio Live: Selected Interviews* (pp. 69–81). London: SAGE Publications. https://doi.org/10.4135/9781446220306.n5

Dickinson, J., & Lumsdon, L. (2010). *Slow Travel and Tourism*. London & Washington, DC: Earthscan.

Ekinsmyth, C. (2011). Challenging the Boundaries of Entrepreneurship: The Spatialities and Practices of UK 'Mumpreneurs'. *Geoforum*, *42*(1), 104–114. https://doi.org/10.1016/J.GEOFORUM.2010.10.005

Ekinsmyth, C. (2014). Mothers' Business, Work/life and the Politics of 'Mumpreneurship'. *Gender, Place & Culture*, *21*(10), 1230–1248. https://doi.org/10.1080/0966369X.2013.817975

Fitzsimons, P., & O'Gorman, C. (2013). *Global Entrepreneurship Monitor: Entrepreneurship in Ireland 2013*. Dublin.

Flaherty, M. G. (2003). Time Work: Customizing Temporal Experience. *Social Psychology Quarterly*, *66*(1), 17–33.

Freeman, E. (2010). *Time Binds: Queer Temporalities, Queer Histories*. Durham, NC: Duke University Press.

Gerstel, N., & Clawson, D. (2018). *Studying Gender and Class: A Multiple Methods Approach to Analyzing Time*. London: SAGE Publications. https://doi.org/10.4135/9781526439581

Gupta, V. K., Turban, D. B., Wasti, S. A., & Sikdar, A. (2009). The Role of Gender Stereotypes in Perceptions of Entrepreneurs and Intentions to Become an Entrepreneur. *Entrepreneurship Theory and Practice*, *33*(2), 397–417. https://doi.org/10.1111/j.1540-6520.2009.00296.x

Hart, M., Bonner, K., Levie, J., & Heery, L. (2017). *Global Entrepreneurship Monitor: United Kingdom 2017 Monitoring Report*. London.

Hochschild, A. R. (1997). *The Time Bind: When Work Becomes Home and Home Becomes Work*. New York: Metropolitan Books.

Huffington, A. (2016). *The Sleep Revolution: Transforming Your Life, One Night at a Time*. New York: Harmony Books.

Joseph, M. (2014). *Debt to Society: Accounting for Life under Capitalism*. Minneapolis, MN: University of Minnesota Press.

Lash, S. M., & Urry, J. (1994). *Economies of Signs and Space*. London: Sage.

Lindley, S. E. (2015). Making Time. In *Proceedings of the 18th ACM Conference on Computer Supported Cooperative Work & Social Computing – CSCW '15* (pp. 1442–1452). New York: ACM Press. https://doi.org/10.1145/2675133.2675157

Luckman, S. (2015). Women's Micro-Entrepreneurial Homeworking. *Australian Feminist Studies*, *30*(84), 146–160. https://doi.org/10.1080/08164649.2015.1038117

Lutz, J.-F. (2012). Slow Science. *Nature Chemistry*, *4*(8), 588–589. https://doi.org/10.1038/nchem.1415

Lynch, K. (2007). Love Labour as a Distinct and Non-Commodifiable Form of Care Labour. *The Sociological Review*, *55*(3), 550–570. https://doi.org/10.1111/j.1467-954X.2007.00714.x

Macnaghten, P., & Urry, J. (1998). *Contested Natures*. London: Sage.

Mazmanian, M., & Erickson, I. (2014). The Product of Availability: Understanding the Economic Underpinnings of Constant Connectivity. In *Proceedings of the 32nd Annual ACM Conference on Human Factors in Computing Systems – CHI '14* (pp. 763–772). New York: ACM Press. https://doi.org/10.1145/2556288.2557381

Moen, P., Lam, J., Ammons, S., & Kelly, E. L. (2013). Time Work by Overworked Professionals. *Work and Occupations*, *40*(2), 79–114. https://doi.org/10.1177/0730888413481482

Mountz, A., Bonds, A., Mansfield, B., Loyd, J., Hyndman, J., Walton-Roberts, M., … Curran, W. (2015). For Slow Scholarship: A Feminist Politics of Resistance through Collective Action in the Neoliberal University. *ACME: An International Journal for Critical Geographies*, *14*(4), 1235–1259. Retrieved from https://acme-journal.org/index.php/acme/article/view/1058

Müller, R. (2014). Racing for What? Anticipation and Acceleration in the Work and Career Practices of Academic Life Science Postdocs. *Forum Qualitative Sozialforschung/ Forum: Qualitative Social Research*, *15*(3). https://doi.org/10.17169/FQS-15.3.2245

O'Neill, M., Martell, L., Mendick, H., & Müller, R. (2014). Slow Movement/Slow University: Critical Engagements. Introduction to the Thematic Section. *Forum Qualitative Sozialforschung, 15*(16). Retrieved from http://nbn-resolving.de/urn:nbn:de:0114-fqs1403166

Orlikowski, W. J. (2007). Sociomaterial Practices: Exploring Technology at Work. *Organization Studies, 28*(9), 1435–1448. https://doi.org/10.1177/0170840607081138

Raval, N., & Dourish, P. (2016). Standing Out from the Crowd: Emotional Labor, Body Labor, and Temporal Labor in Ridesharing. In *Proceedings of the 19th ACM Conference on Computer-Supported Cooperative Work & Social Computing – CSCW '16* (pp. 97–107). New York: ACM Press. https://doi.org/10.1145/2818048.2820026

Rosa, H. (2013). *Social Acceleration: A New Theory of Modernity*. New York: Columbia University Press.

Ross, A. (2004). *No-collar: The Humane Workplace and Its Hidden Costs*. Philadelphia: Temple University Press.

Rottenberg, C. (2017). Neoliberal Feminism and the Future of Human Capital. *Signs: Journal of Women in Culture and Society, 42*(2), 329–348. https://doi.org/10.1086/688182

Sandberg, S. (2013). *Lean in: Women, Work, and the Will to Lead*. New York: Knopf.

Sharma, R. (2013). *Enterprise Mobility Simplified. Siliconindia*. https://doi.org/10.1057/9780230306202

Slaughter, A.-M. (2012). Why Women Still Can't Have It All. *The Atlantic*. Retrieved from www.theatlantic.com/magazine/archive/2012/07/why-women-still-cant-have-it-all/309020/

Suchman, L. (2007). *Human-Machine Reconfigurations: Plans and Situated Actions* (2nd ed.). Cambridge: Cambridge University Press. https://doi.org/10.1002/asi.20714

Sutherland, W., & Jarrahi, M. H. (2017). The Gig Economy and Information Infrastructure. *Proceedings of the ACM on Human-Computer Interaction, 1*(CSCW), 1–24. https://doi.org/10.1145/3134732

Virilio, P. (2010). *The Futurism of the Instant: Stop-Eject*. Cambridge: Polity Press.

Wajcman, J. (2015). *Pressed for Time: The Acceleration of Life in Digital Capitalism*. Chicago & London: University of Chicago Press.

Wajcman, J. (2018). How Silicon Valley Sets Time. *New Media & Society, 21*(6), 1272–1289. https://doi.org/10.1177/1461444818820073

Wajcman, J. (2019). The Digital Architecture of Time Management. *Science, Technology, & Human Values, 44*(2), 315–337. https://doi.org/10.1177/0162243918795041

Wheadon, M., & Duval-Couetil, N. (2017). Entrepreneuring Gender Diversity in Entrepreneurship through Critical Theory and Reflexivity. *International Journal of Gender and Entrepreneurship, 9*(2), 188–202. https://doi.org/10.1108/IJGE-02-2017-0010

Ylijoki, O.-H. (2013). Boundary-work between Work and Life in the High-speed University. *Studies in Higher Education, 38*(2), 242–255. https://doi.org/10.1080/03075079.2011.577524

Chapter 5

'Reflexive rhythmicity' and the making of academic worklives

> [My fiancée works in] academia in (...) Dublin (...) she'll be in between half eight and nine, and she'll work through to maybe six in the evening, and sometimes later (...) she will work through lunch if the experiment is going well ... overall, she works for herself really (...). She can finish at three o'clock on a Friday if she wants to. (...) it's *very flexible and it comes down to the quality of work, not how many hours you're putting in.* Whereas, in (...) a situation *where you're providing somebody with a service, you always need to be available* to deal with that customer, because they could ring you at six o'clock in the evening. They might ring you at ten to nine in the morning (...) so there's no stopping (...) I'm not going to leave work until I have X, Y and Z done (...) I'm just trying to squeeze things in as much as I can. So it's different.
>
> (Damien, ICTM)

* * * *

> We were set up at the same time as [a university research centre working on similar project] (...). They focused on research and developing new technologies, so they ended up working with large companies (...). They're about developing technologies – big R, little D – whereas we're an application centre, so we are little R, big D. So we worked a lot more with entrepreneurs, start-up companies, small companies, indigenous companies (...) if you're a start-up, you don't have the money to have a long *time to market* (...) to have somebody actually buying it off the shelf somewhere. (...) *time to market* is the key predictor of profitability and success (...) *academia works to a different heartbeat.* (...) Whereas in business, if a potential customer wants something, and they say they want it at nine o'clock tomorrow morning, they actually mean that. Five past nine, you're gone. You're dead. You're not going to get it (...). So what we find is the university's very good for dealing with people on certain types of consultancies, either design, architecture design, maybe research.... But for the nitty gritty, get down there and get it working, not so good.
>
> (Jared, ICTM)

We start the chapter with these 'outside' views of academia because they provoke the question of whether they are mirrored by academics themselves. Damien suggests that academic work is flexible and autonomous when compared with the temporal tyranny of business deadlines and Jared sees academic work as free from the business pressures of 'time to market' and profitability. Yet, contra Jared and Damien's perceptions, recent research points to the emergence of 'academic capitalism' and the associated intensification of work pressure, outputs measurement and pace acceleration (De Angelis & Harvie, 2009; Slaughter & Leslie, 1997; Ylijoki, 2003). For example, Menzies and Newson suggest that 'business–like "deliverables"' are becoming the predominant criteria for deciding '"worthwhile" expenditures of money, time and energy' in academia (Menzies & Newson, 2008, p. 85). Others argue that the temporality of research practice is being reconfigured by funding criteria and tight deadlines (Ylijoki, 2003). These temporal shifts are attributed to multiple factors including: the imperative to win funding, a publish or perish culture, demands for 'immediate impact', the espousal of a 'doctrine of excellence' (Vostal, 2015, p. 74), endless audits and inspections, as well as the commodification and monetisation of knowledge (Lynch, 2012; Olssen & Peters, 2005; Slaughter & Leslie, 1997; Vostal, 2015; Ylijoki, 2003). The proliferation and diversification of job roles and specifications within academia contribute to this time pressure. With these changes come shifts in academic work identities (Osbaldiston, Cannizzo, & Mauri, 2019). Perhaps it is these shifts in academic identity that account for the tendency to go along with rather than resist these new work pressures.[1] For example, Mannevuo observes that researcher-mothers 'do not question why academe is a place where one has to work day and night', but 'take it as a fact' (2016, p. 84). Gill (2009) attributes such acceptance, inaction and silence to the idea of academia as a 'noble' calling or vocation.

In this chapter we argue that unlike the accounts of the ICT managers and digital creatives, which suggest a temporal orientation of *anticipatory availability*, those of academics indicate rhythmic temporal patterns. These are reflexively choreographed and implicated in shifting academic work culture norms. We characterise their temporal orientation as *reflexive rhythmicity* to reflect their accounts of the blending and splicing of worklife rhythms and of reflexive sociomaterial improvisations. As in the previous chapter, we consider the ways in which the repeated doing and re–doing of time through diverse sociomaterial practices produces time itself in particular ways via time work. We ask how the institutionally maintained temporal rhythms of the teaching term and the relatively individualised temporality of research commitments combine or conflict in the forging of academic worklives. As in the previous chapter, we build and extend on Flaherty's (2003, 2013) notion of time work as agentic efforts to align with and shape temporal norms, and Moen et al.'s (2013) emphasis on time work as boundary work in addressing these questions.

By examining academic participants' accounts of everyday time work we consider the extent to which their time work achieves harmony between institutional and personally generated rhythms – what Lefebvre (2004) calls *eurhythmia*, and/or accommodates negative disturbances in rhythmic flow – what Lefebvre calls *arrhythmia*. As such, we attend to the dynamics of eurhythmia and arrhythmia in their accounts and the factors that shape their emergence and negotiation. The chapter is structured as follows: first, we review recent debates about the shifting temporality of academic work. We move on in the second section to address worklife rhythms as emergent in what we call *eurhythmia*. In the third section, we identify the appearance of worklife tensions which we characterise as *ambivalent eurhythmia*. Finally, we discuss those moments when continuous connectivity evokes irreconcilable rhythmic turbulence, or *acute arrhythmia*. We conclude by outlining the specific qualities of *reflexive rhythmicity* and what it can tell us about academia and the temporal corollary work involved.

Reflexive rhythmicity and time work

The work of academics is acknowledged to be complex and marked by 'sometimes competing temporalities relating to the various elements of their roles', including teaching, administration and research (Bailey & Madden, 2017, p. 8). For example, echoing Jared's suggestion that academic work beats to the heartbeat of research rather than 'time to market', Noonan argues that 'the logic of ideas and "thought time" does not pay attention to time as measured by a clock' (2015, p. 116). By juxtaposing 'thought-time' and knowledge production against 'money-time' and the production of 'money value', Noonan (2015, p. 117) argues that the short-term temporal horizons of the latter restrict the former. For example, an increased emphasis on pre-defined outcomes and impacts compromises 'the free play of imagination and intellect upon which creation depends' (2015, p. 123).[2] 'Thought time' is central to both teaching and learning (Lambert, Parker, & Neary, 2007). However, whether in teaching or research, the development of thoughts and ideas resists temporal determination. Thought time also defies calculative efforts insofar as the 'impact' of learning and academic research is always uncertain.

Because contemporary academic culture fosters impact, 'fast' subjectivity, flexibility and entrepreneurial dispositions, questions have been raised about the relationship between these institutional imperatives and the ability, and/or willingness of academics to accommodate them (Menzies & Newson, 2008; Ylijoki & Mäntylä, 2003). For example, the institutional valorisation of accelerated and short-term temporalities has implications 'for social reproduction within the university system', including the under-valued and less visible work of administration and student support (Fairweather, 2009; Fairweather & Rhoads, 1995; O'Keefe & Courtois, 2019; Osbaldiston et al., 2019). Additionally, Gill (2009) argues that the intensification of work and heavy workloads erodes commitment to, but also time for collective projects. Instead, institutions foster individualism by promoting courses on 'time management', 'speed reading' and 'prioritising goals' to help individuals work more efficiently (ibid.). As time is turned into a resource, Vostal suggests that feelings of guilt about the lack of time are exacerbated by 'the competition–excellence nexus' (Vostal, 2015, p. 88).

The temporality of academic worklife is also shaped by lifecycle expectations and norms. As noted in Chapter 4, Freeman (2010) proposes the term 'chrononormativity' to capture the ways in which worklife temporal orders are underpinned by expected heteronormative life trajectories. It works through hegemonic assumptions about the 'right' time for 'life stages' such as partnering, parenting and caring, alongside stages of career development, promotion and retirement. These heteronormative ideas of time 'bind us' to different identities and groups through temporal processes of working, partnering, parenting, caring and other life activities, such as leisure (ibid.). For example, gendered temporal practices underpin the modern separation between work and life by naturalising binary notions of masculinity and femininity and the public private divide (Freeman, 2010). However, these gendered rhythms take on different cadences for dual career heterosexual couples. They are also modulated by a deepening intimacy between workers and mobile devices and the mobility and flexibility of many forms of knowledge work (Gregg, 2011). Furthermore, as demonstrated in Chapter 4, the work-centredness of the post-Fordist economy (Hochschild, 1997) means that the home, assumed to be the site of feminised and 'malleable temporalities' (Tietze & Musson, 2003, p. 440) is increasingly organised via rhythms associated with work, including tight scheduling and close calendar management (Brown & Warner-Smith, 2005; Hochschild, 1997; Roberts, 2008). In spite of such attempts at temporal management, worklife rhythms are constantly improvised; there is no '"script" for this "new normal"' (Mannevuo, 2016).

Flaherty, who adopts a more agentic approach than Freeman, invokes the notion of 'time work' to reference attempts 'to shape the contours of our own temporal experience (…) [and] resist external sources of temporal constraint or structure' (Flaherty, 2013, pp. 250–251). Again, picking up on our discussion in Chapter 4, time work for Flaherty is marked by purposefulness and tends to conform to temporal norms already laid down by 'human improvisation and enterprise' (Flaherty, 2013, p. 251). Accordingly, Flaherty suggests that our efforts to modify temporal experience through time work emerge from and reflect 'a socialized self-discipline' (Flaherty, 2013, p. 248). The self is not understood, therefore, as an autonomous sovereign, nor is time depicted as 'the plaything of our desires', rather Flaherty stresses 'the dialectical character of our temporal experience' (Flaherty, 2013, p. 251). Although Flaherty emphasises a socialised agency that largely complies with temporal norms and aspirations of good citizenship, he also acknowledges temporal deviance or resistance, which are also of course shaped by social context. It is harder to pin down the focus of time work when the temporal norms of the 'new normal' are in flux.

While Flaherty stresses the socially shaped purposefulness and agentic aspects of time work, Moen et al. (2013) emphasise the constraints within which time work takes place. They argue that, for the knowledge workers they studied, time work is generated by the constant pressure to engage with work-related activities and the effort involved in carving out non-work time. They see boundary work as integral to time work and driven by the three considerations of work effectiveness, preservation of mental health and achieving rest. Our discussion in this chapter suggests that although such boundarying emerges, it is also avoided by some participants as the subject/lifeworld and work/life binaries become more fluid.

Time work as discussed below extends beyond the intentional and purposeful into domains of habit, improvisation and into the choreographing of personalised rhythmic worklives. The relationship between what we might call the 'institutional timescape (…) and more internal and subjective temporal subtleties of the academic conduct' (Vostal, 2015, p. 77) is captured by Lefebvre's notion of rhythm. Lefebvre defines rhythm as an unfolding 'between measured, imposed, external time, and a more endogenous time' (Lefebvre, 2004, p. 99); it 'is relational, a site of interaction and instability rather than order' (Nansen, Arnold, Gibbs, & Davis, 2009, p. 184). The focus on rhythms enables the qualities of those elements and relations that come together at the intersection of social worlds, cultural norms and mediating technologies, as well as how they constitute one another, and become legible (ibid.).

Because rhythms involve repetition, and repetition always involves 'something new and unforeseen that introduces itself into the repetitive' (Lefebvre, 2004, p. 6), rhythms create space for the unexpected. But rhythms also instantiate routine and, in this way, they reproduce the familiar and the unreflexive. Worklife rhythms can be understood as personalised temporal arrangements consisting of repetition and variation such that the everyday flow of tasks, activities and interactions take on particular temporal form (Lasén, 2015). They consist not only of a specific combination of durations, but also of temporal intensities (ibid.). They relate to and influence each other, 'sometimes achieving eurhythmia, where stability persists, and sometimes, arrhythmia, where they jar and clash' (Edensor, 2010, p. 14). It is in the dynamic between eurhythmia and arrhythmia in the practices of academics, in what we're calling *reflexive rhythmicity*, that particular qualities of worklife time are made.

The sociological definition of reflexivity as the constant individualised process of reflection, redefinition of social activities and modified action followed by further reflection (Beck, 1994; Giddens, 1994) has been subjected to multiple critiques (Adams, 2003; Adkins, 2002, 2004; Alexander, 1996; Crossley, 2001; Lash, 1994; McNay, 2000). For our purposes in this chapter, we are less concerned with individualised reflexivity than reflexivity as a situated practice that is shaped by communal exchanges and emergent practices and identities. It both reproduces and transforms existing practice patterns, just as it shapes and is shaped by existing social structures, such as those of class, race and gender. With regard to the academics in this study, we might say that it is 'guided by an understanding (…) of what is regarded as substantively good by (…) [the academic] community' (Lash, 1994, p. 157). Reflexivity is not understood as a process that takes place '"in" the subject or "in" the self, but in the shared background practices' of academia (Adkins, 2004, p. 195). Insofar as reflexivity includes evaluation of the very act of knowing; it can be understood as both a process and a stance; 'an activity and its result altogether' (Popoveniuc, 2014, p. 206).

By focusing on what we are calling the *reflexive rhythmicity* in the academic accounts, we avoid reducing their temporal orientations to structurally defined time acceleration and time shortage (Vostal, 2015, p. 84). Structures of time consist of mutually implicated formations of 'tempo, timing, duration, sequence and rhythm' (Adam, 1998, p. 202). These formations are governed by socially embedded temporal 'norms, habits and conventions' (Adam, 1995, p. 66), but also by evolving norms and so involve constant improvisation (Flaherty, 2013). Because we do not see time as a singular universal 'thing', but a process that is marked by multiplicity (Vostal, 2015), we attend to the sociomaterial enactment of temporal practices in these accounts of everyday worklife. Lefebvre describes 'temporality as rhythmed through both the organic and the mechanical, where the demands of each intersect, synchronize and compete, producing forms of eurhythmia, polyrhythmia and arrhythmia' (Nansen et al., 2009, p. 184).

In our discussion of the accounts below we examine how multiple, independent but interrelated rhythms intertwine and influence one another. In some moments these rhythms flow together and across one another via a technologically and socially mediated eurhythmia. At other moments their unfolding is less smooth or choppier, giving rise to more ambivalent rhythmicity. And at others, the rhythmic flow is turbulent and disordered, or arrhythmic, as competing temporalities conflict and are rerouted in particular directions.

Academic worklife eurhythmia

When recounting those moments marked by a simultaneous and relatively smooth movement of attention across diverse activities, our academic participants suggest that practices flow across one another, starting and stopping and interspersing seamlessly. A multiplicity of rhythms is inhabited and negotiated (almost) simultaneously so that instead of chronological order, there is a 'layering of time, the mixing of tenses, the editing of sequences, the splicing together of unrelated events' (Adam, 2004, p. 135). Although the very idea of specific temporal relationships to particular work and life domains is unsettled (Hassan, 2003b), a relatively smooth confluence of rhythms is channelled into eurythmic flow. For example, James (full-time lecturer in his mid-50s, married with no children) celebrates his worklife polychronicity:

> My lifestyle is *organic* (...). To me it's not a difference as such [between work and life], it's just *the continuation of different things*. So, while I might be working on a calculation in a spreadsheet, I might be answering an email etc., I might also be trying to pick a few nice photos taken with a digital camera to build a little book (...) to send to relatives for Christmas. It's the *same tools but used for different purposes and there's no difference in that activity more than my own attention* (...). The only limit is *how many things you can juggle in your head*. So, I might be using my iPad to look up a recipe for how to cook salmon, interweaving that with replying to an email

> to you about a lecture (...) while having a conversation on the telephone with someone else.
>
> (James, A)

James' connected kitchen enables a synchronisation of administration and teaching task rhythms with those of family and social relations as well as domestic activities. He is simultaneously attuned to the networked public spaces of relatives, colleagues, students and friends. Although some of the tasks are negotiated within a shared temporal regime and related to calendar deadlines, James' account suggests a hybrid polyrhythmia; a flowing eurhythmia in which institutional and clock times fall into the background (Ylijoki & Mäntylä, 2003).

The myriad capacities of his mobile devices and connected kitchen as well as proximate and distant connections and relations synchronously enact worklife flow (Hassan, 2003b; Martinez, Aguado, & Tortajada, 2012). James embraces the apparently seamless ebb and flow and splicing of tasks and rhythms as organic and unremarkable. He suggests that the potential for simultaneity of activities is limited only by own mental ability to juggle multiple activities at once. Although represented as an autonomous achievement, of course this rhythmic flow is enacted via the entangled sociomaterial practices of technological devices, networked infrastructures, and institutional expectations, including those of the university and family.

Claus (who is a lecturer in his mid-30s, single with no children) also reports a hybrid polyrhythmic worklife routine based on going to the university every day:

> *Personal and work life are concepts*. When my grandfathers worked on the farm, their personal life was their work life [laughs]. They didn't have the distinction (...). If I go on Facebook I have all my school friends, my colleagues there, so I may get people from different times of my life connected discussing something (...) I don't have a family so for me (...) *it's not a very big issue to mix them.*
>
> (Claus, A)

Claus continues:

> I don't have a whole pile of hobbies besides what I do on the internet and technology. I mean, that's just my passion and that's what makes it easy for me. I guess I'm lucky that way (...) *I can stay at home and work from home, but it actually disrupts the daily routine, the rhythm of life, some sort of rhythm that you wake up, you go to work.*
>
> (Claus, A)

The temporal and spatial mobility of work enables the emergence of a personalised worklife rhythm that is not required by institutional scheduled work time or requirements. A eurhythmic confluence of rhythms is aided by the daily rhythm of leaving home for work in the mornings. So, just as this rhythm enables work-life confluence, it simultaneously instantiates a differentiation between home and work within this conjoining.

The qualities of time devoted to research must be made and sustained in and through everyday academic worklives (Spurling, 2015). The rhythms of research work are highly personalised and often rely on creating those (often unique) conditions that will stimulate creativity and inspiration. Research requires high degrees of time autonomy and is often associated with slow temporalities and rhythms. However, some academics identify enlivened, 'accelerative moments' of intuitive insight, 'brainstorming' and points when 'research pathways [are] ... sparked, *accelerated*, by "eureka" moments' (Vostal, 2015, p. 85, emphasis original). These are moments 'when insight comes suddenly and seemingly from somewhere else' (Levy, 2007, p. 246). However, these moments also rely on the more general everyday sustenance of optimal conditions for enabling the unexpected as well as for reflection and thinking. Such conditions are (re)created in Tom's account via rhythmic physical movement through diverse environments and contexts:

> I'll get up in the morning and do a few hours of work (...) over breakfast and coffee, and then I'll (short laugh) either take a break and I'll go to a café and work a little further or come here [to the university] and work. (...) I frequently get really good ideas on my morning commute. Because I have already started the workday, and then I've got this *20-minute bike ride where I'm actually not able to do anything but think (...) that turns out to be really productive in terms of generating new ideas, or solving problems*. So, the fact that I can work from home as easily as I can work from [the university] means that I have this (...) *more elastic workday* (...). It's more like, 'what's that I'm doing right now?' And if I want that to be interrupted or not.
>
> (Tom, A)

In this account, '*timing* is emphasised over time per se' (Lindley, 2015, p. 1445, emphasis original). The movement between rhythms and reflexivity about their relative effectiveness is highlighted. Tom clearly values 'certain kinds of rhythms and times are more highly (...) than others' (Spurling, 2015, p. 372) because of the kind of work they make possible. This eurhythmic confluence facilitates an engaged state of mind cultivated by movement between generative and less generative places (see Chapter 3). Tom orients to these different settings with a view to sustaining optimal working atmosphere. Lefebvre argues that '[e]verywhere where there is interaction between a place, a time, and an expenditure of energy, there is *rhythm*' (2004, p. 15). These accounts suggest that worklife is achieved through repetition of movements and relationships to place in specific configurations of rhythms that are always dynamic and are reflexively engaged with to sustain conducive conditions for work. They show how what Mason calls 'atmos*pherics*' ('not just the aura or feeling of what is going on, but the goings themselves ...') are reproduced via rhythms and relationships as affective and lively in making of worklives (2018, p. 179).

Specific work atmospheres are created in the intermingling of places, people, materials, mobility and other aspects of Tom's environment (Pink & Leder Mackley, 2016). He is constantly improvising as he interacts with 'a world of active materials' in creating work-friendly atmospheres (Ingold, 2012). A sense of flow is achieved by the pace and intensity of engagement with the places inhabited and activities being performed (Wunderlich, 2013, p. 388). The research pathway is made up of 'fast' moments, but also 'the "slow" processes of systematization, articulation, measurement, patient investigations and careful revisions' (Vostal, 2015, p. 87). Tom's routine involves creating 'task sympathetic atmospheres' and potential 'eureka' moments by shifting context, movement and daily rhythm (Böhme, 1993). This helps produce the right atmosphere for knowledge production. 'Thought time' is (re)made via the reflexive rhythm of constantly maximising sociomaterial conditions for thought.

Jenny also describes a relatively fluid, organic worklife, lived across locations and relationships.

> *I live my work (...) I do it at home, I do it in the office, even if I'm travelling I have at least my email. I'm constantly working (...) I work at home and I play at home. I work in the office and I'll play in the office too. If I need a break (...) I'm not afraid to step out and do something else for an hour because I know I'm working just as often at home as I am here* (…) [technologies are] completely and totally integrated and unavoidable in my life (…) *I wake up and have a laptop. I have to force myself to put the laptop away* because I realise I'm on it too much (…) have to get all my news and updates on the computer, on the internet, but the nice thing about that is I can do that whenever, and so if I'm addicted to the internet it hasn't really become a problem in my life [laughs].
>
> (Jenny, A)

By bundling different times, activities and relationships together, a kind of rhythmicity is created that displaces chronology, or any notion of successive events. Relationships and activities are reworked and refashioned in the rhythms of everyday worklife through which multiple work and non-work activities occur in overlapping ways. Yet, the omnipresence of the laptop and its multiple worklife capacities give Jenny pause for thought which is then quickly dismissed as simply the way it has to be.

Digitally mediated eurythmic moments are articulated with a sense of personal achievement and enjoyment in Shannon's account:

> I would *post things to Facebook that are for the students to see, but I would also post silly things* (…) I'm interacting socially. So the boundaries are very blurred there (…) at the same time, because you are at home and keeping an eye on the food cooking on the cooker and you're typing something…. *Complete separation? I don't think it can happen anymore.*
>
> (Shannon, A)

Shannon continues:

> *I tend to work all the time* (...) I came in this morning and I called my mum because I remembered I didn't call her in a few days and by the time I go home she will be asleep. And then you want to make up for that time and you work in the evenings. Or in the evenings at home things are more quiet [*sic*] and I can read; the same on Saturday or Sunday morning. But *I don't really want to limit things* (...) I don't mind working from my holidays or working when I'm travelling.... If *there's something that needs to be done I'm doing it right then and right there.*
>
> (Shannon, A)

As work comes to incorporate wider elements of life such as friendship, family connection and creative activities there is less a reversal of home and work, as Hochschild (1997) suggests, than a blending and splicing of these via emergent worklife rhythms. Yet, Shannon's account suggests being driven by events, there is no 'outside' when she is off.

The differently choreographed academic worklives discussed so far suggest a more varied relationship to time than that of the recent literature on the accelerated temporality of academia and fast subjectivity. A multiplicity of temporalised sociomaterial practices are articulated in and through 'a variety of processes, techniques, understandings and experiences' (Hassan, 2003a, p. 227). There is less evidence of accelerated or short-term rhythms than personalised repetitive rhythms that are subject to improvisation. Some rhythms are more open-ended, contingent and generative than others which (re)produce worklife predictability. Overall, these rhythms interact to achieve what Lefebvre calls eurhythmia, i.e. where a certain level of stability is achieved. As such, these rhythms provide a stable backdrop for both repetition and reflexive improvisation. Time work in these accounts sustains hybridised worklife eurhythmia. To some extent, the accounts discussed so far echo Damien and Jared's differentiation between the profit and customer-driven time pressure of business work and the relative temporal autonomy and flexibility of academic knowledge production. If the technologically and socially mediated blurring of practices and domains produce eurhythmia in the above accounts, we consider the more strained and ambivalent achievement of eurhythmia shaped by exogenous factors in the following section.

Ambivalent eurhythmia: rerouting worklife rhythms

Unlike the previous section where a relatively smooth and hybridised polyrhythmic worklife is reported, in this section worklife rhythms come into tension, giving rise to an ambivalent and sometimes anxious rerouting of worklife rhythms. It addresses those rhythmic tensions that arise in relation to the dominance of work rhythms. The practices described resemble Moen et al.'s characterisation of time work as 'drawing personal boundaries based on a desire to work more effectively' (2013, p. 101). Work goals and commitments emerge as the dominant factors in addressing rhythmic tensions. In these accounts family/friends/colleagues and even devices are looked to as potentially enabling of more effective worklife rhythm through sociomaterial practices of boundarying work. For example, their accounts point to how outside work commitments, such as family, are often appealed to as triggers for shifting gears or pulling back on work.

While ICT managers, such as Damien and Jared, must be constantly available to customers, academics juggle the demands and expectations of multiple stakeholders, from students to research participants, and conference organisers to funders. Although academic timelines are tightening, different values are at stake than in business. To date at least, most academics are salaried, even if employment conditions are becoming more precarious. Whether tenured or not, the difficulty for most academics is how to create 'off' work time. The associated rhythmicity of academic work can produce dissonance between worklife rhythms. For example, Aoife points to the multiplicity of tasks involved and their different temporal qualities:

> I think a lot of the time you have (…) *immediate deadlines* (…) you have to fix a class (…) *short-term deadlines* and things that you have to do quickly, but an awful lot of the rest of our work (…) it's just you who has to do it and there's *nobody standing over you.*
>
> (Aoife, A)

Regardless of the autonomy assumed and embraced by many of the academic participants, this is constrained by compliance with institutional scheduling and academic calendars. Even research, although often presented as the autonomous and homogenous activity of 'thought work', involves the rhythms of many other domains and actors. Aoife continues:

> I'm working on a couple of research projects at the moment. We've just finished doing a whole lot of focus groups and interviews (…) so doing that work and transcriptions (…) *an awful lot of research work is calling people, answering phone calls, trying to get hold of people, (...) and trying to arrange interviews* and focus groups and all of this kind of stuff, which is very *time consuming*, but you have to do it. So it can take up an awful lot of time (…) then of course the writing up….
>
> (Aoife, A)

The rhythms of Aoife's research fieldwork are shaped by the field, which intersects with other research processes such as writing up. It seems that personalised rhythms of unstructured time, because they are ostensibly controlled by academics themselves, often involve long work hours and a struggle to incorporate other life rhythms as Aoife goes on to suggest:

> I suppose just having the luxury (…) where the only thing that you have to do is be present physically in your class and the rest of the work (…) most people don't care where you do it, when you do it, how you do it, so long as it gets done (…). But, *in an ideal world, (…) you would be able to switch off from work at six o'clock on a Friday and switch back on at eight o'clock on a Monday*.
>
> (Aoife, A)

The rhythms of unstructured time and associated subjective experiences of autonomy and flexibility can, as Aoife suggests, take on a juggernaut quality insofar as they cannot be switched off. There is a sense of being out of control.

Even Jenny's relatively smooth worklife rhythmicity described in the previous section is haunted by a sense of losing control, or becoming addicted. Reflecting on worklife blending she notes:

> *My best friends are from my job. I don't have any friends outside. My boyfriend is in the office next door* (laughs) (…) that's very helpful to me (…) *when I have something really eating at me* (…) [they] know what's going on in my personal life and know enough to be able to say, *'Stop. Go home, you need the break', or to say to other people, 'don't mess with her right now, give her a couple of days'*. So that's really useful because they know my personal life.…
>
> (Jenny, A)

Jenny looks to her colleagues/friends to legitimate time off work and links her work rhythms to the temporal socialisation that underpinned her academic training:

> *I know that I live an unhealthy lifestyle* (…) *including my work-life boundary. I just don't know how not to live that way*. One thing that teaches an academic to live that way is postgrad. I mean you live your work (…) to do to get your masters, to get your PhD, you work 16-hour days. But it's also spent with your colleagues and it's spent with the informal meetings and everything else so where do you draw the line there between life and work? *I never learned to draw the line after postgrad* (…) I don't know how to get to a healthy relationship between work and life.
>
> (Jenny, A)

Tensions emerge between habits developed during postgraduate study and public health messages about healthy lifestyles. They effect an ambivalent eurhythmia in Jenny's account which describes her work-oriented hybridised worklife as the only way of life she knows.

Similarly, Philip states:

> I am trying to impose a *discipline (...) because I do feel that I'm spending more time at work than I was five years ago*. There is an element that *my job is a vocation* so I accept that (…) but there has been creep (…) and *creep then is at a cost*, right? You'll either be tired the next day because you're there at half 11 at night answering an email.
>
> (Philip, A)

The term vocation suggests work that is motivated primarily by 'other-oriented values and goals' (Dik & Duffy, 2009, p. 427) and the association of work with personal fulfilment, human worth and dignity (Dawson, 2005). Yet, the rhythm of 'work creep' tests Philip's vocational dedication to his job. He reconsiders his work commitment in response to negative media attitudes to public service workers following the recession:

> There is a culture of (…) public servants who are *overpaid and underworked and not really appreciated for the work that they do. Interestingly, this has given me pause for reflection* (…) in terms of the need for cuts and a cuts agenda….
>
> (Philip A)

The entanglement of personalised academic temporalities with the wider cultural demonising of the public sector as non-productive and a drain on government resources is evident in Philip's account (Coulter & Nagle, 2015; Roche, 2017). This negative external culture punctuates Philip's worklife rhythms, provoking pause for reflection.

Maeve combines work and family rhythms by turning family waiting time into 'thought time':

> If I am sitting in *the car waiting for my kids to come out from something* (…) I do find the advent portable technologies, as hugely significant for me (…) I open in *a notebook* (…) I have got *a screen in front of me that I can, I can edit it* instead of my own horrible scribbling … I am working on two articles at the moment and I have them both on it.
>
> (Maeve, A)

It is not just the grabbed 'thought time' in the interstices of Maeve's daily routine, but the designation of her mobile device for this purpose that frames this as 'thought time':

> And I don't use it for any admin because I kind of think *I don't want to contaminate this space of mine, with administrative stuff* (…) I just find that really, really incredibly useful device and (…) I like to keep it only for that

> activity, because I think, no matter where I am, I mean I *sometimes walk up to the [local café] with my notebook in my bag and I sit in the front area there and I just do my own thing*, and doesn't matter how busy it is, I can engage with it.
>
> (Maeve, A)

It is to her device that Maeve turns to demarcate the rhythms of research and prevent the intrusion of administration or teaching rhythms. Because the work is located on this particular device it can be pursued when the opportunity arises, unaffected by the temporal pressures of administration, or family. Maeve's device is part of a sociomaterial assemblage of temporality, spatiality, task at hand and mood that emerges in this rhythm.

If Maeve's worklife rhythms include grabbing time and designating devices for research work when waiting for her children, Shannon's account suggests that the rhythms of family life potentially boundary or deflect the rhythmic dominance of work:

> Not having a family here I *don't have any obligations*. I don't need to feed anyone or pick up from the kindergarten (…) I don't mind working from my holidays or working when I'm travelling (…). Of course, I take time off and I enjoy my time off and *I'm forcing myself not to look up the email or anything* (…) if you never stop and if you're not taking any time off there's a danger. I was reading the other day – 'Take a day a week without technology, or take a day of silence….' *We need to recharge our batteries.*
>
> (Shannon, A)

'Time off' work does not take on a quality in itself. It is legitimised by having family obligations and in the absence of such obligations it is justified via discourses of health promotion and how it might optimise work time.

When the temporal rhythms of weekends, nine-to-five workdays or holiday times are undone by the 'extreme flexibility' of networked time (Hassan, 2003a, p. 236),[3] the problem becomes when and how to switch off:

> I would work on a Sunday, or I would work on a Saturday whereas maybe something would happen on a Tuesday during normal working hours that I wouldn't get work done when I should be theoretically at work, but then I will do it all on Sunday (…) *nine weekends out of ten I will do some work.* It might only be an hour or it might be two full days just depending on what's coming up….
>
> (Aoife, A)

Like Shannon, Aoife looks to family commitments via her future baby as potentially shifting the rhythmicity of worklife:

> Things will change *when there's a baby in the equation....* Maybe it will *make me be more organised.* Many people say that it does because you have to compartmentalise.
>
> (Aoife, A)

In a different way, Claus sees family life, not as an aspiration or life goal, but as potentially enhancing work performance via distraction:

> I don't have a family (...) It's probably good for my worklife, probably not so good because I *have to have the proper rest as well to be more efficient at work.* Also (...) you need your distraction....
>
> (Claus, A).

In Claus' account, family life might provide the distraction and rest he needs to make work time more effective.

In contrast, for Marc (lecturer, single man in early 40s without children), home life potentially interferes with his work time:

> I would reckon that *life creeping into work can affect your work productivity (...) I fight this battle all the time.* There are things that I can do in the morning time when I'm at home – life related activities, right, that might mean that I get to work at nine-thirty in the morning. Disaster, right? When I start work at eight o'clock in the morning, much more productive day ... if it's life creeping into work (...) like, receiving phone calls; they are obviously distraction but that is life, isn't it?
>
> (Marc, A)

This visceral reaction to any encroachment upon work rhythms by those of life is not typical but reflects the extent to which work priorities prevail in most of these accounts.

For Lucy (lecturer, mid-30s, living with partner without children), it is her relationship with her partner that helps redress the dominance of work rhythmicities:

> My partner is not (...) [an] academic and his work is much more fixed. So when he comes home, he is not required to do any more work and I try not to do more work myself (...) and maybe do things together. *Sometimes that doesn't work out (...) I have a deadline (...) and I have to work, and he ends up (...) talking to himself or watching TV (...) sometimes you can't help it (...)* last night I was working doing reviews because the deadline was already this morning and yesterday during the day I had too many other things to do and I ended up doing a lot of work last night at home.
>
> (Lucy, A)

A temporal quandary arises as being a good partner and meeting work deadlines come into conflict. The momentum of work creates a sense of being out of control – 'you can't help it'. Yet, the social norms of coupledom and intimate relationships also shape how time should be allocated (Flaherty, 2013, p. 248). Flaherty (2013) emphasises temporal agency in such contexts insofar, he would argue, that these specific temporal arrangements are not imposed on Lucy, but created by her. Both Lucy and her partner's intimate temporal structures are shaped by her efforts to reconcile temporal demands and their negotiation of different work rhythms. It is when the normative temporal rhythms of contemporary academic work come into conflict with those of Lucy's intimate relationship that arrhythmia emerges. When the rhythmicity of coupledom comes up against that of work, the latter wins out in the example given by Lucy.

The worklife rhythms discussed in this section do not flow smoothly – they are choppy. Those tensions or ambivalent disturbances thrown up in the everyday rhythmic emergence of worklife are variously reconciled by prioritising work rhythms or appealing to family obligation, health promotion messages, specific device 'fixes' and socio-political contextual factors. Rhythms of family, personal and social relationships are ambivalently engaged with, variously protecting the dominance of work rhythmicity or moving towards undermining its dominance. However, considerable time work goes into protecting the flow of work rhythmicity against disturbance.

Acute arrhythmia

Although ICT managers and digital creatives positively emphasise connectivity as enabling productivity, the academics frame connectivity primarily in relation to rhythmic disruption. Constant accessibility, continuous unwanted demands and annoyance at being interrupted (Lasén, 2015) create rhythmic dissonance. Some describe particular moments of acute arrhythmia and their visceral effects. It is mostly in relation to student email communication and associated expectations of availability and speedy response that the coercive effects of ubiquitous connectivity are articulated. The normalisation of work's presence through connectivity means in some cases that disconnection can create visceral stress. For example, Tom notes:

> Being an academic (…) offers a tremendous amount of *flexibility and freedom* to be able to sort of *combine holiday activities and work* (…) but the drop back is I never really get my (…) holidays because I'm always able to work and I tend to (…) so I don't divorce those two [work and life] anymore (…) but sometimes that can get in the way (…) I don't say this is my holiday and I'm not going to do any work (…) it's actually *very stressful to think of all that stuff sitting there and I'm not making any progress on it.* So it's got

> plusses and minuses (…) on balance I would say it's very positive (…) but sometimes it can intrude.
>
> (Tom, A)

Because he can do work anywhere and anytime, Tom does. Indeed, his account suggests a sense of being impelled to do so. So when, for whatever reason, he can't, he experiences disruption and arrhythmia. He reflects on his previous relationship with a nurse who 'could never understand why I always had my notes and laptop' (Tom, A). His account suggests a reflexive rhythmicity insofar as he anticipates the arrhythmia produced by disconnection from work. For example, he reflects on how his constant proximity to his laptop caused tensions in a previous intimate relationship.

In contrast, Philip describes his efforts to resist the expectation of constant availability, which he experiences as coercive:

> I think people have determined that they need a certain response to emails or a certain response time to voicemails, that perhaps isn't fair (…) *expecting emails at all hours of the evening* in response to stuff which before took days (…) *you end up spending, despite yourself (…) more time looking at them than you should do just because you haven't physically turned off an application* (…). And I know you can stop the alerts (…) but you just tend to click, have a look (…) you're now online and dealing with emails at ten, 11 o'clock at night, which you wouldn't have dreamt of doing or being part of ten years ago.
>
> (Philip, A)

Philip's resentfulness about work extensification via continuous connectivity is augmented by the sense that the agentic power of emails supersedes his inclination to turn off alerts. As the 'obligation to communicate has become an unstated expectation' (Hörning, Ahrens, & Gerhard, 1999, p. 300) the effect is often to 'fall back on learned routines and unconscious cognitive biases'; in short to 'perform' (Menzies & Newson, 2008, p. 93). Moreover, because willingness to communicate is presumed, abstention becomes impossible (Hörning et al., 1999, p. 300). Indeed, 'refusal [is] subjected to massive pressure for justification' (ibid.).

The 'connectivity imperative' (Gregg, 2011) also emerges in Kate's (lecturer, mid-30s, married with toddler) account of the time work generated by it. She describes a sense of undergoing email practice rather than shaping it:

> I think *technology is part of my problem*, because *I find myself (…) checking my email, maybe late at night,* and then (…) if a student is having terrible difficulties uploading a project late at night *I end up worrying* (…) that that student is under pressure and *I end up responding* late at night when I should not respond until the day after. So they *start eating into my boundaries*. It's

> my fault now. I *shouldn't, I should just pretend* I didn't get the message until the day after but I have a kind of an *overriding concern for the welfare of my students so even though it inconveniences* (…) I do tend to do that and it's because technology facilitates that.
>
> (Kate, A)

Kate's account suggests a ceding of agentic control to technology as her own 'fault', yet her email practice is also shaped by her vocational approach to her work. Although rhythmic turbulence is created by the emergent 'cultural norm of speedy responsiveness' (Wajcman, 2015, p. 107), Kate reflexively engages this norm to reconsider the conventions of student/lecturer communication:

> Sometimes I'll *answer emails late at night, other times, I don't want students knowing I'm that accessible so I don't answer them until the day after* (…). We've all created this kind of environment now (…) And, of course, once you've seen an email you feel compelled to reply (…). Once I know about it I *feel I should (...) but I'm not going to, but I should, but I should.* You lose more time thinking about those (…) there's a lot more pressure on you all the time to respond automatically. I like responding quickly. I don't like things hanging over me, but it means I'm always chasing my tail.
>
> (Kate, A)

Action and reaction are collapsed by the technological rhythms of instant communication and the social norms that reproduce these. Yet, through the intra-action of all these actors – the university, student, lecturer, ICT infrastructures and email – a form of potential resistance emerges as Kate is afforded the possibility of 'pretending' she didn't receive the email. Yet, her experience is one of rhythmic turbulence and throws up dilemmas regarding when and how to respond. Kate describes the time work involved as she reflexively deliberates on the communicative impact and appropriateness of each option.

Jenny reflects on the work occasioned by the presencing effects of her devices:

> I *didn't get the devices in order to work wherever I want.* (…) *I didn't think, 'oh God I'd love to be able to work while at the pub'* (…) the disadvantage to being online all the time (…) there's an expectation level that goes up (…) I would say that's not important enough to do right now and that person specially needs to think that I won't jump back (…) *replies are just presence….*
>
> (Jenny, A)

As in Kate's case, Jenny also re-evaluates her academic work practice in light of how work is made present by her mobile device. It is clear, therefore, that the rhythmic norms of digital communication are not just 'out there' but everywhere emergent in the everyday rhythmic arrhythmia reported in the above accounts.

The time work of reflexive rhythmicity evolves through the potentiality of hybridised organic worklife, but also in the arrhythmic flows of information, communication and relationality that undermine this potential. The time work described above involves the reflexive mobilisation of sociomaterial and temporal practices in the incessant (re)making of academic worklives.

Conclusions

In this chapter we give texture to the time work engaged in by academics and its centrality to the corollary work that underpins contemporary academic worklife. Because academic life is marked by the coexistence of predictable and contingent, defined and non-defined temporalities, there is considerable leeway in generating personalised worklife rhythms. However, at a time of change in this work sector, shifting work norms and expectations put personalised rhythms under pressure. In the accounts presented above, rhythmic reflexivity is reproduced through dynamic sociotechnical engagements with multiple environments, technologies, conventions and relationships and in interaction with institutional rhythms and those of the international academic milieu. By emphasising rhythmicity we identify how practices become connected in complex patterns with the effect of reproducing worklives and academic institutions (Blue, 2019). Rhythms of contact, (un)availability and (in)accessibility (Lasén, 2015) are central to academic time work. Beyond Moen et al.'s (2013) characterisation of time work as promoting or supressing particular temporal experiences, these accounts suggest a *reflexive rhythmicity* in which myriad levels and scales of worklife rhythms shimmy or sputter along together sometimes assuming a eurhythmic quality albeit ambivalent, and at other times an arrhythmic quality.

There is no doubt that in academic work 'the imperative of shortening the cycle between ideas-generation and their application – has become one of the most repeated policy mantras of governments, research councils and universities themselves' (Vostal, 2015, p. 74). However, much of the recent research on temporal acceleration and short-termism in academia assumes conformity with these policy and institutional imperatives. As such, it supports Flaherty's definition of time work as producing 'conformity with cultural prescriptions' (Flaherty, 2013). In this chapter, we nuance this human centred and agentic notion of time work to show how, through their sociomaterial temporal practices, academics reproduce and rework institutional/sector rhythms via their emergent personalised polyrhythmic worklives. Through their rhythmic blending and splicing of worklife rhythms and reflexive sociomaterial improvisations, they rework contemporary networked academic worklife temporalities. Their constant striving for optimal working environments and rhythms emerges as a strong theme. As such, the 'fast subjectivity' of contemporary academic culture is not all-determining. Instead, these academics engage in a reflexive process of reproducing customised worklife rhythmicities to some extent at least. And it is to this extent that they support Damien and Jared's perceptions of academic life in the opening quotes of this chapter.

However, it is also evident that work-oriented rhythms and practices take precedence in these accounts. Although pleasurable sociomaterial worklife blending is articulated by some, many also suggest a struggle to pull extra work activities/demands into alignment with availability for work, and often give priority to work. Expectations of work availability are intensified by emergent norms of constant connectivity and changing conventions of lecturer-student interaction. Moreover, as academic work surveillance devolves to students, not least via student evaluation and satisfaction surveys, it is likely that these temporal pressures will intensify. It is clear that temporal dedication to teaching, student support and research is bound up with notions of work as vocation. The relatively autonomous daily worklife rhythms articulated above are improvised in order to sustain work meaningfulness, often blurring boundaries between self and occupation, and bolstering willingness to work long hours (Bailey & Madden, 2017, p. 12). When this autonomy is threatened (by the encroachments of constant connectivity, or media criticism of public sector workers), work commitment is eroded (ibid.). As such, academics' time work goes into generating worklife rhythms that sustain the personal and professional meaningfulness of the work itself.

Notes

1 More and more of these jobs are unstable and insecure (Archer, 2008; Kuhling, 2017), and are shaped by formal and informal exploitative gendered practices (Gray, 1994; O'Connor et al., 2017; O'Keefe & Courtois, 2019).

2 This short-termism is augmented by the replacement of full-time tenured academic positions by short-term and sessional contracts (Hey, 2001; Noonan, 2015; O'Keefe & Courtois, 2019; Spurling, 2015).

3 A defining feature of Castells' network society is the significance of networked communication technologies, information processing and globalised economic and social interdependence (Castells, 2000). This society is characterised by a reworking of time and space in which logical sequences of biological and social time are broken down so that time is reconfigured as timeless time. This temporality is facilitated by the space of flows in which physical distances are overcome by the instantaneous communication enabled by new technologies (ibid.).

References

Adam, B. (1995). *Timewatch: The Social Analysis of Time*. Cambridge: Polity.

Adam, B. (1998). *Timescapes of Modernity: The Environment and Invisible Hazards*. London: Routledge.

Adam, B. (2004). *Time*. Cambridge: Polity.

Adams, M. (2003). The Reflexive Self and Culture: A Critique. *British Journal of Sociology*, *54*(2), 221–238. https://doi.org/10.1080/0007131032000080212

Adkins, L. (2002). *Revisions: Gender and Sexuality in Late Modernity*. Buckingham: Open University Press.

Adkins, L. (2004). Reflexivity: Freedom or Habit of Gender? *The Sociological Review, 52*(2_suppl), 191–210. https://doi.org/10.1111/j.1467-954X.2005.00531.x
Alexander, J. C. (1996). Critical Reflections on "Reflexive Modernization". *Theory, Culture & Society, 13*(4), 133–138.
Archer, L. (2008). The New Neoliberal Subjects? Young/Er Academics' Constructions of Professional Identity. *Journal of Education Policy, 23*(3), 265–285. https://doi.org/10.1080/02680930701754047
Bailey, C., & Madden, A. (2017). Time Reclaimed: Temporality and the Experience of Meaningful Work. *Work, Employment and Society, 31*(1), 3–18. https://doi.org/10.1177/0950017015604100
Beck, U. (1994). Living in a Post-traditional Society. In U. Beck, A. Giddens, & S. Lash (Eds.), *Reflexive Modernization: Politics, Tradition and Aesthetics in the Modern Social Order* (pp. 56–109). Cambridge: Polity Press.
Blue, S. (2019). Institutional Rhythms: Combining Practice Theory and Rhythmanalysis to Conceptualise Processes of Institutionalisation. *Time & Society, 28*(3), 922–950. https://doi.org/10.1177/0961463X17702165
Böhme, G. (1993). Atmosphere as the Fundamental Concept of a New Aesthetics. *Thesis Eleven, 36*(1), 113–126. https://doi.org/10.1177/072551369303600107
Brown, P., & Warner-Smith, P. (2005). The Taylorisation of Family Time: An Effective Strategy in the Struggle to 'Manage' Work and Life? *Annals of Leisure Research, 8*(2–3), 75–90. https://doi.org/10.1080/11745398.2005.10600963
Castells, M. (2000). *The Rise of the Network Society*. Oxford: Blackwell Publishers.
Coulter, C., & Nagle, A. (2015). *Ireland under Austerity: Neoliberal Crisis, Neoliberal Solutions*. Manchester & New York: Manchester University Press.
Crossley, N. (2001). The Phenomenological Habitus and Its Construction. *Theory and Society, 30*(1), 81–120. https://doi.org/10.1023/A:1011070710987
Dawson, J. (2005). A History of Vocation: Tracing a Keyword of Work, Meaning, and Moral Purpose. *Adult Education Quarterly, 55*(3), 220–231. https://doi.org/10.1177/0741713605274606
De Angelis, M., & Harvie, D. (2009). "Cognitive Capitalism" and the Rat-Race: How Capital Measures Immaterial Labour in British Universities. *Historical Materialism, 17*(3), 3–30. https://doi.org/10.1163/146544609X12469428108420
Dik, B. J., & Duffy, R. D. (2009). Calling and Vocation at Work: Definitions and Prospects for Research and Practice. *The Counseling Psychologist, 37*(3), 424–450. https://doi.org/10.1177/0011000008316430
Edensor, T. (2010). Introduction: Thinking about Rhythm and Space. In T. Edensor (Ed.), *Geographies of Rhythm: Nature, Place, Mobilities and Bodies* (p. 1). Famham: Ashgate.
Fairweather, J. S. (2009). Work Allocation and Rewards in Shaping Academic Work. In J. Enders & E. de Weert (Eds.), *The Changing Face of Academic Life: Analytical and Comparative Perspectives* (pp. 171–192). London: Palgrave Macmillan.
Fairweather, J. S., & Rhoads, R. A. (1995). Teaching and the Faculty Role: Enhancing the Commitment to Instruction in American Colleges and Universities. *Educational Evaluation and Policy Analysis, 17*(2), 179–194. https://doi.org/10.3102/01623737017002179
Flaherty, M. G. (2003). Time Work: Customizing Temporal Experience. *Social Psychology Quarterly, 66*(1), 17–33.
Flaherty, M. G. (2013). Age and Agency: Time Work across the Life Course. *Time & Society, 22*(2), 237–253. https://doi.org/10.1177/0961463X12455598

Freeman, E. (2010). *Time Binds: Queer Temporalities, Queer Histories*. Durham, NC: Duke University Press.

Giddens, A. (1994). Self-Dissolution and Self-Endangerment of Industrial Society: What Does This Mean? In U. Beck, A. Giddens, & S. Lash (Eds.), *Reflexive Modernization: Politics, Tradition and Aesthetics in the Modern Social Order*. Cambridge: Polity Press.

Gill, R. (2009). Breaking the Silence: The Hidden Injuries of Neo-Liberal Academia. In R. Ryan-Flood & Gill Rosalind (Eds.), *Secrecy and Silence in the Research Process: Feminist Reflections* (pp. 228–244). London: Routledge. https://doi.org/10.1515/fs-2016-0105

Gray, B. (1994). Women in Higher Education. In S. Davies, C. Lubelska, & J. Quinn (Eds.), *Changing the Subject: Women in Higher Education* (pp. 75–88). London: Taylor & Francis.

Gregg, M. (2011). *Work's Intimacy*. Cambridge: Polity.

Hassan, R. (2003a). Network Time and the New Knowledge Epoch. *Time & Society*, *12*(2–3), 226–241. https://doi.org/10.1177/0961463X030122004

Hassan, R. (2003b). *The Chronoscopic Society: Globalization, Time and Knowledge in the Network Economy*. New York: Peter Lang.

Hey, V. (2001). The Construction of Academic Time: Sub/Contracting Academic Labour in Research. *Journal of Education Policy*, *16*(1), 67–84. https://doi.org/10.1080/02680930010009831

Hochschild, A. R. (1997). *The Time Bind: When Work Becomes Home and Home Becomes Work*. New York: Metropolitan Books.

Hörning, K. H., Ahrens, D., & Gerhard, A. (1999). Do Technologies Have Time? *Time & Society*, *8*(2–3), 293–308. https://doi.org/10.1177/0961463X99008002005

Ingold, T. (2012). Introduction: The Perception of the User-Producer. In W. Gunn & J. Donovan (Eds.), *Design and Anthropology* (pp. 19–33). Surrey, UK & Burlington, VT: Ashgate.

Kuhling, C. (2017). The Hidden Injuries of the 'Accelerated University' in Ireland: "Stretched Subjectivities" and Precarious Academic Work. *Irish Journal of Anthropology*, *20*(2), 77–87.

Lambert, C., Parker, A., & Neary, M. (2007). Entrepreneurialism and Critical Pedagogy: Reinventing the Higher Education Curriculum. *Teaching in Higher Education*, *12*(4), 525–537. https://doi.org/10.1080/13562510701415672

Lasén, A. (2015). Rhythms and Flow. Timing and Spacing the Digitally Mediated Everyday. In *Handbook of Children and Youth Studies* (pp. 749–760). Singapore: Springer Singapore. https://doi.org/10.1007/978-981-4451-15-4_37

Lash, S. (1994). Reflexivity and its Doubles: Structure, Aesthetics, Community. In U. Beck, A. Giddens, & S. Lash (Eds.), *Reflexive Modernization: Politics, Tradition and Aesthetics in the Modern Social Order* (pp. 110–173). Cambridge: Polity Press.

Lefebvre, H. (2004). *Rhythmanalysis: Space, Time, and Everyday Life*. London & New York: Continuum.

Levy, D. M. (2007). No Time to Think: Reflections on Information Technology and Contemplative Scholarship. *Ethics and Information Technology*, *9*(4), 237–249. https://doi.org/10.1007/s10676-007-9142-6

Lindley, S. E. (2015). Making Time. In *Proceedings of the 18th ACM Conference on Computer Supported Cooperative Work & Social Computing – CSCW '15* (pp. 1442–1452). New York: ACM Press. https://doi.org/10.1145/2675133.2675157

Lynch, K. (2012). On the Market: Neoliberalism and New Managerialism in Irish Education. *Social Justice Series*, *12*(5), 88–102.

Mannevuo, M. (2016). Caught in a Bad Romance? Affective Attachments in Contemporary Academia. In L. Adkins & M. Dever (Eds.), *The Post-Fordist Sexual Contract: Working and Living in Contingency* (pp. 71–88). London: Palgrave Macmillan UK.

Martinez, I. J., Aguado, J. M., & Tortajada, I. (2012). Managing the Unbalanced: Gendered Mobile Appropriation, Identity Boundaries and Social Role Coordination. *Feminist Media Studies*, *12*(4), 506–516. https://doi.org/10.1080/14680777.2012.741867

Mason, J. (2018). *Affinities: Potent Connections in Personal Life*. Cambridge: Polity.

McNay, L. (2000). *Gender and Agency: Reconfiguring the Subject in Feminist and Social Theory*. Cambridge: Polity.

Menzies, H., & Newson, J. (2008). Time, Stress and Intellectual Engagement in Academic Work: Exploring Gender Difference. *Gender, Work & Organization*, *15*(5), 504–522. https://doi.org/10.1111/j.1468-0432.2008.00415.x

Moen, P., Lam, J., Ammons, S., & Kelly, E. L. (2013). Time Work by Overworked Professionals. *Work and Occupations*, *40*(2), 79–114. https://doi.org/10.1177/0730888413481482

Nansen, B., Arnold, M., Gibbs, M. R., & Davis, H. (2009). Domestic Orchestration: Rhythms in the Mediated Home. *Time & Society*, *18*(2–3), 181–207. https://doi.org/10.1177/0961463X09338082

Noonan, J. (2015). Thought-Time, Money-Time, and the Temporal Conditions of Academic Freedom. *Time & Society*, *24*(1), 109–128. https://doi.org/10.1177/0961463X14539579

O'Connor, P., López, E. M., O' Hagan, C., Wolffram, A., Aye, M., Chizzola, V., … Çağlayan, H. (2017). Micro-Political Practices in Higher Education: A Challenge to Excellence as a Rationalising Myth? *Critical Studies in Education*, 1–17. https://doi.org/10.1080/17508487.2017.1381629

O'Keefe, T., & Courtois, A. (2019). 'Not One of the Family': Gender and Precarious Work in the Neoliberal University. *Gender, Work & Organization*, *26*(4), 463–479. https://doi.org/10.1111/gwao.12346

Olssen, M., & Peters, M. A. (2005). Neoliberalism, Higher Education and the Knowledge Economy: From the Free Market to Knowledge Capitalism. *Journal of Education Policy*, *20*(3), 313–345. https://doi.org/10.1080/02680930500108718

Osbaldiston, N., Cannizzo, F., & Mauri, C. (2019). 'I Love My Work but I Hate My Job' – Early Career Academic Perspective on Academic Times in Australia. *Time & Society*, *28*(2), 743–762. https://doi.org/10.1177/0961463X16682516

Pink, S., & Leder Mackley, K. (2016). Moving, Making and Atmosphere: Routines of Home as Sites for Mundane Improvisation. *Mobilities*, *11*(2), 171–187. https://doi.org/10.1080/17450101.2014.957066

Popoveniuc, B. (2014). Self Reflexivity: The Ultimate End of Knowledge. *Procedia – Social and Behavioral Sciences*, *163*, 204–213. https://doi.org/10.1016/j.sbspro.2014.12.308

Roberts, E. (2008). Time and Work-Life Balance: The Roles of 'Temporal Customization' and 'Life Temporality'. *Gender, Work & Organization*, *15*(5), 430–453. https://doi.org/10.1111/j.1468-0432.2008.00412.x

Roche, W. K. (2017). Workplaces. In W. K. Roche, P. J. O'Connell, & A. Prothero (Eds.), *Austerity and Recovery in Ireland: Europe's Poster Child and the Great Recession* (pp. 194–213). Oxford: Oxford University Press.

Slaughter, S., & Leslie, L. L. (1997). *Academic Capitalism: Politics, Policies, and the Entrepreneurial University*. Baltimore & London: The Johns Hopkins University Press.

Spurling, N. (2015). Differential Experiences of Time in Academic Work: How Qualities of Time Are Made in Practice. *Time & Society*, *24*(3), 367–389. https://doi.org/10.1177/0961463X15575842

Tietze, S., & Musson, G. (2003). The Times and Temporalities of Home-Based Telework. *Personnel Review*, *32*(4), 438–455. https://doi.org/10.1108/00483480310477524

Vostal, F. (2015). Academic Life in the Fast Lane: The Experience of Time and Speed in British Academia. *Time & Society*, *24*(1), 71–95. https://doi.org/10.1177/0961463X13517537

Wajcman, J. (2015). *Pressed for Time: The Acceleration of Life in Digital Capitalism*. Chicago & London: University of Chicago Press.

Wunderlich, F. M. (2013). Place-Temporality and Urban Place-Rhythms in Urban Analysis and Design: An Aesthetic Akin to Music. *Journal of Urban Design*, *18*(3), 383–408. https://doi.org/10.1080/13574809.2013.772882

Ylijoki, O.-H. (2003). Entangled in Academic Capitalism? A Case-Study on Changing Ideals and Practices of University Research. *Higher Education*, *45*(3), 307–335. https://doi.org/10.1023/A:1022667923715

Ylijoki, O.-H., & Mäntylä, H. (2003). Conflicting Time Perspectives in Academic Work. *Time & Society*, *12*(1), 55–78. https://doi.org/10.1177/0961463X03012001364

Chapter 6

The productivity quest

> All these tools are supposed to make me more productive (…) but *you actually have to have time to sit down and look at the productive tools to become more productive yourself.* So, it's kind of a vicious circle really. There are so many tools, then you have so many things you have to update, there's so many things you have to log into, so many different passwords, and it actually takes up more time than actually doing the tasks the old-fashioned way.
>
> (Kate, A)

Corollary work extends beyond facilitating the spatialities and temporalities of MKW to the work of nurturing a productive self, generating and sustaining a narrative of productivity. It involves constant improvising to maintain performance 'in the private and public zones that are now equally crucial to displaying competent professional subjectivity' (Gregg, 2018, p. 94). The study participants describe this imperative to 'be productive' not only as striving to perform efficiently and deliver outcomes, but as a constant quest. In this chapter, we unpack this quest for productivity as shaped by three key considerations: defining the elusive knowledge product; crafting and monitoring productivity narratives; and working on the self to nurture and sustain productive subjectivity. This involves constantly improved sociomaterial practices through which products and productivity are mobilised and made to work in MKWrs' lives. In the opening quote, Kate identifies the tensions between the expectation of ever-improving personal productivity and the substantial effort and skill needed to manage those tools that are supposed to boost it. According to Gregg, these (digital) tools embody an infrastructure for achieving productivity as 'a sensibility, a "user experience" of smooth and seamless integration, designed to compensate for a (work)life that, without diligent monitoring, risks falling into disrepair' (2018, p. 86).

In Chapter 4, Dean (a digital creative, who is married, with one child and engaged in demanding leisure activities) described the time work required to counter the tyranny of the temporal orientation of *anticipatory availability* so that he could carve out family and sports time. He judges a week as 'a well spent 30 hours' based not only on income as an indicator of productivity, but also on time spent with family and engaging in sports. For example, although Dean questions some of the productivity indicators commonly adopted by businesses, he sets other productive goals for himself: he describes a customised and personalised narrative of productivity – a productive worklife. Dean's account and Kate's opening quote indicate both the imperative to frame worklife through a narrative of productivity and their efforts to articulate productivity against the grain. There is no alternative legible measure of self-worth.

Both accounts point to the many aspects of worklife invested in via narratives of productivity as a 'mode', a manner of working and living that privileges outcomes and achievements. This concern is shared by participants across the three cohorts. The corollary work of nurturing a productive self, sensibility and narrative, involves finding ways of defining and demonstrating productivity in the face of shifting and changing targets. These productivity narratives and practices are made to work sociomaterially in the intra-action of workers, customers, tools, resources, social networks, markets and economic policies. They require vigilant monitoring, and diligent efforts to prevent breakdown, or failure. In the following section, we review the ways in which productivity and productive selves are addressed in MKW scholarship. The remaining three sections focus first, on how *the product* is constituted in the context of MKW; second, on how *productivity narratives* are crafted and monitored by participants to become an integral aspect of their worklives; and third the *cultivation of a reflexive productive self.*

Discourses of productivity and product in (mobile) knowledge work

Productivity is not univocally defined in knowledge-intensive work (Davenport, 2005; Drucker, 1999). Ways of monitoring and measuring productivity are constantly evolving (Ramírez & Nembhard, 2004), as knowledge workers are often responsible for setting and assessing their own productivity (Bosch-Sijtsema, Ruohomäki, & Vartiainen, 2009; Drucker, 1999). Moreover, indicators of productivity are constructed and reconstructed as demand, trends, organisational structures and branding styles shift and change direction (Davenport, 2005; Gandini, 2016; Haynes, 2007; Lazzarato, 1997; Lehdonvirta, 2018; Perlow, 1999; Teece, 1998).

While organisational culture plays a role in shaping products, productivity narratives and productive subjectivity, those working outside institutions, such as freelancers, look to sectoral cultures of productivity which are frequently characterised by high expectations that normalise overwork and even exploitation (Cohen, 2016). Value is also unstable as it arises via the customisation of solutions for customers so that 'variation is the objective' (Pepitone, 2002, p. 44). Productivity pressures operate via the need to 'feel productive' (Gregg, 2015, p. 188) and through peer competition among the 'creative class' (Leaman & Bordass, 2000). What is needed in the economy tomorrow is difficult to anticipate or predict today (Adkins, 2012). Additionally, productivity is shaped by varying temporal frames, from one day's work to that of an entire working life. Because productivity in MKW emerges in unanticipated times and places, it requires considerable work around managing spatialities and temporalities: i.e. the where and when matters of productivity.

The above trends contribute to the idea of productivity as a mood, process and sensibility (Gregg, 2018). They require constant adjustment to unanticipated work (i.e. customer requests, changes in process, etc.), but also constant performance of productivity as an aspect of self-branding and self-promotion (Arvidsson, Gandini, & Bandinelli, 2016) as well as competitive distinction. This is exemplified by the culture of overwork and constant busyness subscribed to by academics (Berg & Seeber, 2016). The productive self must be constantly alert to opportunity, and cultivated in relation to emergent circumstances.

As an individual responsibility, productivity is also a site of failure to meet goals or to comply with productivity rules and expectations (Gregg, 2015). It is, therefore, closely bound up with experiences of guilt (Berg & Seeber, 2016) and even 'trauma' (Gregg, 2018, p. 17).[1] Indeed, peer evaluations and self-evaluations of failures to maintain productivity can reach quasi-religious tones. Such tones are evident in the search for 'asceticism' in the form of reflective solitude to avoid the temptation of distractions and to reach the 'peak productivity' of uninterrupted creative work (Ames, Rosner, & Erickson, 2015; Gregg, 2018). Self-help is also invoked to overcome and prevent failure (Gregg, 2018). The productive self must cultivate and sustain efficiency, focus and an ability to recover from setbacks (Jeffrey Hill et al., 2008; MacEachen, Polzer, & Clarke, 2008; Tremblay & Genin, 2010). Qualities such as concentration and focus are promoted via the efficient use of certain tools and techniques (from mindfulness apps, to 'brain training' exercises). A kind of athleticism is also associated with the productive subject who keeps training to increase both potential and performance. The end-goal is to reach 'peak productivity', which amounts to being single-mindedly focused on a creative/innovative task without interruptions, and free of the need to worry about anything else (Gregg, 2018). Leisure activities become channelled into servicing individual 'creative powers as a strategy for further economizing the body' (Banks, 2009, p. 673). They are made instrumental to generating new knowledge or skills and augmenting one's economic value. Work 'has pervasively absorbed leisure into its own logic' (Banks, 2009, p. 670). But of course, productivity athleticism (Gregg, 2018) and instrumental leisure (Banks, 2009) are gendered insofar as the care responsibilities that tend to fall to women curtail their access to such performances of the productive self.

Combating counterproductive factors also requires work, such as strategies for dealing with distractions and impediments, and controlling myriad potential interruptions and fragmentations (Lange, 2008; Mark, 2015). The productivity imperative subtly shifts from that of being productive to 'staying productive' and 'feel[ing] productive' (Mark, 2015). Productivity-support tools offer solutions for time management, self-motivation and self-monitoring, but their built-in 'technological optimism' relies on 'the fantasy that time can be managed'

(Gregg, 2018, p. x). The effect is the opposite. Additional work is generated by 'expectations of always more activity' and a 'state of anticipatory achievement' (Gregg, 2018, p. 85). As Kate's opening quote asserts, 'it's a vicious circle'. While digital tools can assist in accomplishing tasks needing a rapid response, better situation awareness and the use of idle time, also require constant monitoring and improvisation (Vuolle, 2010). Additionally, the time saved through productivity software is often used for technology troubleshooting or maintenance (Palvalin, Lönnqvist, & Vuolle, 2013, p. 552).[2] While these imperatives and the underlying context are shared across the three study cohorts, we discuss some of the nuances of the corollary work that sustains the quest for productivity in these MKWrs' lives below.

Elusive products

As well as emerging in constantly shifting contexts, knowledge products are elusive, difficult to articulate, dependent on varying expectations, and part of a web of interrelated and interdependent products. In the case of ICT managers' companies, products are mature, complex and established as there is a company with various capacities behind them. Digital creatives work on products that are manageable by a solo worker or very small team; in the case of start-ups, these products are more novel and still seeking a steady market. Other digital creatives deliver products that are customised for each client and therefore unique every time (for example, a website design). The efforts of academics go into managing diverse products and productive lines simultaneously (teaching, research, admin), each demanding different handling and productivity expectations.

Products are always in the process of becoming, depending on and relating to anticipated and unanticipated networks (i.e. of distribution, competition, etc.), and development possibilities. As knowledge is augmented and expanded, knowledge products are also evolved, updated and re-imagined. For example, products such as software packages need to be constantly updated but also invested in to grow in terms of visibility: 'Developing the product is all very fine (…) *you can have the best product in the world*, but (…) *if people don't see it, there's no point*' (Jared, ICTM). Products need to be 'activated' to become successful in a global ICT sector, so they need to interconnect with other productive lines in the same company, and with other firms and other sectors:

> Previously we would have had a (…) large team here, anything from (…) ten to 20 engineers developing our products. Now we just have three here and we have a team in India who work in development (…). Our product is used to test and debug software. [The software is] developed in (…) companies like Philips, Nokia, whatever. They need tools to develop this software. *If we can get the [recommendation of] semiconductor companies who are supplying the chips for these products for whom the software's being written, then we make sales.*
>
> (Jared, ICTM)

The success of Jared's highly networked product depends on related nodes in several organisational networks. The product is, to some extent at least, the effect of those 'networks of machines, technologies, organizations, texts and actors that constitute various interconnected nodes along which flows can be relayed' (Urry, 2000, p. 193). Jared's account shows that the decentralised and networked nature of the information economy results not only from open software and peer-production (Urry, 2012), but is shaped by how knowledge products relate to one another. It is necessary for Jared to map how his company's product comes into being (in Ireland and India), how it is activated in relation to clients/customers (via key recommendations) and in relation to other products. This market positioning will impact its success and profitability. Flexibility and creative production processes are required so that the product and the company operations that produce it can be adapted quickly: 'we developed some products all the way from (…) idea right through to product. Others, we'd maybe develop the prototype and then [another] company would develop the product. Others we'd do the product, while they did the prototype' (Jared, ICTM).

Furthermore, promotion and development are essential features of a mature product, which must be taken to the 'next level' of success and to be fully realised:

> I would love to (…) partner with somebody in the States (…) that would maybe *take this product on and move it on*. And that's something *we have to look at* (…) because the product is developed and works and (…) it's really lack of marketing and lack of money for marketing really.
>
> (Jerry, ICTM)

Like Jared, Jerry suggests that a product needs to be 'seen' and 'moved on', in order to be effective. Even when the building of it is done, the product itself is not completed without mobilisation and activation within networks. Successful, active and mobile, knowledge products are the stuff of MKW. They require marketing, networking, partnerships and activation as well as product expertise. ICT managers emphasise the fostering of a culture of productivity in their organisations (Akin & Hopelain, 1986), which is not just about setting standards for products and their quality:

> We don't purely look at results. We look at the actual individual as well, and them fitting into the actual organisation and creating a culture in the organisation (…). *The people that work with you are the people that end up deciding whether your business is a success or not.*
>
> (Damien, ICTM)

Good products rely on the right people, and workers who will 'fit' into the company's culture and vision; the human capital of innovative knowledge production. These employees will need not only to deliver specific tasks, but work together closely to achieve 'productive innovation': 'there is a world where you can be (…) task-focused (…). But for (…) the business we're in, where *you're constantly looking for new products and new ideas*, you do need [to be] sparking off one another' (Angela, ICTM).

While also highly networked and processual, product for the digital creatives is more closely identified with the individual. Digital creatives' products are subject to more uncertainty and short-termism compared to those of larger ICT companies. They are often impossible to replicate, as future customers will almost certainly require something different or totally new. Because they are less anchored to environments and schedules for production, digital creatives often manage more than one productive line. Moreover, alongside delivering one or more services they are frequently engaged in upskilling, training and establishing a reputation. The success of their products is more a matter of individual effort and reputational work; they must 'make it happen'. Product for them is the innovative service/platform they are developing as well as becoming their own brand: 'I am what I am and *I am what you're buying and I am my brand*' (Sara, DC).

Product for digital creatives also emerges in relation to the demands and expectations of 'meeting the specific needs of each customer' (Pepitone, 2002, p. 40):

> The *customer will dictate what the product is, not you*. And I think that was the hardest thing (…) the clarity of thinking and carrying it with you all the time and still having no clarity (…) *it's just exhausting* (…) because you are not clear in where you are going.
>
> (Rita, DC)

As these accounts suggest, the digital creatives are constantly shifting their 'productive gear' to meet shifting customer demands which is the primary measure of their productivity. Because 'the customer dictates', clarity about the product and direction is always elusive. Rita experiences the absence of clear direction as exhausting.

Seamus, having worked in ICT companies in the past and now a self-employed digital creative, is keenly aware of the differences between freelancers and entrepreneurs and what they aim to produce. Becoming a self-employed entrepreneur gave Seamus the freedom to adopt innovative and fresh approaches to product development. However, it also enables him to contribute socially as he is designing products to help children with autism and later suggests: 'what I'm doing is hopefully going to generate more jobs and employment' (Seamus, DC). Similarly, Peggy's start-up developing a digital tool for flexible business management was inspired by her own struggle to manage worklife demands in her previous career:

> Life has to be made easier for other people (…) [my company] started from that. I got married two years ago (…) and when I came back from our honeymoon (…) I realised that I didn't want to be in business consultancy anymore and I had this mad urge to set up this business start-up (…). I wanted to look at the digital world (…) I really believe (…) that's where it has to go for

women to have (…) a work-life balance. What [my product] does is it allows you to run your business online…. We also have a shop (…) geared at women in general and we put lots of products in there for women (…) *[My product] is trying to (...) show them that they can run their business online*, that they don't need a fancy office, that they don't need extra staff, that people can do this from home and it also opens up opportunities for women to work from home as well.

(Peggy, digital creative, mid-30s, married with a 3-year-old son)

Managing women's worklife struggle and enabling mobility has become Peggy's product, and she sees the impact on professional women as the eventual outcome of her company. Her product is the lifestyle she represents. Peggy's worklife is not only productive, it is the product itself.

MKW products are rendered even more elusive by the centrality of information, communication, marketing and networking to their production. ICT managers describe the importance of networking to the positioning of the company and the product:

I'm *growing something that may or may not be worth something in the end* (…) I do it because I'm challenged by it. I do it because I get to meet a few people out there, and it's interesting (…). And (…) going out talking to people, networking groups (…) meeting potential customers, developing relationships, befriending people (…) *that's all part of it.*

(Dan, ICTM)

These activities are personally satisfying for Dan (Managing Director of an IT network start-up, single, with no children), but they are also linked to the anticipation of future products (i.e. through new collaborations). Dan also questions his 'good citizen' contributions within the region and Ireland. He reflects that he is not being paid enough for all the relationship building he does. Yet, he is hopeful that it will generate more employment in his company in the long term.

However, digital creatives cannot rely on the backup of an established company and its products as a springboard for networking and have to monitor time devoted to it:

I've stopped doing all of that [networking] because I am at a point now where I don't necessarily need (…) to do that *until I actually have a product* because (…) it came to a point that you go to all these things, 'how's the product?', ah yeah, *you're still developing the product* (…) you don't actually have some [meat].

(Arthur, DC)

For digital creatives, networking in this informal peer-organised way is about ensuring the conditions for productive work and future success (Gandini, 2016).

Arthur is conscious of missing out, but at this stage in his start-up it is more important for him to dedicate himself to building his product.

Compared to ICT managers and digital creatives, the products generated by academics are less identifiable. As noted in Chapter 5, academics deal with conflicting work priorities, temporalities and rhythms. Reputation, ideas, lectures, scientific publications, citations, administrative roles, and well-prepared students are all productive outcomes of academic worklives: 'very busy, constantly on the go. I love the diversity, which I suppose [it] sometimes gives you a very challenging lifestyle because *you're constantly thinking about very different things*' (Elaine, academic, part-time lecturer with a 12-year-old daughter). Academics' productivity is also shaped by policies setting standards for teaching and research.[3] This includes monitoring and assessment of outcomes such as student satisfaction and employability, research success in terms of publications, citation metrics, etc. (Vostal, 2015). Philip (as also discussed in Chapter 5) is concerned with the increased workload and productivity expectations imposed on academics. He feels that academics are pulled in several different directions when it comes to desired productive outcomes (i.e. admin work vs. research innovation) based on escalating expectations of diverse and ambitious outputs generation (e.g. grants, publications, successful graduates, etc.). This is less and less linked to incentives because of austerity culture and cutbacks. Similarly, Kate remarks about juggling many 'productive lines':

> I give lectures and labs. I also have a *huge amount of administration.* Teaching-wise I have maybe seven or eight hours per week but I also do distance teaching and facilitation, so I have to record podcast lectures for students, answer queries they have on the forums (…) I participate in open days (…). Then also (…) *I'm finishing up my PhD, but that's really more in my spare time at the weekends, late at night. It should be part of my day job but there's no time in the day, so PhD is in my hobby time [laughs]. And then I'm doing some research as part of my teaching* which is like the virtual team project, so that would be part of my day research.
>
> (Kate, A)

The collective products of the university devour Kate's time and trump her own career development through the PhD work which is relegated to weekends and night-time. Managing these wildly different productive lines is individually and continuously sculpted. While formally the university allocates academic staff the 40:40:20 workload model (40 per cent of time to each teaching and research, and 20 per cent to administration), this is difficult to maintain in practice (Kenny, 2018). Philip has many responsibilities as a lecturer and course director (including the marketing and promotion of the programme, student recruitment, liaising with schools, attending committee meetings, etc.), with his research outputs suffering as a result:

> *I try my best to keep it to 40:40:20 as per the promotional literature* suggests, but clearly *there's more time spent in teaching now*, there's more time spent

> in research in the summertime. *I try to strike a balance….* What happens, particularly in term time, you find there's *a creep.*
>
> (Philip, A)

Across all three cohorts, therefore, MKW *products are relational and processual*: highly networked, continuously mobilised, dependent myriad connections within networks, and never complete. The elusivity of the product is compounded by shifting expectations in their sectors: for example, the one person/one product model for digital creatives, the diverse productive outcomes for academics, and the organisational interdependency of software products for ICT managers. These products represent: the work and worker who generates them; organisational culture that fosters innovative and responsive workers (Angela, ICTM); the worker's way of working/brand (Sara, DC); or an entire worklife (Peggy, DC). The product escapes precise definition in all cases. As such, the process of producing it and the storying of these processes take on greater significance, as we see in the section that follows.

Developing narratives of productivity

Individual MKWrs construct their own narratives of productivity, including their efforts to define, monitor and evaluate it. These narratives craft productivity and how it is achieved in diverse ways; sometimes they are framed in highly individualised terms and sometimes by managerial discourses. For example, Dan's individualised narrative puts connectivity at the centre of his productivity:

> [My] normal day-to-day (…) mobility (…) works in a different way (…) since I got the *iPhone device (…). We've quite good systems for email and calendar and productivity.* So, I have … *synchronisation* set up with my iPhone and my email and all that. So, I find that, even when I'm moving around, I'm always getting my emails and I'm checking them and I'm always (…) connected to what's going on (…). *My productivity would be massively higher than (…) people who maybe aren't as skilled at IT*, or haven't good systems set up.
>
> (Dan, ICTM)

The mobile devices and systems used by Dan (and his technical ability to do so) ensure higher productivity. He frames productivity in terms of his highly mobile, digitally savvy, and always-connected worklife. In contrast, the narratives of other participants, such as Lily (DC) and Kate (A), suggest that being constantly connected and reachable (and in a state of anticipatory availability) hinders productivity which they associate with focus and concentration: 'I find continually being online can be counterproductive because you're just responding to everything as it happens which is (…) distracting' (Lily, DC).

The ICT sector is the only sector in which managerial narratives of productivity arise. This is not surprising as most of these participants have managerial responsibilities. However, not all of them frame productivity in terms of management, for example, some narrate productivity in terms of employee self-monitoring and the rewarding of independent work (Ekman, 2013). Due to their management roles, ICT managers focus on the productivity of their teams and cultivate particular organisational productivity narratives. For example, Annabel emphasises the active management and monitoring of work:

> I think it's *important that everyone knows what they're doing* at the start of the day so then people are efficient, people then have targets, and they want to meet them (…) because they know *everybody within the company has targets to meet on that day* (…). So, I think it motivates them to not be the only person to come back at the end of the day and say 'oh I haven't that done' (…). They're getting there, they might not have it complete, but they're getting there.
>
> (Annabel, ICTM)

A shared culture of productivity is promoted among Annabel's employees based on shared targets, competition and mutual motivation. She does not detail how these targets are set and monitored by the company, but appeals to traditional corporate productivity attributes: legibility (i.e. each worker knows what they have to do), coherence (i.e. everyone is working on the same assumptions and on interlinked targets), and open-endedness (i.e. workers know how much more they have to do to reach a goal) (Akin & Hopelain, 1986).

Angela's is also a narrative of managed productivity (and product), shaped by manufacturing industry practices:

> *I feel things can be a lot more controlled*, and creativity doesn't have to be this all-inclusive area where you can give an unlimited time, unlimited budget to get a product that is quite vague (…). So [we're] just taking a lot of the practices from manufacturing and bringing them to new product development.
>
> (Angela, ICTM)

While a few adopted a more centralised managerial notion of productivity, most ICT managers narrate productivity in terms of promoting individual talent and initiative: 'we also had a number of very talented individuals who wanted to (…) work two or three days a week and do other things. And my experience with them was such that *they convinced me that that was an excellent way to work*' (Charles, ICTM). Charles, who is a very experienced manager, admits that his (more traditional) productivity narrative was fundamentally challenged by the results of granting independence to 'talented' individuals. His productivity narrative is now one of fostering talented 'capital'. While greater independence promises workers more creative freedom, it also means greater responsibility and pressure for workers to deliver increasingly ambiguous and ever-receding targets. However, this more autonomous productivity culture is often monitored by more covert means of control (Fleming, 2017; Fleming & Sturdy, 2009).

Nearly all of the ICT managers' narratives emphasise the value of face-to-face, co-located interactions, despite a push towards digital communications and collaborations at a distance. For example, Damien's narrative of daily productivity highlights the gentle monitoring and peer competition that takes place in a co-located team:

> When you work as part of a team, everybody feels somewhat compared to the next guy. So, a small bit of competition is healthy. Too much competition is unhealthy. And *I think if you're at home on your own, it has the potential to be (...) less productive* (...). But I think that in terms of productivity (...) probably the ideal situation is to have people coming into the office most of the time (...) because you can talk to them and *less mistakes (...) and less misunderstandings*.
>
> (Damien, ICTM)

In this narrative of productivity, a kind of normative control is at work as peers compete to express their talent and creativity. This is aided by co-location and fostering just the 'right' amount of competition: carefully managing the competitive drive within a team so that it is lively but not unhealthy. This contrasts with Annabel's view that productivity is driven by all team members subscribing to the same targets and monitoring their success or failure in achieving them. Co-location also aids productivity in Damien's view because it enables problems and misunderstandings to be rectified quickly. For Annabel, it is her own presence as a senior team member and expert in the field that ensures: 'I was off for a day, [team members] wouldn't get as much work done (...) because they'll run into an issue and they don't know how to get (...) the server back up and running' (Annabel, ICTM). Although many celebrate the benefits of outsourcing to 'talented' workers, the ICT managers tend to eschew long-distance or frequent mobility of staff in favour of more settled, company-based routines, which are deemed to better enable productive teamwork.

Like Charles, Jared notes that individual talent, autonomy and drive can make a dramatic difference to productivity when innovation and high quality are key company values. As discussed in Chapter 1, his business operates by contracting out work as much as possible and reducing the number of hired personnel. For Jared, 'high-quality' individual talent is key to productivity: 'in high-tech (...) talent really does have an impact (...). Have a talented programmer versus a less talented programmer, and the productivity could be like a thousand per cent' (Jared, ICTM).

Jared defines talent as the ability to generate high-quality outputs, rather than high quantity: 'there's no hiding it (...) great programmers have great output. Bad programmers have bad output...*The talent gets to be converted into valuable outputs more directly*' (Jared, ICTM). But he also remarks that talent is something that can increase overall productivity, a sort of trigger for inspiration and model for others, echoing the view that 'productivity of knowledge work therefore has to aim first at obtaining quality' (Drucker, 1999, p. 84).

Instead, Jonathan's productivity concerns are mainly to do with sales, market penetration and follow-up customer support beyond the release of products. His productivity narrative is driven by company profit and a sensitivity to the interdependencies in the sector:

> We have certain customers who are loyal and actually like our products, and we do a good job for those customers. But we never achieved the scale that some of our competitors have done. And that is I think largely because *we didn't crack the two main drivers of high-tech development tools*, which would be automotive and the mobile telecoms.
>
> (Jonathan, ICT manager, married with two teenage children)

Productivity and a good product require the fostering of good relationships with loyal customers. Jonathan's productivity narrative is also grounded in the ambition of scaling up in order to compete internationally and match the achievements of sector competitors. Indeed, most productivity narratives are cognisant of competitors and associated reputational capital: 'we're *building our name, building our credibility* as a viable partner for somebody who might have a great idea in the future' (Damien, ICTM). No matter how much you are producing, there is an ever-receding horizon of networked and global success to aspire to[4].

The earlier accounts by Charles and Jared show how ICT managers' narratives of productivity are increasingly shaped by the awareness of the successes of digital creatives and start-ups, in particular their flexible and self-driven productivity goals. For example, Seamus notes: 'Everyone has a different pattern of getting their best productivity, and *it mightn't meet the image of what a typical employer thinks it should be* (…). I'd say [ICT managers] are going to have to cop on' (Seamus, DC).

While diverse, the narratives of digital creatives narrate productivity as personally driven and individually focused even if more precarious and difficult to harness into set targets and goals. Their narratives of productivity articulate worklife as a constant productive effort:

> *Working for yourself is you're never off.* You're always thinking about it no matter if (…) you've all your work done, you are wondering 'okay where is the next job going to come from, I need to make some, I need to get some projects lined up' (…) I have no problem working into weekends and late nights (…). From February to June or July I was working, doing an awful lot of late nights because *I'm productive late at night as well.*
>
> (Noel, DC)

When constantly reaching out to seek new business, and thinking about work, 'even over the Christmas, you're thinking "okay, I need to get back to this"' (Noel, DC). When work becomes a way of life, as Noel's account suggests, it reproduces and legitimates a 'post-professional' productivity narrative which extends to periods of unemployment and 'in between job' periods, when workers ensure that they remain connected, efficient and employable (Gregg, 2015). The productivity narratives in the digital creative sector extend beyond daily routines about where and when to work to major long-term life plans. Some digital creatives (such as Seamus, Lily and Noel) have given up previous careers to be their own boss working to their own standards, or to pursue work that they feel is valuable.

These individualised productivity narratives are also a component of their product. Peggy narrates a worklife directed by ambition and hoped-for achievement. However, the success of her business is driven by desire for other achievements in her personal and family life: 'it's not to make a lot of money, to be on the rich list and have a fancy house and a fancy car, [but] *to fulfil the other things that I want to do in my life*' (Peggy, DC). Although a highly motivated and driven worker, Peggy's productivity narrative embraces all aspects of her worklife, including the sharing of leisure activities with her family: 'when I do Kilimanjaro I want [my son], my husband and my family to join me and do a Safari. When *I do the North Pole, I want them to meet me at the other end*' (Peggy, DC).

Seamus thinks that the key to success for digital creatives is to create a 'product that can sell itself when you're asleep'. The ultimate in productivity would be to create 'a business that should be able to (…) run itself (…) So, stop selling your time for money, start selling your product' (Seamus, DC). The 'scope of optimisation' for productivity is potentially unlimited in this model (Adams, Murphy, & Clarke, 2009, p. 256). This is just one example of how new sociotechnical imaginaries are shaping productivity narratives. However, online selling potentially heightens the pace of work insofar as tracking change and adapting products becomes all the more urgent (Alvial-Palavicino, 2015). Beyond productivity for profit, however, some digital creatives aspire to contribute to society in some way: Seamus by helping children with autism and by creating jobs and employment; Lily by developing a product to support children with dyslexia; Kathy by 'creating something that inspires kids'. These represent some of the few points in the accounts that extend the value of work beyond productivity into a wider sense of their contribution to society and wider well-being. It is in relation to these alternative narrations of work's significance, that MKWrs escape the compulsory monitoring of self, product and progress in terms of the productivity imperative.

The productivity narratives of academics are the most variegated, but like the digital creatives, they construct narratives of customised individual productivity. Creative productivity is a major concern. For example, research ideas require flexibility to achieve the necessary 'flow' enabled by place, time and mood (Wunderlich, 2013). But enjoyment of their work is central to their productivity narratives (and identities, see Chapter 7): 'if you're not enjoying it, then you won't be productive' (Philip, A).

Productivity is constructed by specific time and place frames for each of the activities that academics need to deliver. 'Elasticity' in the way work is done underpins this (Erickson, Menezes, Raheja, & Shetty, 2019). But it requires planning and work on the self to know which conditions will be productive for which task. These productivity narratives are marked by a tension between individual productivity and external demands:

> I'm *checking my email at night-time*, but in my head I'm telling myself, '*well I'll have less to do tomorrow*', but it means I've carried it home with me. So maybe (…) I've become more efficient because of the tools, but in other ways maybe work and home are not being distinguished enough because of the tools either. It's too easy to work at home.
>
> (Kate, A)

Kate's opening quote in this chapter highlights the counterproductive effects of connectivity and productivity-support tools. In describing how she makes herself productive, there is a tension between wanting to be productive by anticipating the next day's work (i.e. checking emails at night) and not getting enough rest. Kate also expresses a concern in terms of relational demands on her productivity (i.e. responding to others' demands). This also arises in the productivity narratives of other academics: 'I would reckon *that life creeping into work can affect your work productivity*, that would be the biggest thing for me, because *I fight this battle all the time*' (Marc, A).

While creativity free of other demands ('peak creativity' in Gregg's words) is seen as the prize activity leading to prize outcomes, there is also a tension between seeking concentration and focus and maintaining dialogues and interactions with others – as both are central to academic productivity.

> Sometimes I close myself and I'm not online anywhere so I don't get distractions, but most of the time I prefer to keep open so I'm available for interaction, which in many cases is work-oriented interaction. Because (…) we want to keep interaction with the world. *The moment you stop the interaction with the world it's difficult to progress in research* as well.
>
> (Claus, A)

Claus describes the contrasting needs to 'close himself' to interruptions – the 'productive reclusion' described by Gregg (2018) – for some tasks, and to open up to social interaction for others. Putting oneself away from distractions (Haynes, 2007) is needed in order to concentrate. However, Claus needs to deliver both individual productivity and relational productivity in research and teaching, so contact with others is required.

For Claus and others, their narratives of productivity are often ambivalent, because productivity in some aspects of their work can have counterproductive effects on others. They need to plan different productive efforts, although this often means adopting a mode of constant productivity such that work becomes a way of life. Several academics (for example Tom and Josh) describe the work they do to identify productivity conducive workspaces (see Chapter 3 and Chapter 5). Despite mounting pressure to achieve multiple forms of productivity, many academics see this additional work as an acceptable trade-off for doing work that they value and which enables relative flexibility and autonomy. In many ways, therefore, the productivity of academics is more elusive as it relates to different aspects of their jobs (i.e. teaching vs. research and administration). However, the productivity narratives of all MKWrs discussed above highlight their myriad practices of working and reworking themselves and their products in relation to the imperative of achieving all-encompassing productive lives.

Cultivating a productive self

Narratives of productivity are implicated in the reproduction of a productive subject and this section addresses the kinds of work these workers do on themselves to foster productive subjectivity. It is increasingly clear that while qualifications and expertise are important, more and more value is placed upon those who can demonstrate a productive self. A premium is put on the potential of MKWrs to deliver, and their willingness to develop and even reinvent themselves in these terms. For example, Dean defines digital creatives as: 'focused (…) with belief in themselves and (…) taking a sequential approach to it. If I look back, (…) college gave me the ability to think sequentially. I think people can follow their dreams really, you know. It's *only ourselves stopping us*' (Dean, DC). Beyond any qualifications or accumulated knowledge, Dean emphasises potential, and a willingness to take responsibility for one's own success.

However, productivity and potential continue to be linked to educational achievement. For example, Kelly (ICT manager, chief engineer in a telecom software firm, married with two children) states that her parents believed that education was key. She was raised to strive to educate herself in the best possible way and now she applies the same standards to her kids. She decided to work part-time, thus supporting the development of her children as productive students. The quest for productivity is about becoming and forming productive subjects. Individuals get socialised into productivity from an early age, and into the evaluation of self as productive or not: 'I'm sure I'm not as productive as I could be but I'm definitely being very productive so that's the best you can do' (Kate, A). Kate is always anxious about meeting elusive productivity ideals even while conscious that she is, after all, doing her best and 'definitely very productive'.

Digital creatives' work on themselves often focuses on resolving the tension between the imperative to be productive (i.e. efficient, organised, creative, skilled, knowledgeable about productivity barriers and opportunities), and the struggle to develop original ideas and products in a sector rife with competition and precarity. They promote themselves as innovators, original thinkers to the extent that moments of reflective productivity are rare and fleeting:

> I'm at my *most creative (…) when I'm driving on my own in the car* (…) before the pregnancy I would have ran a lot (…). And it was on those runs that I would have (…) the time out. I find it very hard, I couldn't sit in this office

> now and be creative (…). It would be on a run, on a walk, in the car (…) lying in the bed in an empty house if you're tired, or just talking to people (…), but usually talking to people is because you have something in your head and you're trying to figure it out or they plant a seed in your head.
>
> (Peggy, DC)

Creative productivity is mobile across worklife and cannot be accounted for in relation to specific times, places or activities. Making themselves creatively productive is difficult and challenging, but a 'normalised' part of worklife. 'Peak productivity' (Gregg, 2018) usually needs solitary, focused time but this can be scarce, as Peggy suggests, particularly mothers and those with caring responsibilities. Several academics recount their struggle with becoming and remaining productive. Tom describes his efforts to foster productivity by seeking out favourable circumstances:

> I've got this *20-minute bike ride where I'm actually not able to do anything but think about what I was just doing* and what I'm gonna do when I get here. That turns out to be *really productive in terms of generating new ideas or solving problems*. So, the fact that I can work from home as easily as I can work from here means that *I have this more elastic workday but it also means different environments give me different kinds of (...) creative stimuli.*
>
> (Tom, A)

The ability to generate innovative ideas, products and services is seen as an elastic process as career trajectories in a fast-changing economy are all about constant personal improvement, agility, flexibility and resilience. Such personal qualities can be honed and improved by investing in oneself as the primary currency of productivity: 'the self is the what to invest and enhance in terms of economic value' (Fleming, 2017, p. 692). This occasions internal conversations about 'how am I doing in my worklife?', as well as setting and re-setting personal rules, indicators, goals in one's own terms:

> *I'm very organised and very efficient and it was almost expected* that (…) I be the perfect mother and the perfect housewife and the perfect this, that and the other (…) and that's one of the things that I don't want [my product] (laughs) to be about. It actually isn't about perfection, it's about being comfortable and having time for whatever it is that you need it for (…). *You feel that pressure from everywhere*, you feel it from the people around you most because, if you were somewhat of a perfectionist before, they expect it to continue or they expect you to fall, one or the other. And then you get it from the media. You get it from online sites. You get it from mother and toddler groups. And there's this *constant pressure* that your child is ahead of everybody else or that you're immaculately turned out, or if you're not that there is a horror story as to why your makeup is not on that morning [laughter].
>
> (Peggy, DC)

Peggy has turned her work on herself into a product. Even though her product is all about relieving working mothers in particular from this 'constant pressure', she describes herself in terms of her own level of efficiency and organisation. Thus both her product and her worker self are shaped by the productivity imperative even if in contradictory ways.

Many MKWrs are concerned with performing a self that looks competent, lean and mean, not only able to deliver good results at work, but also to engage in sports, go to the gym and organise family activities – all without losing track of work:

> I'm in the pool at about 8.30 a.m. and then I train until ten or ten-thirty (...) from 11.00 on usually I work (...) solid until about maybe five or six. Then I'll go and probably get dinner and then I'll be doing more [triathlon] training (...) it's more relaxed (...) *because what I'm doing, even when I'm training, I'm thinking about stuff that I've been doing in the day and I'm generating ideas.*
>
> (Dean, DC)

All-round productive selves are achieved via incessant self-improvement and self-development efforts. Dean is training for a cycling competition and a triathlon, something that also channels his focused creativity for work. Angela did a lot of research to help her son when he was diagnosed with dyslexia: '[I've] come across (...) the whole idea of where the brain can relearn and be retrained. *I would do a lot with software with him* and (...) retraining (...) so that took up a lot of the last year in terms of doing extra work for him at home' (Angela, ICTM). Both Dean's and Angela's examples resonate with Banks' notion of instrumental leisure (Banks, 2009), where time outside work is put to productive use: leisure time is invested in to become instrumental in achieving a useful (often professional) purpose or generating a particular outcome. Angela, by drawing on research findings to care for her son, ensures a productive present and future for him. Dean's account of productivity beyond work generates value that is not just professional: he embodies 'productivity athleticism' (Gregg, 2018), as an approach to his work and in personal competitive athletic pursuits. These in turn require management, focus and dedication. Dean even had to adjust his training regimen to sustain productivity: 'Last year like it became chaotic in that I was doing triathlon, cycling and long-distance running separate to just triathlon, I was competing in all of them. And that was ultimately counterproductive' (Dean, DC).

The value associated with being a productive person, striving to achieve an outcome or even seeking the right conditions to become productive requires preparatory work and getting in the right mood:

> Some days (...) you might try and you sit there for eight hours (...) but you won't get anything done. I will try and step away from it, I might talk to [fiancée], we might go out for dinner or something (...) and I'll literally forget about

> everything. I won't even think about it, and *I could wake up the following morning and (...) I get around that problem (...) and do it* (...). I think sport helps as well (...). I've rugby training on a Tuesday, I might be having a crap day and I won't even want to go training, but I know it's getting me out of the house, it's getting me active and (...) the last thing you're thinking of when you're stuck at the bottom of a ruck is what's some client said to you in an email.
>
> (Noel, DC)

Outside work activities are articulated as a form of work on the self to reboot productivity and creativity. The more experienced the workers, the more skilful they become in staying productive, overcoming disruptions, and finding ways of reigniting productivity. As well as reigniting or boosting productivity, Noel describes the complex sociomaterial everyday practices of constructing a productive self in relation to spaces, times, routines, activities, people and relationships. These accounts respond to a perceived pressure to prove personal value: 'busy and high energy is required in terms of lifestyle' (Elaine, A).

Peers, colleagues and their experiences can also become models for personal productivity development: 'one of my other colleagues at work (...) also worked three days a week and she had a girl, but *she was very organised in her personal life and very organised in her worklife*. And when she was in the office, *I did notice, she wouldn't have the luxury of going for a second coffee break* if that's what other people were doing' (Nancy, ICTM).

Other accomplishments not necessarily to do with one's own self-improvement are constitutive of the productive self. These include cultivating children as productive selves. For example, Cathal states:

> I have a 12-year-old son, a 10-year-old son (...) and a 7-year-old daughter. The whole computing thing affects their life (...) they go to CoderDojo [programming club for youngsters] (...) all three of them are in the Khan academy [online maths and science education platform] (...) I hold ambitions that my kids will be all maths nerds.
>
> (Cathal, A)

If productivity and product are processual and emerging in narratives that are unique to each individual (i.e. personal creativity, imagination, resilience, autonomy, efficiency, etc.), the productive self is an ongoing project – a work-in-progress. But this self-project is also relational insofar as it is performed as part of networks:

> This is where you project this image (...) *I can put up a website saying my company does this – it's all 'we'*, 'we', 'there's ten of us here in the office' but it's not true and I think *you can very easily disguise*, and because that's the industry I'm in I don't trust it so I'm willing to (...) put myself out there on it as well in a strange way.
>
> (Kathy, DC)

The projection of the business can involve a certain amount of subterfuge insofar as the aim is to engender trust in the product and its delivery. Kathy describes her ambivalence about putting herself 'out there' but without doing so she can't be productive. The productive self is mobilised, therefore, through sociomaterial practices of self/product imaging, branding, collaboration, competition. More and more of the reputational aspects of MKW occur online. It is not just the self and product that are communicated online, but also the work done on the self to become more productive. For example, digital creatives Kathy, Betty and Sara are particularly conscious of the importance of performing productive and ever-improving personal selves online. For Kathy this is a particular challenge as her previous career was in companies that communicated as an (impersonal) brand. Now, as a self-employed entrepreneur, she is conscious that she has to put herself forward as the figurehead of her business: 'I was the only one that said "(...) get your brand out there, it's all about your brand". And they were all – and even the experts were like "No! Get yourself!" [out there] [laughing]' (Kathy, DC).

Working on the productive self is also relational insofar as family responsibilities both add demands and might impose constraints on worklives. This concern (shared across cohorts) is particularly felt by digital creatives due to their more precarious and fluid work situation, and even more keenly felt by mothers. Although Sharon's husband does an equal share of childcare in support of her fledgling new business, she characterises this as helping her out. She also remains acutely aware of the needs of her family and of the limited time that she has with her children:

> If I need to go to a meeting, to go see clients, I can ask [my husband] to work from home. And he has done that, *he's been very obliging*, even sometimes if work has gotten on top of me I've asked him to take the kids away to his parents for the weekend and things like that, and he's obliged and given me a free run at it but (...) *the juggling is very much on my part.*
>
> (Sharon, DC)

The sociomaterial accomplishment of locating people, changing routines, finding resources falls to mothers, such as Sharon, who simultaneously tries to be her most productive self.

Furthermore, as MKWrs work from home a great deal of the time, being in a domestic place can bring different demands (as we saw in Chapter 3), often for a different kind of productivity – to do with housekeeping, or with children's homework. For example, many mothers in particular describe attending to family or domestic needs, which constitute another form of productivity. However, this is often backgrounded or downplayed even in the accounts of mothers themselves. Instead, they work on portraying professional productivity in ways that often conceal their other priorities:

> There might be fighting [between the kids] or they might need to tell you something, or sometimes it's not even attention-seeking it's just interaction (...). And

> then the garden, and this and that. Yes, I actually feel if I could find someone that could help me organise, because my husband says to me, '*You're always very busy but you're not productive*' and it's true, sometimes I'm so busy but I'm not productive.
>
> (Betty, DC)

Betty and her husband call this being 'busy' rather than 'productive', with a hint of (self) blame about diverting potentially productive time and effort away from her business. Yet, by working from home, Betty saves the family a significant amount of money in childcare costs. Betty is as productive as she can be given her and her family's current situation:

> I mean you can't equate children to money *but it is a question of money, regardless, a question of time*.... It's not about being selfish and 'I want my own life'.
>
> (Betty, DC)

Betty is 'productive' insofar as she created a job to combine childcare, household care, and income, but this goes unrecognised. Her circumstances contributed to a clash with the innovation programme director, and is a source of tension with her husband: 'I'm sure if my husband was here he'd say "You're not in it for the money because you're not getting any"' (Betty, DC). Productive selves and recognised business outcomes are deeply gendered and little value is given to all the life and care work (social reproduction) upon which productivity ultimately relies.

As shown in some earlier examples (such as Dan and Dean), many of the participants fully embrace and embody the ever-productive, ever-ready disposition that is expected in their field and in related economic policy. They characterise themselves in terms of their steady, reliable professional productivity, their individual productive personality and internalised drive and ambition. This applies particularly to digital creatives who constantly work on themselves to be productive subjects, products of their work and the optimal embodiment of their productivity narrative.[5] To be productive means '*to project and protect the self in one's work – to be in the work and be at work*' (Petriglieri, Ashford, & Wrzesniewski, 2019, p. 139, emphasis added).

Conclusions

The imperative of productivity pervades the accounts of these MKWrs. As the MKW product is so elusive, much emphasis is put on crafting a personalised (or company) productivity narrative. The sense of being at work is replaced by constantly optimising productive activity anywhere and everywhere, from cycling to resting, and plane journeys to the kitchen table. Productive subjects are potentially always productive with some aspiring to sustain productivity while sleeping via product availability online. MKW is about the performance of productive subjectivity. Therefore, work becomes a way of life, not work and/or life, but worklife. The promise of freedom and flexibility through MKW 'is, perversely, the freedom to work' (Gregg, 2018, p. 93). While most of the practices discussed in this chapter are the stuff of MKW, they also rely on the corollary work of crafting a sustainable productive self and legible narratives of productivity. Unsurprisingly, productivity becomes 'a conduit for intense and conflicting emotions' (Petriglieri et al., 2019, p. 139). For example, these accounts highlight the work involved in managing the tensions between the productivity imperative and the demands of childcare, or the perception that productivity and working from home are incompatible. Tensions between partners and between workers based on conflicting narratives of productivity must be managed by workers themselves. When it operates as an imperative, productivity is highly charged. As these accounts indicate, it generates emotions of guilt about not doing enough, even when conscious of the evidence to the contrary; it gives rise to resentment within families and workplaces and sometimes fraught internal conversations about one's own performance. For example, Seán berates himself: '*The determinant of my productivity now is me*, so the only battle is with me and my laziness or tendency to just get distracted' (Seán, ICTM).

It is academics who most often criticise the productivity drives and imperatives imposed on them. Yet, they tend to comply with these in order to benefit from highly valued aspects of their job, such as its security and flexibility. Moreover, the promotion of a productive culture based on the approval of projects and acquisitions of soft-money by universities means that academics are beginning to deploy entrepreneurial discourses by branding themselves and describing their work in terms of personal achievements and success. Across all three sectors, these accounts describe the processual, performative and relational aspects of product, productivity and productive subjectivity. From productivity as accomplishing tasks and delivering outputs, to productivity as a sensibility towards opportunities for achievement, and as a production and reproduction of efficient, driven, skilled selves, the worklives of MKWrs are characterised by the quest to sustain productivity as a way of life. The corollary work of navigating the productivity imperative, and negotiating consequent worklife tensions, is evident across all accounts. This work requires constant improvisation and self-evaluation, which is conducted in interaction with the monitoring that takes place online and via other technological and non-technological means. It also involves negotiating relationships with family members, colleagues and competitors regarding productivity and how it is interpreted. While these accounts suggest that it is very difficult to evade the productivity imperative, they also suggest that work is at the same time valued by many for its contribution to wider social ends and the common good.

Notes

1 Presenteeism, e.g. attending work while ill, is an increasing concern for workers who feel the need to perform attending work despite being unwell (Johns, 2010). It is also

a concern for organisations as it does in fact lead to productivity loss (Bevan, 2018; Johns, 2010).

2 Moreover, those tools that support team productivity by mediating the 'presence' and activity of others to colleagues (for example, instant messaging platforms) can also be used for monitoring and surveillance (Nardi, Whittaker, & Bradner, 2000), thus generating further performance pressure.
3 In Ireland, policies in relation to teaching quality are set by the HEA, the Higher Education Authority. Research quality guidelines and policies include those set by the European Commission (2019) or developed by national initiatives such as the Irish Research Council in Ireland and the Research Excellence Framework (REF) in the UK (Vostal, 2015).
4 Nonetheless, in ICT companies, the existence of an organisational infrastructure in support of productivity means that other forms of productive work (and of products) are possible for the managers who took part in our study. They might not be leading to direct outcomes but they are part of their overall narrative of productivity. Examples are occasional lecturing at the university (as it is the case for Dominic and Jonathan, both managers of scientific software companies), participation in research projects (i.e. Jared, Angela), and networking.
5 There were only a few instances of MKWrs (Philip and Kathy, for example) who distanced themselves from this discourse and imperative of constant productivity and expected personal traits to go with it.

References

Adams, V., Murphy, M., & Clarke, A. E. (2009). Anticipation: Technoscience, Life, Affect, Temporality. *Subjectivity*, *28*(1), 246–265. https://doi.org/10.1057/sub.2009.18

Adkins, L. (2012). Out of Work or Out of Time? Rethinking Labor after the Financial Crisis. *South Atlantic Quarterly*, *111*(4), 621–641. https://doi.org/10.1215/00382876-1724111

Akin, G., & Hopelain, D. (1986). Finding the Culture of Productivity. *Organizational Dynamics*, *14*(3), 19–32. https://doi.org/10.1016/0090-2616(86)90029-X

Alvial-Palavicino, C. (2015). The Future as Practice: A Framework to Understand Anticipation in Science and Technology. *Italian Journal of Science & Technology Studies (Tecnoscienza)*, *6*(2), 135–172. Retrieved from www.tecnoscienza.net/index.php/tsj/article/view/239

Ames, M. G., Rosner, D. K., & Erickson, I. (2015). Worship, Faith, and Evangelism: Religion as an Ideological Lens for Engineering Worlds. In *Proceedings of the 18th ACM Conference on Computer Supported Cooperative Work & Social Computing – CSCW '15* (pp. 69–81). New York: ACM Press. https://doi.org/10.1145/2675133.2675282

Arvidsson, A., Gandini, A., & Bandinelli, C. (2016). Self-Branding among Freelance Knowledge Workers. In M. Crain, W. R. Poster, & M. A. Cherry (Eds.), *Invisible Labor: Hidden Work in the Contemporary World* (pp. 239–256). Oakland, CA: University of California Press.

Banks, M. (2009). Fit and Working Again? The Instrumental Leisure of the 'Creative Class'. *Environment and Planning A: Economy and Space*, *41*(3), 668–681. https://doi.org/10.1068/a40333

Berg, M., & Seeber, B. K. (2016). *The Slow Professor: Challenging the Culture of Speed in the Academy*. Toronto, Buffalo & London: University of Toronto Press.

Bevan, S. (2018). The Productivity Puzzle: Are We Looking in the Right Place? *Institute for Employment Studies*. Retrieved from www.employment-studies.co.uk/news/productivity-puzzle-are-we-looking-right-place

Bosch-Sijtsema, P. M., Ruohomäki, V., & Vartiainen, M. (2009). Knowledge Work Productivity in Distributed Teams. *Journal of Knowledge Management*, *13*(6), 533–546. https://doi.org/10.1108/13673270910997178

Cohen, N. S. (2016). Cultural Work as a Site of Struggle: Freelancers and Exploitation. In *Marx and the Political Economy of the Media* (pp. 36–64). Leiden & Boston, MA: Brill.

Davenport, T. H. (2005). *Thinking for a Living: How to Get Better Performance and Results from Knowledge Workers*. Boston, MA: Harvard Business School Press.

Drucker, P. F. (1999). Knowledge-Worker Productivity: The Biggest Challenge. *California Management Review*, *41*(2), 79–94. https://doi.org/10.2307/41165987

Ekman, S. (2013). Fantasies about Work as Limitless Potential: How Managers and Employees Seduce Each Other through Dynamics of Mutual Recognition. *Human Relations*, *66*(9), 1159–1181. https://doi.org/10.1177/0018726712461812

Erickson, I., Menezes, D., Raheja, R., & Shetty, T. (2019). Flexible Turtles and Elastic Octopi: Exploring Agile Practice in Knowledge Work. *Computer Supported Cooperative Work (CSCW)*, *28*(3–4), 627–653. https://doi.org/10.1007/s10606-019-09360-1

European Commission. (2019). Research and Innovation. Retrieved 11 October 2019, from https://ec.europa.eu/info/research-and-innovation_en

Fleming, P. (2017). The Human Capital Hoax: Work, Debt and Insecurity in the Era of Uberization. *Organization Studies*, *38*(5), 691–709. https://doi.org/10.1177/0170840616686129

Fleming, P., & Sturdy, A. (2009). "Just Be Yourself!": Towards Neo-Normative Control in Organisations? *Employee Relations*, *31*(6), 569–583. https://doi.org/10.1108/01425450910991730

Gandini, A. (2016). Digital Work: Self-branding and Social Capital in the Freelance Knowledge Economy. *Marketing Theory*, *16*(1), 123–141. https://doi.org/10.1177/1470593115607942

Gregg, M. (2015). Getting Things Done: Productivity, Self-Management and the Order of Things. In K. Hills, S. Paasonen, & M. Petit (Eds.), *Networked Affect* (pp. 187–202). Boston, MA: MIT Press.

Gregg, M. (2018). *Counterproductive: Time Management in the Knowledge Economy*. Durham, NC & London: Duke University Press.

Haynes, B. P. (2007). Office Productivity: A Theoretical Framework. *Journal of Corporate Real Estate*, *9*(2), 97–110. https://doi.org/10.1108/14630010710828108

Jeffrey Hill, E., Grzywacz, J. G., Allen, S., Blanchard, V. L., Matz-Costa, C., Shulkin, S., & Pitt-Catsouphes, M. (2008). Defining and Conceptualizing Workplace Flexibility. *Community, Work & Family*, *11*(2), 149–163. https://doi.org/10.1080/13668800802024678

Johns, G. (2010). Presenteeism in the Workplace: A Review and Research Agenda. *Journal of Organizational Behavior*, *31*(4), 519–542. https://doi.org/10.1002/job.630

Kenny, J. (2018). Re-Empowering Academics in a Corporate Culture: An Exploration of Workload and Performativity in a University. *Higher Education*, *75*(2), 365–380. https://doi.org/10.1007/s10734-017-0143-z

Lange, P. G. (2008). Interruptions and Intertasking in Distributed Knowledge Work. *NAPA Bulletin*, *30*(1), 128–147. https://doi.org/10.1111/j.1556-4797.2008.00024.x

Lazzarato, M. (1997). *Lavoro Immateriale: Forme di Vita e Produzione di Soggettività*. Ombre Corte.

Leaman, A., & Bordass, B. (2000). Productivity in Buildings: The 'Killer' Variables. In D. Clements-Croome (Ed.), *Creating the Productive Workplace* (pp. 167–191). London & New York: E & FN Spon.

Lehdonvirta, V. (2018). Flexibility in the Gig Economy: Managing Time on Three Online Piecework Platforms. *New Technology, Work and Employment*, *33*(1), 13–29. https://doi.org/10.1111/ntwe.12102

MacEachen, E., Polzer, J., & Clarke, J. (2008). "You Are Free to Set Your Own Hours": Governing Worker Productivity and Health through Flexibility and Resilience. *Social Science & Medicine*, *66*(5), 1019–1033. https://doi.org/10.1016/J.SOCSCIMED.2007.11.013

Mark, G. (2015). Multitasking in the Digital Age. *Synthesis Lectures on Human-Centered Informatics*, *8*(3), 1–113. https://doi.org/10.2200/S00635ED1V01Y201503HCI029

Nardi, B. A., Whittaker, S., & Bradner, E. (2000). Interaction and Outeraction: Instant Messaging in Action. In *Proceedings of the 2000 ACM Conference on Computer Supported Cooperative Work – CSCW '00* (pp. 79–88). New York: ACM Press. https://doi.org/10.1145/358916.358975

Palvalin, M., Lönnqvist, A., & Vuolle, M. (2013). Analysing the Impacts of ICT on Knowledge Work Productivity. *Journal of Knowledge Management*, *17*(4), 545–557. https://doi.org/10.1108/JKM-03-2013-0113

Pepitone, J. S. (2002). A Case for Humaneering: People Are Not Machines, That's Why Applying Engineered Work Design to Knowledge Jobs Can Be a Mistake. *IIE Solutions*, *34*(5), 39–45. Retrieved from https://go.galegroup.com/ps/anonymous?id=GALE%7CA86761511&sid=googleScholar&v=2.1&it=r&linkaccess=abs&issn=10851259&p=AONE&sw=w

Perlow, L. A. (1999). The Time Famine: Toward a Sociology of Work Time. *Administrative Science Quarterly*, *44*(1), 57. https://doi.org/10.2307/2667031

Petriglieri, G., Ashford, S. J., & Wrzesniewski, A. (2019). Agony and Ecstasy in the Gig Economy: Cultivating Holding Environments for Precarious and Personalized Work Identities. *Administrative Science Quarterly*, *64*(1), 124–170. https://doi.org/10.1177/0001839218759646

Ramírez, Y. W., & Nembhard, D. A. (2004). Measuring Knowledge Worker Productivity: A Taxonomy. *Journal of Intellectual Capital*, *5*(4), 602–628. https://doi.org/10.1108/14691930410567040

Teece, D. J. (1998). Capturing Value from Knowledge Assets: The New Economy, Markets for Know-How, and Intangible Assets. *California Management Review*, *40*(3), 55–79. https://doi.org/10.2307/41165943

Tremblay, D.-G., & Genin, E. (2010). IT Self-Employed Workers between Constraint and Flexibility. *New Technology, Work and Employment*, *25*(1), 34–48. https://doi.org/10.1111/j.1468-005X.2009.00237.x

Urry, J. (2000). *Sociology Beyond Societies*. London: Routledge.

Urry, J. (2012). Social Networks, Mobile Lives and Social Inequalities. *Journal of Transport Geography*, *21*, 24–30. https://doi.org/10.1016/J.JTRANGEO.2011.10.003

Vostal, F. (2015). Academic Life in the Fast Lane: The Experience of Time and Speed in British Academia. *Time & Society*, *24*(1), 71–95. https://doi.org/10.1177/0961463X13517537

Vuolle, M. (2010). Productivity Impacts of Mobile Office Service. *International Journal of Services Technology and Management*, *14*(4), 326. https://doi.org/10.1504/IJSTM.2010.035782

Wunderlich, F. M. (2013). Place-Temporality and Urban Place-Rhythms in Urban Analysis and Design: An Aesthetic Akin to Music. *Journal of Urban Design*, *18*(3), 383–408. https://doi.org/10.1080/13574809.2013.772882

Chapter 7

Identity work

Animating the mobile knowledge worklife

> I just got fed up (...) not being able to (...) direct my own affairs and be my own boss (...) I had (...) gone from one job to another (...) [and] each job better than the last in terms of salary and conditions (...) I was young, having a good time (...) and I still *wasn't quite happy* (...) so I (...) started to analyse it and wanted to work for myself, or to be my own boss (...) *I wanted to love my work* (...) let's face it work is the biggest part of our lives (...) you might as well try and find something that you're *passionate* about (...) I think that's the word, *passionate*. I feel like I'm *passionate* about what I'm doing now and I wasn't in the past, so it doesn't feel like work (...) I'm just a *tech geek* (laughter) and just *enjoy technology* (laughs) that's one part of it (...) if I wasn't doing it for work I'd probably be reading up about it (...) because it's *a hobby, a passion*. And the *flexibility* is something I certainly enjoy (...) I earned a lot more ten years ago (...) but (...) I'm just *happier* doing what I really want to do (...) *I do really love it*. You could say, 'Well weren't you doing IT when you were in [two multinational tech companies]'? And I was, but there's quite a difference in the types of IT (...) so now I'm just really focused in on the *kind of technology that I'm really interested in....*
>
> (Seamus, DC)

Seamus' account mirrors the usual trajectory of start-ups, in which founders leave full-time employment to establish a business and produce a particular product or service (Cockayne, 2016). He can now fully express his identification as a 'tech geek' by doing what he is passionate about, and by putting his tech employee identity in the past.[1] Salaried employment might provide pay security and organisational support, but it is experienced as constraining, inflexible and unfulfilling. Seamus has gained back control for himself. As 'a claim about what is most desirable and worthwhile in a person's life' (Walker & Kavedžija, 2015, p. 1), happiness gives Seamus' worklife direction. The indicators of Seamus' potential happiness or proximity to it are located in the dissolving of worklife boundaries, the achievement of personal autonomy and the meaningfulness of work.

Many have noted that appeals to passion and intimacy are increasingly migrating into the domain of work (Gill, 2014; Gregg, 2011), having been associated predominantly with heterosexual 'romantic love' (Jackson, 1995; Pearce & Stacey, 1995). Recent studies identify passion and love of work as particularly important to entrepreneurship because they provide 'the fire that fuels innovation, persistence, and ultimate success' (Cardon, Glauser, & Murnieks, 2017, p. 25). They are also deemed central to the work experience of academics (Byrne & MacDonagh, 2017; Clarke, Knights, & Jarvis, 2012). Yet, we know very little about these as worker attributes beyond their connection to positive work experiences (Perrewé, Hochwarter, Ferris, McAllister, & Harris, 2014).[2]

Gregg (2011) links a deepening passion for work among the middle classes to technological developments and an intensified compulsion towards constant online connection. Driven by desire, but also by anxieties about missing out, the 'enticing and seductive dimensions' of contemporary MKW are intensified by constant connectivity (2011, pp. 142–143). For example, identities such as 'tech geek' rely on the entanglement of myriad practices and enhanced connectivity (Symon & Pritchard, 2015). Because such workers are 'conscious of the always-present potential for engaging with work', they are always negotiating their affective relationship to it (Gregg, 2011).

In this chapter we investigate the ways in which Seamus and participants across all three sectors strive to establish and maintain happy and fulfilled selves through 'identity work'. Debates about 'identity work' in psychology and organisational studies frame it around transitional moments in which threats to identity are addressed and resolved. For example, Alvesson and Willmott define identity work as 'forming, repairing, maintaining, strengthening or revising the constructions that are productive of a precarious sense of coherence and distinctiveness' (2002, p. 626). Although crafted in the 'now', identity work 'is connected strongly to past, remembered and future projected selves' (Brown, 2015, p. 24). As such, it is always a performance in the present that is linked to specific points in a life course and a projected future.

Most identity work scholarship defines it as transitional work that is done to salvage a sense of self 'by resolving tensions and restoring consistency' (Beech, Gilmore, Hibbert, & Ybema, 2016, p. 506). However, Beech et al. call for an approach that focuses more on 'continuing struggles which do not achieve a secure sense of self' (ibid.). They propose an angle on identity work that emphasises ongoing '"self-questioning" rather than "self-affirming" identity work' (Beech et al., 2016, p. 507). This form of identity work is continuous rather than transitory because it involves perpetual engagement with struggles that are never resolved. The focus is shifted away from the transitionary resolving of tensions and emotions of anxiety, frustration and worry (Winkler, 2018) towards identity work that sustains more positive emotions, such as happiness.

We begin our discussion by locating the promise of happiness through work in relation to recent debates regarding identity work. We consider how materiality, 'technology' (e.g. the specific kinds of technology and 'tech geek' identity suggested in Seamus' account) and particular sociomaterial practices intersect to constitute work as a site of passion and happiness. The three central sections are dedicated to the particular emphasis of identity work for each worker cohort: i.e. the *dissolving of worklife boundaries* as the dominant route to happiness in the accounts of digital creatives; the association of happiness primarily with *autonomy* in the accounts of the ICT managers; and the pre-eminence of *work's meaningfulness* for the academics.

Identity work: worklife, autonomy, meaningfulness and the promise of happiness

Theorists of identity work argue that identity must be achieved in order to exist and be maintained. It has to be worked at (Schwartz, 1987 cited in Knights & Clarke, 2014) – hence the term identity work. This approach emphasises human agency by privileging 'the meanings that individuals attach reflexively to themselves (…) [as] (…) developed and sustained through processes of social interaction' (Brown, 2015, p. 23).[3] It addresses the questions: 'who am I?', 'how should I act?', 'who are we?' and 'how do we act?' Identity is achieved via appeals to those knowledges and truths that render particular identities legible and recognisable. It involves internalising 'a given identity as a (partial) definition of self', for example, 'I am an academic' (Ashforth & Schinoff, 2016, p. 113). Specific stories or ways of talking, thinking and enacting identity are regulated through the complex sociomaterial reproduction of practices, rules and norms that are variously taken up, reproduced or subverted. However, the burden of identity work is uneven as structures of inequality, racism, sexism, xenophobia and heteronormativity shape potential identifications and therefore identity work.[4]

Building on this work, but adopting a more performative approach, we see identity as a 'doing' rather than a 'being'; as constituted in and through what we repeatedly do (Butler, 1990). Butler calls the doing of identity 'performativity'. To see identity as performatively reproduced is to attend to how it is repeatedly enacted to achieve the effect of a naturalised identity. As such, the obligation to 'do' identity is not as an intentional act but an already (pre)scripted 'performance' that is always different insofar as it is repeated (ibid.). This is the paradox of identity – it looks fixed but is inherently unstable so that it requires continual maintenance if it is to materialise. The materialisation of identities are the effects of multiple intermeshed sociomaterial institutions, relations, practices and discourses.

All of these sociomaterial processes are shaped by specific feelings rules. For example, Seamus' account above points to the feeling rules of contemporary digital creative work, which simultaneously rely on, generate and reward emotions of passion and love for work. Passion and the promise of happiness are constitutive of his sense of self, both enabling and constraining his performance of worklife identity. 'Emotion work' can be understood as the work done on the self 'to affect the self, by the self upon others, and others upon the self' (Messer, 2013, p. 15). It does not pre-exist discourse and practice, but is constituted in and through these and the power relations that shape them (Zembylas, 2003).

Like those concerned with identity work, Hochschild's (1983) analysis of emotional labour emphasises workers' attempts to achieve harmony both within themselves and in relation to other workers. She argues that the work that goes into emotional labour and feeling management requires 'an appreciation of display rules, feeling rules and a capacity for deep acting' (Hochschild, 2003, p. 102). Therefore, emotions are not natural responses to situations but are relationally negotiated and worked at through 'emotional management' to comply with culturally specific 'feeling rules' (Hochschild, 1983). These feeling rules 'define what we imagine we should and shouldn't feel and (…) would like to feel over a range of circumstances …' (Hochschild, 1983, p. 86). Emotions then are not just felt or expressed, they are 'elicited, invoked, regulated and managed through a variety of expectations, patterns and anticipations' which specify the kinds and forms of the emotions that should be experienced or displayed (Sheller, 2004, p. 226). For example, by expecting to achieve happiness through work identification, Seamus performs work as enjoyable and enhancing of his well-being (Ashforth & Humphrey, 1993, p. 107). While Hochschild is concerned with the emotional labour that underpins service work, we address the ways in which identity work mediates and performs the 'feeling rules' of contemporary MKW. The more that happiness is politically and culturally identified 'with productivity, functionality, goodness and even normality' (Cabanas & Illouz, 2019, p. 10), the more it moves centre stage in cultivating committed workers as the accounts discussed in this chapter suggest.

Emotions, according to Ahmed (2004), can be understood as cultural practices that connect the psychic and the social. As they circulate between individuals and collectivities, they serve to align them with hegemonic norms. So, happiness can be seen as entrenching the contemporary norm of work as the site of self-fulfilment and enjoyment (Ahmed, 2010). Emotional investment and attachment to work-based happiness are cultivated and sustained by the promise of benefits and rewards. As such, the promise of happiness through work binds and orientates individuals towards specific worklife norms. The happy worklife symbolises a socially acceptable goal, identity and lifestyle. However, as a component of identity work, the incessant emotional work done to follow these emotional norms or feeling rules is often invisible or at least made to appear effortless.

Based on our data, we argue that the identity work of MKWrs is driven by the promise of happiness and is rationalised and performed in three different ways: first by striving for the *conjoining of work and life* so that they become synonymous; second, via the *autonomous* pursuit of goals, and third, by making and sustaining *work as a meaningful activity*. By making work and life interchangeable, modern divisions between production and social reproduction become dispersed across social domains and times such that it is impossible to distinguish any limits to work (Morini & Fumagalli 2010). For some participants, this represents efforts to achieve a confluence of all aspects of work and life so that they are conjoined as worklife. For the digital creative study participants in particular, the promise of happiness is invested in the potential to inhabit worklife authentically. This means eradicating any distinction between the quality of the experience that marks work and life as separate domains (Morini & Fumagalli, 2010; Weeks, 2007).

The promise of happiness is also located in the pursuit of autonomy; a 'normatively loaded term' linked to 'liberal (and neoliberal) ideals of self-government and self-direction' (Madhok, Phillips, & Wilson, 2013, p. 5).[5] Cabanas and Illouz argue that 'individualism and the autonomous and independent pursuit of goals' are presented as the most natural way of achieving a happy life (2019, pp. 52–54). Understood as 'regulation by the self', the notion of autonomy relies on notions of individual will, choice and freedom (Ryan & Deci, 2006, p. 1557). The autonomous pursuit of goals is closely linked to the generation of human capital, well-being and productivity (Ryan & Deci, 2006, p. 1558). Seamus makes this link by suggesting that he can optimise these by moving from salaried employment to the relative autonomy of self-employment. But, while autonomy may form 'the bedrock of contemporary identity projects', for Seamus and many other study participants, it also generates 'burdens and anxieties' (Gabriel, 2015, p. 27). These anxieties are often related to getting it wrong or fear of falling out of the game. However, autonomy and relatedness are interconnected as they are both identified as human needs and individuals 'feel most related to those who support their autonomy' (Ryan & Deci, 2006, p. 1565). Yet, as we see later in the chapter, the ways in which autonomy and relatedness are inhabited and performed emerges differently in the accounts of women and men participants.

The meaningfulness of work also emerges as a route to personal happiness in many accounts. Indeed, much of the positive psychology literature on happiness links happiness with meaningfulness (Seligman, Parks, & Steen, 2004). For Viktor Frankl, meaning and meaningfulness can be 'discovered through creative, experiential, and attitudinal values that are motivated by self-transcendence rather than by self-interest' (Wong, 2014, p. 149). Similarly, Bellah et al. (1985) link meaning with the importance given to the subjective experience of work as a job, career or calling. Relatedly, the term vocation is associated with work motivated primarily by 'other-oriented values and goals' and thus seen as meaningful (Dik & Duffy, 2009, p. 427). Thus, the identity work linked to the pursuit of meaningful worklives is often driven by a search for 'genuine' connection between self and work and the idea of engaging in work 'of "real" value' (Symon & Whiting, 2019, p. 676). Because meaningfulness relates to the significance something holds for an individual, it is closely linked to personal identity (Rosso, Dekas, & Wrzesniewski, 2010). For some, meaningfulness contributes to very long work hours and a 'diffuse boundary between self and occupation' (Bailey & Madden, 2017, p. 10; Symon & Whiting, 2019). Sharing activities with both colleagues and friends can deepen worklife connections in meaningful ways, but it also involves considerable identity management work (Symon & Whiting, 2019). In the sections that follow we unravel the ongoing identity work that sustains deep work commitment across each of the worker cohorts.

Digital creatives' worklives: the identity work of making work and life synonymous

Returning to Seamus' opening account, his identity work, although framed by work aspirations and the cultivation of a happy self through work, is inextricable from life.

> I wanted to run my own business. I just didn't *feel fulfilled* (…) working for other people (…) *I decided I'm not going to spend the money on a house*, I'm going to invest in business instead (…) I'm not earning anything as much as what I was earning ten years ago (…) *I'm not having anything like the lifestyle* (…) but I'm still *a lot happier* doing what I'm doing because I'm doing it for myself. And I feel like (…) I'm really *achieving things for myself* and not for other people.
>
> (Seamus, DC)

Happiness in work is less an addition than a precondition for work success; '[q]uestions of pay, working hours and social security assume a secondary place' (Sandoval, 2018, p. 115). For Seamus, investing in a house and enjoying a non-work-oriented lifestyle must be postponed, or moved down the priority list. Instead, he has devoted himself to work, but happiness through love of work often goes 'hand in hand with rather unlovable working conditions' (Sandoval, 2018, p. 113):

> Part of the problem for people like myself is, of course, the problem that *we work 24/7* a lot of the time – *365 days a year* if you're an entrepreneur (…) that *doesn't exactly chime with your family*. So, if you wanted to go on a break with your family, *are there facilities for you to continue working* so that you can be with your family in the evening …?
>
> (Seamus, DC)

Although Seamus is single, it is only the absence of connectivity infrastructures on his hypothetical family break that throws up potential worklife boundaries.[6]

However, even when doing what you love, anxieties and disappointments arise as a result of long hours, exhaustion and other factors. So there can be no 'pure' happiness because both positive and negative emotions and '[a]mbivalent feelings colour any event in life' (Cabanas & Illouz, 2019, p. 158). Although it is his passion, running his own business also has downsides for Seamus:

> When you're doing books or accounts (…) (laughter) (…) *it feels like work then for sure (…) if business goes badly, or you let down a client, or a customer* and business goes that way, *it can be very tough*. Sometimes you do want to separate it, even though I say it's great because it's a *passion, it's a hobby* (…) there are *times when you would like to be able to separate it from your personal life and you can't* and that is a problem….
>
> (Seamus, DC)

Precisely because work is a passion and hobby, because it is so elemental to personal identity, it is impossible to disentangle work and personal life even when there is a strong desire to do so. Indeed, the desire to do so is backgrounded in Seamus' account. Yet, the paradox of well-being and happiness is that the positive experiences commonly associated with happiness 'often rely for their meaning and significance on negative events in our lives' (Cieslik, 2015, p. 429). It seems, however, that a key aspect of identity work is the playing down of such negative experiences. Much identity work is also focused on backgrounding non-work related life aspirations, especially those unrelated to cultivating a productive self.

However, Seamus' business is not solely an individualised happiness project. It is also motivated by a wider social mission: 'part of the reason I'm in it (...) is surely because *[nephew] is autistic* (...). I do want to make a living (...) [but] I want to (...) feel *I can make a real difference to education, to children with special needs, to parents*, to a lot of different people'. Identity work for Seamus aligns with contemporary capitalist 'feeling rules' of work-related happiness and passion. Yet, insofar as he foregrounds a happy and committed work persona, he backgrounds his personal commitment to helping children like his nephew. He also downplays anxieties about how he might separate work from life given his passionate work commitment.

Kathy describes a similar journey towards finding work that will bring her self-fulfilment and happiness:

> I (...) steadily worked myself up into positions where I was earning quite good money (...) but recognising that *was never [emphasis] going to make me happy* (...) they were challenging to a degree, but *the inspiration wasn't there*. There wasn't *real passion for the work* (...) I just feel that if you find something you *truly love*, you'll *be productive* at it because you can be actively engaged and interested in it, and the money will come then afterwards....
>
> (Kathy, DC)

Like Seamus, Kathy's identity work involves a projective worklife quest for work that inspires passion and personal happiness. Happiness is productive both in enabling Kathy's self-realisation and as the basis for work success. As such, it works as a kind of 'hope technology' (Franklin, 1997, p. 203) because it is by hoping for something that we attribute happiness to it (Ahmed, 2010, p. 181). This 'projective narrative' of the happy self 'develops as it strives to catch up with the best version of itself' (Cabanas & Illouz, 2019, p. 139). Thus the projective narrative of hope for the happy worklife keeps workers engaged – investing in work in the present as a buffer against the uncertainty of the future. It necessitates constant identity work, whether in justifying past worklife decisions or work commitment in the present as an investment in future happiness. Kathy continues:

> I've always been *career driven* (...) years ago, I (...) made choices between the guy I was with (...) [for] a long, long time and the choice was, am I

> really going to (…) try make a career of it, or am I going to do what *makes you happy*? And *I chose the career* (…) and that makes me sound so cold but I know I *wouldn't have been happy* any other way. And I tried it for long enough to know that *if I'm not happy* in my career or doing something I really want to do and have *that passion for it* then I'm not going to be happy anyway so (…) *I'm not going to rely on someone, the partner I'm with to make me happy*. It has to come from somewhere else so….
>
> (Kathy, DC)

As something that she '*should* be inclined toward', happiness (understood as available through work) guides Kathy's decisions about how to live well (Ahmed, 2010, p. 199, emphasis original). The promise of happiness via an intimate relationship is forfeited in favour of career, which is more likely to deliver. Referring to the person she is currently seeing, who is also self-employed, she reflects:

> The great thing about seeing *someone who has that* [self-employment] as well, *they just understand* (…) if I say, look if I can't make that dinner I promised you I'd be at, that's okay.
>
> (Kathy, DC)

When meaningfulness and self-identity are invested in work, it is 'work's intimacy' that prevails (Gregg, 2011). Yet, this passionate and intimate relationship to work, as Kathy suggests, must be worked at:

> After about a year I had really burnt out. I *wasn't being c*reative (…) there was no head space for it whatsoever (…) to be creative you kind of have to give yourself (…) a complete break away (…) *it's a thing between doing a job and being inspired* (…). *You need something inspirational in your life* (…) that (…) keeps the passion there.
>
> (Kathy, DC)

When passionate work exhausts its potential to deliver inspiration, Kathy looks outside of work for respite. It is necessary to escape work in search of other sources of inspiration. Life is mined to rekindle work passion. Her conjoined worklife must be disjoined. Like Seamus, Kathy also struggles against those aspects of work that do not bolster her passion:

> Doing *something I love has kind of suffered* in the last while (…) I've become far more selective about the kind of projects I will do (…) when I'm actually working on (…) *my own stuff*, stuff that I want to develop *in my own name*, yeah, *it's work of passion* (…) but it has been *so rare* that I get that time….
>
> (Kathy, DC)

Ironically, it is the very promise of doing what she loves that creates the dissatisfaction that work is supposed to overcome (Cabanas & Illouz, 2019). When self-fulfilment and happiness are the yardsticks against which relationships to self and to work are measured, identity work pushes towards sustaining these. Yet, the performance of the happy MKWr is riddled with moments of doubt. For Kathy, it includes tracking her progress and making opportunities to pursue 'her own stuff', in her 'own name'. She must strive to sustain her passion even when work circumstances militate against this – her happiness depends on keeping going. Meanwhile, the close identification of life and work renders those aspects of work that compromise this extra burdensome.

Sara invests in the idea of 'doing what you love' (DWYL) for both herself and her husband:

> I do what I do because *I love doing it* and *I'm passionate about doing it well.* (…) I'm pretty sure I could land a salary [sic] job that would probably earn more money (…) but I *wouldn't be as happy.*
>
> (Sara, DC)

Sara's work commitment is also in support of her husband's pursuit of worklife happiness:

> My husband runs (…) a non-partisan political website (…) and he's been working on that for about 18 months. But it's unpaid (…) he's doing what *he is doing because he loves doing it* and I'm working 18 hours a day because *I love what I do* and because *somebody has to be earning an income in our household* (…) that's not him because he is in start-up phase (…) he definitely feels very strongly about, *working at what you love to do* (…) he's not making any money doing it (…) he's doing it because *he loves it….*
>
> (Sara, DC)

Via the imbricated capacities of networked connectivity and their knowledge skills, as well as a grocery delivery service and the help of a cleaner, Sara and her husband are able to pursue work projects they love. Her husband's potential happiness through work is invested in through Sara's long hours of work, but also via his free work. As Bousquet (2009) argues, contemporary work arrangements, particularly in MKW, induce workers to freely downplay the significance of their wage and make much of the pay-offs in terms of passion and happiness. Indeed, because the notion of happiness is subjective and elusive, it translates relatively easily across diverse worklife ends (Walker & Kavedžija, 2015).

Betty, whose previous employment was as a journalist, PR executive and fashion magazine editor in Sweden, recently started her own business – an online parenting magazine for first- and second-time mothers in Ireland. Her decision was related to finding a way of combining 'work with minding my own children [as well as addressing the absence of] information (…) for mothers'. Because becoming a self-employed digital entrepreneur is not driven primarily by a quest for happiness, she is all the more conscious of the cultural imperative to be passionate about work:

> The creative job (…) it's expected [that] it's such *a passion within you*, it's almost like *you're not working, you're doing a hobby* (…) sometimes I wake up and I ask myself, Jesus, am I going to be writing about kids forever?
>
> (Betty, DC)

Later in the interview, Betty draws attention to the work involved in appearing happy when a friend commented on her blog: 'she said (…) "I was (…) saying to myself *she can't be this chirpy the whole time*, I know her, she's not this chirpy the whole time!" – and I said (…) "*You write as if you were*" '. Like Hochschild's flight attendants, Betty feigns 'chirpiness' – a form of surface acting that suppresses 'resentment and anxiety' (Coupland & Spedale, 2020, p. 838).

In common with many other participants, Noel reflexively engages with the assumed connection between setting up a business and love of the work: 'you need extreme self-motivation to do it and you *need to love what you're doing*' (Noel, DC). Self-employment, although promising, means that Noel has to work on his sense of self to achieve it: 'I almost made *a conscious decision to make myself unemployable* (…) so that I could never go back …'.

Happiness is connected with a feeling of being headed in the right direction, but this involves Noel in the work of sustaining this direction. Indeed, the obligation to be happy makes it difficult to articulate the unhappy effects of the work in which happiness is invested. For example, Noel notes that: 'although *I love the flexibility of working for myself*, I mean if I want to go for lunch with someone, I can do that (…) [but] I never do because I'm *always worried* about work' (Noel, DC). So, even when the promise of happiness doesn't deliver, it works to sustain an orientation towards work and work commitment. Because they feel entirely accountable for their own choices, when fulfilment or happiness eludes these workers it is often interpreted as a 'sign of flawed will and dysfunctional psyches, and even as marks of failed biographies' (Cabanas & Illouz, 2019, p. 71).

Although she had a good job with a large salary, Peggy describes her journey towards self-employment as a 'soul searching' experience; 'almost like a *burning desire, it's like I can't help it*' (Peggy, DC). Reflecting on a previous employed position, she notes that 'it *wouldn't have been a passion*', it was simply satisfaction with a job well done. However, since starting her own business: 'even the people that fall in front of me are the right people (…) it's almost *like it has a life of its own*, if that makes sense'. Yet, pursuit of personal desire through work turns out to be only part of the story for Peggy:

> I think [I am] *happy* when [everything is] balanced, it's keeping it balanced (…). It *does take work. It really does take work to keep it balanced.* It's very easy to get sucked into different things (…) I'll just check my email at seven (…) but

> once it's on a balance, it *works really, really well for everybody* not just for me and [family] but even just for work, or for the business and everything as well.
>
> (Peggy, DC)

Because work is always present and accessible via Peggy's mobile devices, its seductiveness has to be 'balanced' against her caring and dutiful relationship to family members and colleagues (Cieslik, 2015; Thin, 2012). In fact, by achieving such balance, she suggests that the business benefits too. However, there is a sense from her interview that these moments of 'balance' are few and are constantly worked at.

Lily's business idea (as for Seamus and some other participants) is linked to her son's learning needs:

> I *love working and I love working creatively* but I wanted, firstly to do something that was more *meaningful to me personally* rather than purely driven by commercial (…) (hesitates) (…) motives (…) through the *learning needs of my son* (…) I hit upon (…) the perfect solution which was working on something that was *meaningful but also creative*….
>
> (Lily, DC)

Lily's ability to invest in happiness through work is reliant on doing something that is personally meaningful which for her meant developing a product that might meet her son's learning needs. Her relationship to work is also embedded in managing her children's care and well-being. For example, she notes that her 'most valuable asset' now is 'a really, really fantastic child minder'. She points out that when her daughter was 'in a crèche full-time and she hated it (…) it was heart breaking (…) a huge emotional pressure on me'. Now she has the '*emotional freedom* to know that *they're perfectly happy* (…) that is a huge stress release' (Lily, DC).

Like most of the mothers in our study, Lily narrates a personal love of work and simultaneous love and care for her children. These must be creatively combined. But what is at stake in this gendered promise of happiness by 'balancing' work and family for mothers? Slaughter's (2012) essay 'Why Women Still Can't Have It All' suggests that happiness might be achieved by finding 'a satisfying balance between family and work' and poses this as a feminist goal. This 'invocation of happiness as a highly — if not the most highly — valued social good' is held out as a normative model for all middle-class women (Rottenberg, 2014, p. 147). It reorients liberal feminism 'away from notions of freedom, equal rights, and social justice and toward the importance of well-roundedness and well-being' (ibid.). Similarly, Facebook CEO Sandberg's bestselling book, *Lean In*, 'presents women who are "competent professionals and happy mothers — or (…) happy professionals and competent mothers" as its progressive and feminist ideal' (2013, p. 154). As well as celebrating an unobtainable ideal, this promise of smooth worklife blending or 'balance' as a route to happiness erases the worklives of working-class and racialised women upon whose work it relies.

In brief, the identity work that goes into meeting the deinstitutionalised ideal of an autonomous and happy work-identified digital creative meets its limits when customer demands do not align with work goals, when relatively boring administration and business tasks must be done, and at times of burnout and exhaustion. It is at these moments that the promise of happiness through a seamless conjoining of worklife starts to look disingenuous. Yet, only a few of the digital creative participants distance themselves from this ideal, mainly by pointing out the extent to which it is a performance that has to be sustained. This promise also looks disingenuous from the perspectives of differently positioned workers because it is predicated on the assumption of middle-class lives. Moreover, by making middle-class women its most emblematic champions, it disguises the class and gender inequalities that continue to shape paid and unpaid work. When workers are self-employed, as in the case of these digital creatives, passion and love of work ensure the vitality that bolsters the working self in the absence of organisational scaffolding and support (Petriglieri, Ashford, & Wrzesniewski, 2019). The identity work that goes into sustaining this vitality relies on the resourcefulness of workers themselves.

ICT managers: towards an autonomous worklife

For the ICT managers, their identity work is closely linked to the success of their companies and the pursuit of happiness through a quest for autonomy. But this requires emotional investment. For example, Dan observes that 'any *high skilled job has to marry passion*'. His commitment is to his work. He founded an IT network start-up in 2006 and is managing director with one co-director who owns half the company. This position enables him autonomy over this worklife:

> I'm the boss really in terms of running the company (…) at least half my time is spent managing the business and growing business and dealing with customers and that's what I'm interested in (…) half the reason for setting up my own business was so that I could *have control over things like where I live (...) or what I want to do….*
>
> (Dan, ICTM)

Autonomous subjects are assumed to have 'the ability to determine the pattern and shape of their own lives' (Boris & Parreñas, 2010, p. 253), and it is towards this goal that many of the ICT managers aspire. Autonomy, understood as enjoying control over one's life and desires tends to be presented as 'an undoubted good' (Madhok et al., 2013, p. 5). For example, Damien worked for multinational companies and was half owner of a software company for eight years when living in South Africa. He recently set up a new consulting business which has two employees and three freelance workers based in Poland and Ireland.

> It's like being a race car driver or an artist (…) *the passion* is the number one reason, the *interest, the excitement* (…). It doesn't feel like work (…) I would hate it very much to give up what I'm doing for a living (…) and have to work for someone again.
>
> (Damien, ICTM)

Damien's self-identity is bound up with the success of the company: 'this is your own business (…) *your own baby, it's your own love, it's everything* (…) you want it to work so you will always put everything into it (…) the day that stops is the day that your company is going to be in decline' (Damien, ICTM). However, Damien's identification with his company and its project is not shared with his fiancée or wider family: 'my fiancée has no interest in either the internet or the business, so that's a complete disconnect. And my family has no interest'.

Damien's dedication to the business means less time for his partner: 'we just kind of *keep on tipping along*. So in terms of work-life balance and the busy schedule, *you kind of sometimes ask yourself "is it all worth it?"*'. Reflecting on his highly mobile lifestyle he notes: 'you're travelling, you're in different time zones, *you have no real circle of friends, relationships would be shallow (...) it's a young man's job*'. He goes on to suggest that this is only possible for 'a certain period of your life, and eventually (…) you're *looking more for the actual life-style, less work, as you get older*'. This shift towards combining work dedication with lifestyle is evident in the accounts of two middle-aged men ICT managers discussed later.

Jared worked as a chartered accountant with large multinationals but, like Damien, he was not 'keen on working in big companies':

> I much prefer being more *entrepreneurial and innovative* (…) high-tech people tend to be driven much more by the *inherent motivation* (…) it isn't about getting any sort of pensionable job, hanging in there until you retire (…) if you're doing it at a very high level, it's very abstract and it's *highly motivating, highly motivating.*
>
> (Jared, ICTM)

By running 'a small high-tech company like this' Jared achieves autonomy: 'we are *in control of our own destiny. We make all our own decisions*'.

Similarly, Seán, who works from home but as part of a remotely networked company, cherishes his work autonomy: 'I try to *treat myself as sort of a business in itself* and do that as efficiently as I can (…) it wouldn't occur to me to not be able (…) to work wherever I was (…) I like people (…) but I'm (…) better as sort of a lone warrior. It's the ideal way to do things' (Seán, ICTM). By identifying as a lone warrior and mobile worker, Seán performs an autonomous self that is in control of his work process and expectations.

As well as defining themselves as passionate and autonomous workers through their companies, many of the ICT managers described how they also foster the autonomy of their workers (whether employed or contracted). For example, Dominic (owner/general manager of a small ICT company, married with a 3-year-old son) refers to the autonomous working conditions his company promotes:

> We *prefer that people work on their own initiative*, so we kind of *give them a lot of freedom* (…) we get a much better outcome out of that, people not being stressed and they like the work they do. And that provides (…) *a good environment in the company* (…). So if they have to stay later, they stay themselves, *nobody tells them 'oh, you have to stay another hour to do that work'. So they know they have to.*
>
> (Dominic, ICTM)

Work-based autonomy has in the past been defined in terms of employee discretion and freedom in carrying out assigned work tasks (Langfred & Rockmann, 2016). However, in the context of technologically mediated mobile work, and MKW in particular, worker 'discretion and freedom has expanded in many different ways' (Langfred & Rockmann, 2016, p. 638). Because MKW involves indefinable inputs of creativity and innovative problem-solving, as well as self-defined productivity (see Chapter 6), workers are 'granted control over a far greater scope of their work' (2016, p. 639). Managing this work, as Dominic's account indicates, involves cultivating autonomy as a foundational value (Banks, 2010). Worker autonomy is a normative principle for both the employer and employee and reinforces the economic profit-making interests of the company (Banks, 2010). Individualised work practices even as members of collaborative project work teams, reproduce autonomy as a work norm.

Like individuals, companies have lifecycles. Moreover, the trajectory and identity of the company is closely bound up with the personal reputation and identity of owners and managers. For example, Jonathan (CEO of software firm, married with two teenage children) notes that his company was thriving in the 1990s but stagnated in the 2000s:

> *Companies reach plateaus* and then they need (…) a boost (…) to bring companies to the next stage (…) the second plateau would have been to break sort of ten million in sales (…) you can have the best product in the world, but *if (…) people don't see it, there's no point….*
>
> (Jonathan, ICTM)

Because the company identity work (in the form of marketing) wasn't well targeted, the company didn't scale up and was acquired by a foreign company. Those who started it, including Jonathan, '*lost the intellectual property*' but also the autonomy gained by owning the company when they became employees.

It is noteworthy that worklife style emerged as a central concern for only two middle-aged men participants (one married with children and the other single).

For example, Charles, who lives in a rural area with his wife and children and works from home, observes that:

> Work, especially when you enjoy it (...) can become addictive (...) I am conscious of that. I *make a very conscious effort not to get stuck in the workaholic track* (...) I embed it [work] in my lifestyle (...). It is different than I used to do things (...) that's because I am a company owner now (...). *Technologies allow us to work remotely (...) and an attitude that is required.*
>
> (Charles, ICTM)

Charles' home-based worklife represents a shift in priorities as he describes a bucolic daily routine: 'I usually *drop my kids at school, sometimes we take the bicycle, otherwise the car, then I go to my home office, and use things like email and Skype* (...) social media tools like Twitter and LinkedIn ...' (Charles, ICMT). The sociomateriality of his identity work is emphasised in Charles' account of maintaining connections to work and sustaining his remote worklife style. His identity performances as an ICT manager rely heavily on social media and ICT.

The mobility of his work skills, finances and digital environment enable Martin, who is a 'data architect', to move to Ireland from the USA because it is easier for him to keep horses and go riding (as discussed in Chapter 2):

> *I'm awfully content at my level.* I have the very good fortune of having the trust and respect of my CEO and the board. I have the *money* I need to do my job. I have very good people around me.
>
> (Martin, ICTM)

For Martin, as for all of the other men ICT managers quoted above, personal autonomy is imbued with intrinsic value and endows them with a sense of well-being (Mill, 1975). The decisions they made along their career trajectories are articulated as 'their' decisions (even if motivated by diverse concerns), thus constituting themselves as having the capacity of autonomy; a capacity that attaches to them as individuals (Christman, 2003), even as this autonomy is capacitated by multiple actors, including mobile devices, horses, infrastructures and financial resources. It is what enables them to pursue their own work agendas and to move towards realising an 'authentic' self that is uninhibited by external constraints or demands (Christman, 2004).[7]

While Charles' claim to autonomy in crafting his own worklife style is relationally recounted, it is framed as taking control. In contrast, the accounts of women ICT managers claim a more relational autonomy. Relational approaches to autonomy as a sociomaterial constituted capacity recognise the ways in which 'practical identities and value commitments are constituted in and by our interpersonal relationships and social[material] environment' (Mackenzie, 2008, p. 519). For example, Angela, managing director of a small programming company, couches her role in relation to the gendered sensibilities of customers with regard to technology:

> I found the people who (...) are very *good technical programmers*, you can't [let] near a client as in they *don't have the good skills in terms of dealing with the client* (...) they can be very *defensive* of some things they have written, which may be technically correct, but I would take the view that *if the customer can't use it, it's as much a fault in the design or the delivery....*
>
> (Angela, ICTM)

She does 'a lot of the customer work because *I tend to speak less technical with them* [than men technical programmers]' (Angela, ICMT). This is important, she notes, because customers will '*accept that from a woman,* whereas they expect sometimes the man to be more (...) technical speak (...) *they feel more comfortable* (...) if they're not as up to speed on the technology as some of the guys in the company here would be'. Angela takes on the work of translating technological projects and services to customers thus gifting time to her colleagues to focus on technical work. She also suggests that her contribution of 90 per cent of the work in the home is by agreement with her family because it is most important to her: '*if the people living there are happy and if I'm happy*, that's the important thing' (Angela, ICTM).

Like many of the women digital creatives, Angela's worklife is framed by her own career success in conjunction with the happiness and well-being of family. This is not easy and is not helped by the promise that contemporary 'career women' can 'have it all':

> Although you supposedly *have it all now* (...) you can go out to work, you have choices (...) it's a case of *balancing* (...) just because more is available to you, do you really need (...) all those extra choices? (...) *with choices comes expectations*, so it's (...) *managing those expectations and managing those choices.*
>
> (Angela, ICTM)

The expectation of living one's life freely, according to one's choices as a sovereign individual, is modelled on the 'construction of a male, white bourgeois subject' (Lorey, 2015, p. 30). Because the ideal MKWr is constructed in terms of unencumbered individuality, individuality itself becomes the 'very instrument' of MKWr 'self-making' (Butler, 2015, p. x). This involves the identity work of mediating high-tech products to customers and trying to smooth the way to happiness at home by doing most of the domestic and care work. Like the accounts of the digital creatives, Peggy and Lily, Angela works towards simultaneously inhabiting the positions of a public worker subject and a present mother who strives for the simultaneous achievement of work and family happiness.

Kelly also struggles with the conflicting ideals of career and motherhood, noting that when she worked full-time she did 'everything' at work, often staying on till late in the evening. She continues:

> I have *worked part-time since my second child was born* (...) it was more my decision (...) *I would have seen it as a duty* (...) the income thing wouldn't have come into it (...) because it probably *would have been financially better for us if I had stayed full-time* and he had worked part-time (...) *I felt it was important to give time to my children.*
>
> (Kelly, ICTM)

Kelly goes on to say that she is 'in the nice position in that being a cofounder, that can never be taken away from me'; it enables her to scale back on work to care for her children. Even so, she describes working 'after nine o'clock, once they've [children] gone to bed (...) you'd finish the report that you were working on' (Kelly, ICTM). Women ICT managers who were not mothers referred to the struggles of colleagues, almost as cautionary tales. For example, Nancy refers to the struggles of a number of women colleagues, and one in particular who is pregnant: 'she has to work late and *she's already stressing about what she's going to do when the child comes* (...) how will she manage? (...) you (...) really have to adapt your life to your work' (Nancy, ICTM).

The identity work described by the ICT managers focuses mostly on the pursuit of autonomy both as a route to happiness and as a normative principle that has deeply gendered implications. The identity work of mothers in particular focused on negotiating family and work, while fathers' identity work (with only one exception) suggested little association of work identity and parental status (Annink & den Dulk, 2012). Yet, some of the younger men, such as Damien, suggested concerns about combining their high level of autonomous work investment with establishing long-term intimate relationships and family lives in the future.

Sustaining meaningful academic worklives

In common with the digital creatives and ICT managers, the academic cohort articulate a love of work but this is primarily in relation to work's meaningfulness. Work's meaningfulness emerges in the day-to-day doing of the work and in the concern for doing it well. Although a quest for happiness and autonomy is present in their accounts, they describe more convoluted routes into academia, often prompted by chance events, with only a third seeking out academia as a desired career. For example, Elaine describes how she became an academic as follows:

> It *wasn't something that I planned*, but I had done an MSc here at [the university] (...) and they asked me to come back and do some work, and

> *I found out I loved it* (…) particularly the teaching and the class dynamic and working with students (…) and *I love it* (…) *I love the diversity.*
>
> (Elaine, A)

While she loves her work, Elaine describes her lifestyle as 'challenging (…) frenetic (…) busy and high energy …'. This includes combining work with mothering:

> If I get a call from the school to say my *daughter's sick (…) to know that I can go home and my office can come with me*, so I can be at home and I can still effectively work and do what's required of me (…) the fact that you can stay in touch (…) you know what's been going on when you get in the next day, that's useful.
>
> (Elaine, A)

For Elaine, 'identity performances of connection are an emergent product of an entanglement of social and material agencies' (Symon & Pritchard, 2015, p. 258) that enable the simultaneous meeting of work and mothering commitments.

Like Elaine, Marc describes the way he 'fell' into an academic career:

> *It wasn't planned* (…) I didn't really think about teaching at third level (…) many of life's starting roads (…) can lead you in different directions, *some things are decisions you make yourself, some things are things that happen.*
>
> (Marc, A)

He goes on to describe his undergraduate degree in science, and loving maths without any sense of 'where that was going to lead me'. After graduation he was contacted by a lecturer in his current department inviting him to do a research master's project: 'So, I jumped to the unknown (…) so, that influenced taking a PhD and so on' (Marc, A).

Kate's journey into academia was prompted during her undergraduate studies: 'When I started here as a student (…) I knew I'd like to become a lecturer'. When doing her master's, she was offered teaching hours 'and then *I got a six-month contract post when somebody was on sabbatical*, so I got official lecturing experience (…) then I pretty much went for this job and I've been working since'. Noting that she is a relatively young lecturer, Kate reflexively cultivates her relationship with students:

> I like to try and show them how *I'm learning as well and I'm trying to improve what I'm doing* and how this was done properly today but yesterday's class wasn't. So, *I want them to know that I'm actively making efforts to teach more effectively* but that I don't always get it right.
>
> (Kate, A)

Like the academics participating in Byrne and McDonagh's study, Kate invests high levels of care and effort in her work and goes 'to great lengths to prepare for lectures and teach in ways that would be most effective for students' (2017, p. 196). Later in the interview she describes the conflict between mothering and her high standards of performance at work, as when her daughter became ill at crèche. This created:

> … a lot of extra stress in my life (…) because I hadn't had sleep for about a week and I had to tell the class, 'I am really tired. I have had no sleep'. (…) because *I felt they would just think I was disinterested and not motivated….*
>
> (Kate, A)

As for mothers in the other sectors, Kate's identity work is shaped by family demands and their impact on work performance in a job. She is also concerned about preserving personal time and privacy in a job that requires high levels of personal exposure. For example, she reflects on how she has become 'a little bit addicted to' social media, which she uses for work, and notes that 'I'm trying *to keep one little bit for me for myself (...) I like to keep a bit of myself private*' (Kate, A).

Like many others, Cathal describes his journey into academia as a chance happening:

> I am *absolutely lucky in programming, I am just good at it* (…) it has just happened (…) [he travelled globally working for international companies and on financial IT systems for a bank] (…) then *I got sort of serious about studying and came back and did a master's part-time in the evening* (…) [I] was then offered the scholarship for full-time PhD and that was one of the crossroads events (…) So I *give up this nice job with a big banker and lots of money, everything that your mother wanted stuff,* to go back to academia (…) to be a PhD student.
>
> (Cathal, A)

After his PhD, Cathal worked in Sweden, Australia and elsewhere in Ireland before taking up his current position. Reflecting on his career, Cathal is conscious of work being everywhere in his life and notes: 'I recognise that it's unhealthy (…) but at the same time, is it unhealthy to *be doing what you love* all the time?'. When work is experienced as personally enriching it becomes central to identity formation (Clarke et al., 2012), and a labour of love in Cathal's account.

Like Cathal, Shannon moved into academia from a company role in IT when a new university opened in her city in Romania:

> *They asked me to teach part-time* and I got involved in teaching groups of students and also lecturing for new and final students (…) *I started enjoying preparing lectures* and (…) they offered me a position full-time (…) I was

> very reluctant to be honest because *I loved software development*, but *because family circumstances, so two little kids (...) I accepted it* (...) I needed to get a PhD to get a permanent job, so that was a delight (...) *it was exciting, an exciting time. I'm glad I did that step.*
>
> (Shannon, A)

Work is considered to be meaningful when there is a sense of pride and achievement in work well done, but also when there is 'an authentic connection between (...) work and a broader transcendent life purpose beyond the self' (Bailey & Madden, 2016, p. 55). Despite entering the profession on the basis that it suited her family circumstances, academic research is now an integral part of Shannon's life and identity. She is able to work on 'pet projects' that she's really interested in and uses social media to communicate her findings. She notes that 'if you try to completely disconnect work from your other life (...) I don't think it works' (Shannon, A).

Work's meaningfulness can also involve struggle insofar as it involves negotiation between competing sites of meaning (Symon & Whiting, 2019). For example, Claus describes how he manages the complex relationship between the research and teaching aspects of his work:

> Sometimes I close myself and I'm not online anywhere so I don't get distractions (...) because we are researchers as well, we are not only teachers (...) *I feel that if I demonstrate technological skills (...) they* [students] *can be more involved (...). They may feel, 'okay this lecturer knows how to use computers.* Maybe he can teach me something about computing?'. So, they can be more attentive....
>
> (Claus, A)

While Claus emphasises the importance of 'disconnected time' for research, he also tries to put himself in the position of his students so that he can inspire confidence by showing his competence and experience. Briefly referring to family and work, Claus couches it in abstract terms: 'if you want to have a balance in your life, *work-life balance they call it*, it can be dis-balanced without technology (...) maybe I actually don't want to pay attention to my family, I want to work? Is it advantage or disadvantage? *Depends what priority you put on life*' (Claus, A). The tone of his account contrasts with the sense of struggle evident in the accounts of mothers above. Claus is one of those who sought out academia as a preferred career: 'I *didn't imagine another option* [than becoming an academic]. *This was what I wanted to do* (...) I already had some connections here so I chose to come here to do a PhD' (Claus, A).

Jenny, also reflecting on her decision to become an academic, notes that:

> It was *planned*. I am a composer and there are a variety of paths a composer of new and experimental music can take but *the strongest path is to become an*

> *academic*, which supports you [to] (…) do your experimental music within the academic domain. *I'm just lucky in that I also really do enjoy working with students and I really enjoy teaching.*
>
> (Jenny, A)

For Jenny, academia is an all-consuming vocation, to the extent that she locates her academic self at the centre of her life (Clarke et al., 2012, p. 9):

> *I live my work*. I see what I do as a *vocation* not a job. I do it at home, I do it in the office, even if I'm travelling (…) I'm constantly working. And when I'm not working on specifically class-orientated or academic work, I'm composing (…). That's why I say it's more of a *vocation*.
>
> (Jenny, A)

Aoife also sees her work as omnipresent insofar as it relies on ideas and inspiration which can emerge at any time:

> *It's always with me (...) I'm always working* (…) it's an *unfortunate aspect* of what we do (…) you could possibly work all your week hours, and, you know, *inspiration comes when it comes* (…) I find it very difficult just to exclude certain parts of the day from work.
>
> (Aoife, A)

Similarly, Gabriel (a full-time lecturer, single with no children) notes that it is 'very difficult' to say when he's working or not 'because most of the time what *you teach it's what you love* (…) people say, all you get loads of holiday and blah blah blah (…) but, it's *a constant engagement of your mental energy*' (Gabriel, A). While Lucy is also conscious of always being connected to work, because her partner is not an academic and works fixed hours, she reflects:

> *My former partner was an academic too and we ended up (...) working all the time, always – evenings, Sundays* – I think it was one of the reasons why it didn't last (…) the fact that my [current] partner's job is different from mine, I try and respect that.
>
> (Lucy, A)

Because it is highly engaging, academia can become all-consuming. For example, Philip suggests that '*my job is a vocation*, so I accept that, as in all vocations, one can't be cut and dried like turning off at one minute past five on a weekday evening'. He goes on to emphasise his enjoyment of work:

> The academic lifestyle is one that if you're not engaged by it, *if you're not enjoying it* (…) if there's even the slightest resentment in your mind about being there, *you might as well just turn off the machine and walk away*

> because unless you are totally open and totally engaged there will be no progress, there will be nothing interesting.
>
> (Philip A)

Yet, later in his account he expresses some resentment:

> The *creeping increase in workload and productivity* (…) you're now online and dealing with emails at ten, 11 o'clock at night (…) I have reflected on that, particularly in the culture (…) where we're being paid less for what we do (…) *[the idea that] public servants (…) are not really appreciated for the work that they do* (…) it has made me *reflect more*, particularly in the last couple of months. There are times when *I have specifically said, 'no actually that email will wait until tomorrow morning'*.
>
> (Philip, A)

Philip's commitment to work as a 'labour of love' is stretched by a loveless public cultural attitude to public service work (Clarke et al., 2012). Referring more to changes in academic organisational culture, Byrne and McDonagh found that the quality of academics' relationship with their employing university had deteriorated based on a perceived incongruence between their values and the university's increasingly structured and standardised environment (2017, p. 197). Amongst the academics in this study, dissatisfaction arises more with regard to work creep, austerity policies and the associated public discrediting of public sector workers, as in Philip's account above. When work is experienced and conducted as a 'labour of love' and a meaningful activity in itself, subjection to market values of instrumental productivity undermine this work orientation (Byrne & MacDonagh, 2017; Clarke et al., 2012; Lynch, 2010; Lynch, Grummell, & Devine, 2012). As noted in Chapter 5, work's personal meaningfulness underpins the identity work and work dedication of academics. The accounts of mothers (as in the other sectors) suggests both an embracing of work's mobility in enabling the combination of work and family and a persistent struggle to make these identities compatible. Although the sociomaterial mobility of work holds out the promise of combining work and motherhood, tensions and contradictions arise in the everyday simultaneous practice of both that are not evident in the accounts of fathers. A few in the academic cohort also alluded to discomfort with shifting values within the sector away from scholarly values towards a business and market-oriented culture.

Conclusions

In this chapter we unravel the identity work of sustaining a happy relationship to MKW and the backgrounding of those anxieties relating to its costs. Work as a site of happiness instils hope and sustains work commitment. As an aspect of corollary work, identity work is undertaken in the managing of worklife trajectories, cultivating agility and flexibility, constant vigilance around making work enjoyable and striving for worklife confluence, autonomy and/or meaning through work. This identity work also requires backgrounding the costs of work dedication variously by feigning enthusiasm, managing potential loss of privacy and seeking out resources to address exhaustion and achieve respite.

A heavy load of identity work goes into cultivating a happy and fulfilled self through finding the right work and then sustaining work dedication and commitment. A specific labour market niche or career is sociomaterially configured and sustained across and within relationships, place, time, cultural scripts, social networks and mobile devices. Happiness, precisely because of its elusivity and its definition in subjective terms, does considerable work in these relationships. All aspects of life and human capital are mobilised in pursuit of happiness through work, which is in turn the measure of success and optimal individual functioning (Cabanas & Illouz, 2019).

However, this optimal individual functioning 'creates burdens and anxieties. Questioning persists: Have we made the right choices? Have we missed out on hidden possibilities?' (Gabriel, 2015, p. 27). The precariousness of worklife trajectories specific to knowledge workers is related to the expectation that 'they must know how to make choices' (Armano & Murgia, 2013, p. 497). Yet, the benefits of autonomy and 'choice' that accrue, do so unevenly across gender in the above accounts. Men ICT managers and digital creatives seek out work autonomy articulated in terms of taking command of worklife even as their accounts also indicate that they are consumed by work (Petriglieri et al., 2019). Happiness via work autonomy is both an expectation and simultaneously a site of potential failure in the accounts of mothers. Indeed, the attachment to work articulated in these accounts can be read as cruelly optimistic because investment in work as a labour of love is often at the same time an obstacle to achieving this (Berlant, 2011). The particularly heavy weight of identity work involved in making motherhood part of a liveable MKWlife arises for all three cohorts of women workers.

It is because these workers occupy privileged positions in the contemporary labour market that they seem able to sustain optimistic attachments to their worklives despite concerns and disappointments (Berlant, 2011). It is this optimism that keeps them going as they repeatedly invest in the identity work of cultivating the happy MKWr persona. Like Adkins, however, we question the assumption that creative work (and MKW in general) is paradigmatically individualised labour. Many if not most of the above accounts combine the pursuit of individual autonomy with a social mission and an orientation towards the wellbeing of others. Their identity work and love of work, although individualised and dependent upon privileged access to resources, are often expressed as socially oriented, caring and dutiful relations.

For most of these workers, 'unhappy' worklife experiences are addressed by taking time out to rejuvenate, or working on becoming a better or more efficient worker. Yet, such unhappy experiences could potentially be viewed more as '[p]edagogic lessons on the limits of the promise of happiness' (Ahmed, 2010, p. 217). Such an analysis might unravel the ways in which the promise of happiness binds workers to both individualised privilege and injurious conditions and practices, including practices of self-exploitation (Gill, 2014; McRobbie, 2010; Neilson, 2013), or accepting conditions that ostensibly reward self-exploitation. It might also reveal the ways in which this promise obscures the worklives of those workers that facilitate MKW in advanced capitalist economies. For example, the working conditions of those who manufacture MKW tools and who do the domestic and care work that enables such high levels of work dedication remain outside the frame.[8] The identity work described in this chapter points to the ceaseless work done to make vital and viable MKWlives via an imperative to downplay the costs.[9] The investment in worklife happiness underpinning this identity work is the animus that channels the flow of corollary work that enacts MKWlife.

Notes

1 The 'high-tech' worklife package promises a relatively humane working environment that enables personal autonomy (Coupland & Spedale, 2020; Kunda, 2009).

2 Based on their qualitative study of 80 entrepreneurs and focusing on the words '"passion", "love", "excitement", and "who or what I am"(identity)' (2017, p. 28), Cardon et al. identify six key sources of entrepreneurial passion: 'passion for growth, passion for people, passion for the product or service, passion for inventing, passion for competition, and passion for a social cause' (2017, p. 24).

3 The focus in this chapter is on identity rather than subjectivity although these are closely related. The notion of subjectivity assumes no pre-existing self outside of its enactment in the imbricated material (technologies, institutions, infrastructures/environments) and social (discourses, enactments, routines, relations) practices. The experience of being a subject is an outcome of these entangled practices; it does not have 'an independent, self-contained existence' (Barad, 2007, p. ix). Subjectivity involves, therefore, the continuous historical and contextual constitution of individuals, which is never completed and is always multiple, contradictory and shaped by multiple sociomaterial practices. In contrast, identity is located within the more conscious context of how individuals construct themselves as coherent and distinct selves.

4 Positioned as 'outsiders' in the workforce, these workers must engage in 'performative activities' that facilitate 'fitting in' and 'emulate the behaviors of insiders' (Poster, Crain, & Cherry, 2016, p. 281). This 'extra' work is in addition to normal work-based tasks (ibid.). As well as 'acting like' whites or men, individuals falling into discriminated groups have to work harder to demonstrate competence (Poster et al., 2016, p. 282). For example, women are often assumed to be less technologically competent than men and have to work harder to be seen to be competent.

5 The opposite of autonomy is constraint, coercion or oppression by forces external to the self which cannot be authentically embraced (Christman, 2003). Although often used interchangeably, autonomy and freedom are not the same. Freedom relates to 'the ability to act, without external or internal constraints' while autonomy 'concerns the independence and authenticity of the desires (values, emotions, etc.) that move one to act in the first place' (ibid.).

6 A combination of family activities and the related absence of connectivity throw up boundaries around work and life in similar ways in Tom's account in Chapter 5.

7 Christman (2003, 2004) reminds us that the very notion of authenticity is itself a socially constructed notion.

8 Indeed, this 'economics of happiness' prioritises 'well-being over wealth' (Frawley, 2015, p. 63). Monetary value is downplayed in conditions of deepening inequality for fear of politicising issues of social injustice and inequalities (Thin, 2012; Walker & Kavedžija, 2015). The attributing of value to happiness and well-being pushes questions of equality, redistribution and social justice off the political agenda.

9 For many contemporary workers a split between optimism and expectation leading to a kind of hopelessness arises as a result of relentless disappointment (Berlant, 2011). If the exhaustion that arises from this gives rise to a search for 'a condition of stasis, of being able to *be somewhere* and make a life exercising existence as a fact, not a project' – finding resting places (Berlant, 2007, p. 291, emphasis original), then this was only fleetingly evident in our data.

References

Ahmed, S. (2004). *The Cultural Politics of Emotion*. New York & London: Routledge.

Ahmed, S. (2010). *The Promise of Happiness*. Durham, NC & London: Duke University Press.

Alvesson, M., & Willmott, H. (2002). Identity Regulation as Organizational Control: Producing the Appropriate Individual. *Journal of Management Studies*, *39*(5), 619–644. https://doi.org/10.1111/1467-6486.00305

Annink, A., & den Dulk, L. (2012). Autonomy: The Panacea for Self-Employed Women's Work-Life Balance? *Community, Work & Family*, *15*(4), 383–402. https://doi.org/10.1080/13668803.2012.723901

Armano, E., & Murgia, A. (2013). The Precariousnesses of Young Knowledge Workers: A Subject-Oriented Approach. *Global Discourse*, *3*(3), 486–501. https://doi.org/10.1080/23269995.2013.865313

Ashforth, B. E., & Humphrey, R. H. (1993). Emotional Labor in Service Roles: The Influence of Identity. *The Academy of Management Review*, *18*(1), 88–115. https://doi.org/10.2307/258824

Ashforth, B. E., & Schinoff, B. S. (2016). Identity under Construction: How Individuals Come to Define Themselves in Organizations. *Annual Review of Organizational Psychology and Organizational Behavior*, *3*(1), 111–137. https://doi.org/10.1146/annurev-orgpsych-041015-062322

Bailey, C., & Madden, A. (2016). What Makes Work Meaningful – Or Meaningless. *MIT Sloan Management Review*, *27*(4).

Bailey, C., & Madden, A. (2017). Time Reclaimed: Temporality and the Experience of Meaningful Work. *Work, Employment and Society*, *31*(1), 3–18. https://doi.org/10.1177/0950017015604100

Banks, M. (2010). Autonomy Guaranteed? Cultural Work and the "Art–Commerce Relation". *Journal for Cultural Research*, *14*(3), 251–269. https://doi.org/10.1080/14797581003791487

Barad, K. M. (2007). *Meeting the Universe: Halfway Quantum Physics and the Entanglement of Matter and Meaning*. Durham, NC: Duke University Press.

Beech, N., Gilmore, C., Hibbert, P., & Ybema, S. (2016). Identity-in-the-Work and Musicians' Struggles: The Production of Self-Questioning Identity Work. *Work, Employment and Society*, *30*(3), 506–522. https://doi.org/10.1177/0950017015620767

Bellah, R. N., Madsen, R., Sullivan, W. M., Swidler, A., & Tipton, S. M. (1985). *Habits of the Heart: Individualism and Commitment in American Life*. Berkeley, CA: University of California Press.

Berlant, L. G. (2007). Nearly Utopian, Nearly Normal: Post-Fordist Affect in La Promesse and Rosetta. *Public Culture*, *19*(2), 273–301. https://doi.org/10.1215/08992363-2006-036

Berlant, L. G. (2011). *Cruel Optimism*. Durham, NC: Duke University Press.

Boris, E., & Parreñas, R. S. (2010). *Intimate Labors: Cultures, Technologies, and the Politics of Care*. Stanford, CA: Stanford Social Sciences.

Bousquet, M. (2009). We Work. *The Minnesota Review*, (71–72), 145–152. https://doi.org/10.1215/00265667-2009-71-72-145

Brown, A. D. (2015). Identities and Identity Work in Organizations. *International Journal of Management Reviews*, *17*(1), 20–40. https://doi.org/10.1111/ijmr.12035

Butler, J. (1990). *Gender Trouble: Feminism and the Subversion of Identity*. New York: Routledge.

Butler, J. (2015). *Senses of the Subject*. New York: Fordham University Press.

Byrne, O., & MacDonagh, J. (2017). What's Love Got to Do with It? Employee Engagement amongst Higher Education Workers. *The Irish Journal of Management*, *36*(3), 189–205. https://doi.org/10.1515/ijm-2017-0019

Cabanas, E., & Illouz, E. (2019). *Manufacturing Happy Citizens: How the Science and Industry of Happiness Control our Lives*. Cambridge: Polity Press.

Cardon, M. S., Glauser, M., & Murnieks, C. Y. (2017). Passion for What? Expanding the Domains of Entrepreneurial Passion. *Journal of Business Venturing Insights*, *8*, 24–32. https://doi.org/10.1016/J.JBVI.2017.05.004

Christman, J. (2003). Autonomy in Moral and Political Philosophy. In *Stanford Encyclopedia of Philosophy*. Stanford, CA: Stanford University Press. Retrieved from https://plato.stanford.edu/entries/autonomy-moral/

Christman, J. (2004). Relational Autonomy, Liberal Individualism, and the Social Constitution of Selves. *Philosophical Studies*, *117*(1/2), 143–164.

Cieslik, M. (2015). 'Not Smiling but Frowning': Sociology and the 'Problem of Happiness'. *Sociology*, *49*(3), 422–437. https://doi.org/10.1177/0038038514543297

Clarke, C., Knights, D., & Jarvis, C. (2012). A Labour of Love? Academics in Business Schools. *Scandinavian Journal of Management*, *28*(1), 5–15. https://doi.org/10.1016/j.scaman.2011.12.003

Cockayne, D. G. (2016). Sharing and Neoliberal Discourse: The Economic Function of Sharing in the Digital On-Demand Economy. *Geoforum*, *77*, 73–82. https://doi.org/10.1016/J.GEOFORUM.2016.10.005

Coupland, C., & Spedale, S. (2020). Agile Identities: Fragile Humans? In *Oxford Handbook of Identities in Organizations* (pp. 833–846). Oxford: Oxford University Press.

Dik, B. J., & Duffy, R. D. (2009). Calling and Vocation at Work: Definitions and Prospects for Research and Practice. *The Counseling Psychologist*, *37*(3), 424–450. https://doi.org/10.1177/0011000008316430

Franklin, S. (1997). *Embodied Progress: A Cultural Account of Reproduction*. London: Routledge.

Frawley, A. (2015). Happiness Research: A Review of Critiques. *Sociology Compass*, *9*(1), 62–77. https://doi.org/10.1111/soc4.12236

Gabriel, Y. (2015). Identity, Choice and Consumer Freedom – The New Opiates? A Psychoanalytic Interrogation. *Marketing Theory*, *15*(1), 25–30.

Gill, R. (2014). Academics, Cultural Workers and Critical Labour Studies. *Journal of Cultural Economy*, *7*(1), 12–30. https://doi.org/10.1080/17530350.2013.861763
Gregg, M. (2011). *Work's Intimacy*. Cambridge: Polity.
Hochschild, A. R. (1983). *The Managed Heart: Communication of Human Feeling*. Berkeley, CA: University of California Press.
Hochschild, A. R. (2003). *The Commercialization of Intimate Life: Notes from Home and Work*. Berkeley, CA & London: University of California Press. Retrieved from www.ucpress.edu/book/9780520214880/the-commercialization-of-intimate-life
Jackson, S. (1995). Women and Heterosexual Love: Complicity, Resistance and Change. In L. Pearce & J. Stacey (Eds.) (pp. 49–62). London: Lawrence and Wishart.
Knights, D., & Clarke, C. A. (2014). It's a Bittersweet Symphony, This Life: Fragile Academic Selves and Insecure Identities at Work. *Organization Studies*, *35*(3), 335–357. https://doi.org/10.1177/0170840613508396
Kunda, G. (2009). *Engineering Culture: Control and Commitment in a High-tech Corporation*. Philadelphia, PA: Temple University Press.
Langfred, C. W., & Rockmann, K. W. (2016). The Push and Pull of Autonomy. *Group & Organization Management*, *41*(5), 629–657. https://doi.org/10.1177/1059601116668971
Lorey, I. (2015). *State of Insecurity: Government of the Precarious*. London: Verso.
Lynch, K. (2010). Carelessness: A Hidden Doxa of Higher Education. *Arts and Humanities in Higher Education*, *9*(1), 54–67. https://doi.org/10.1177/1474022209350104
Lynch, K., Grummell, B., & Devine, D. (2012). *New Managerialism in Education: Commercialization, Carelessness, and Gender*. Basingstoke: Palgrave Macmillan.
Mackenzie, C. (2008). Relational Autonomy, Normative Authority and Perfectionism. *Journal of Social Philosophy*, *39*(4), 512–533. https://doi.org/10.1111/j.1467-9833.2008.00440.x
Madhok, S., Phillips, A., & Wilson, K. (2013). Introduction. In S. Madhok, A. Phillips, & K. Wilson (Eds.), *Gender, Agency, and Coercion* (pp. 1–13). London: Palgrave Macmillan UK. https://doi.org/10.1057/9781137295613_1
McRobbie, A. (2010). *Top Girls: Feminismus und der Aufstieg des neolieberalen Geschlechterregimes*. Heidelberg: VS Verlag.
Messer, J. (2013). Reconceptualizing Maternal Work: Dejours, Ruddick and Lionel Shriver's We Need to Talk About Kevin. *Women's Studies International Forum*, *38*, 11–20. https://doi.org/10.1016/J.WSIF.2013.01.015
Mill, J. S. (1975). *On Liberty*. New York: Norton.
Morini, C., & Fumagalli, A. (2010). Life Put to Work: Towards a Life Theory of Value. *Ephemera*, *10*(3/4), 234–252.
Neilson, B. (2013). Logistics of Cultural Work. In M. Banks, R. Gill, & S. Taylor (Eds.), *Theorizing Cultural Work: Labour, Continuity and Change in the Cultural and Creative Industries* (pp. 99–112). London: Routledge.
Pearce, L., & Stacey, J. (Eds.). (1995). *Romance Revisited*. London: Lawrence and Wishart.
Perrewé, P. L., Hochwarter, W. A., Ferris, G. R., McAllister, C. P., & Harris, J. N. (2014). Developing a Passion for Work Passion: Future Directions on an Emerging Construct. *Journal of Organizational Behavior*, *35*(1), 145–150. https://doi.org/10.1002/job.1902
Petriglieri, G., Ashford, S. J., & Wrzesniewski, A. (2019). Agony and Ecstasy in the Gig Economy: Cultivating Holding Environments for Precarious and Personalized Work Identities. *Administrative Science Quarterly*, *64*(1), 124–170. https://doi.org/10.1177/0001839218759646

Poster, W. R., Crain, M., & Cherry, M. A. (2016). Conceptualizing Invisible Labor. In M. Crain, W. R. Poster, & M. A. Cherry (Eds.), *Invisible Labor: Hidden Work in the Contemporary World* (pp. 3–27). Oakland, CA: University of California Press.

Rosso, B. D., Dekas, K. H., & Wrzesniewski, A. (2010). On the Meaning of Work: A Theoretical Integration and Review. *Research in Organizational Behavior*, *30*, 91–127. https://doi.org/10.1016/J.RIOB.2010.09.001

Rottenberg, C. (2014). Happiness and the Liberal Imagination: How Superwoman Became Balanced. *Feminist Studies*, *40*(1), 144–168. https://doi.org/10.15767/feministstudies.40.1.144

Ryan, R. M., & Deci, E. L. (2006). Self-Regulation and the Problem of Human Autonomy: Does Psychology Need Choice, Self-Determination, and Will? *Journal of Personality*, *74*(6), 1557–1586. https://doi.org/10.1111/j.1467-6494.2006.00420.x

Sandberg, S. (2013). *Lean in: Women, Work, and the Will to Lead*. New York: Knopf.

Sandoval, M. (2018). From Passionate Labour to Compassionate Work: Cultural Co-Ops, Do What You Love and Social Change. *European Journal of Cultural Studies*, *21*(2), 113–129. https://doi.org/10.1177/1367549417719011

Seligman, M. E. P., Parks, A. C., & Steen, T. (2004). A Balanced Psychology and a Full Life. *Philosophical Transactions of the Royal Society of London. Series B, Biological Sciences*, *359*(1449), 1379–1381. https://doi.org/10.1098/rstb.2004.1513

Sheller, M. (2004). Automotive Emotions: Feeling the Car. *Theory, Culture & Society*, *21*(4–5), 221–242. https://doi.org/10.1177/0263276404046068

Slaughter, A.-M. (2012). Why Women Still Can't Have It All. *The Atlantic*. Retrieved from www.theatlantic.com/magazine/archive/2012/07/why-women-still-cant-have-it-all/309020/

Symon, G., & Pritchard, K. (2015). Performing the Responsive and Committed Employee through the Sociomaterial Mangle of Connection. *Organization Studies*, *36*(2), 241–263. https://doi.org/10.1177/0170840614556914

Symon, G., & Whiting, R. (2019). The Sociomaterial Negotiation of Social Entrepreneurs' Meaningful Work. *Journal of Management Studies*, *56*(3), 655–684. https://doi.org/10.1111/joms.12421

Thin, N. (2012). *Social Happiness: Theory into Policy and Practice*. Bristol: Policy Press. https://doi.org/10.1017/S0047279414000117

Walker, H., & Kavedžija, I. (2015). Values of Happiness. *HAU: Journal of Ethnographic Theory*, *5*(3), 1–23. https://doi.org/10.14318/hau5.3.002

Weeks, K. (2007). Life within and Against Work: Affective Labor, Feminist Critique, and Post-Fordist Politics. *Ephemera*, *7*(1), 233–249.

Winkler, I. (2018). Identity Work and Emotions: A Review. *International Journal of Management Reviews*, *20*(1), 120–133. https://doi.org/10.1111/ijmr.12119

Wong, P. T. P. (2014). Viktor Frankl's Meaning-Seeking Model and Positive Psychology. In A. Batthyany & P. Russo-Netzer (Eds.), *Meaning in Positive and Existential Psychology* (pp. 149–184). New York: Springer New York. https://doi.org/10.1007/978-1-4939-0308-5_10

Zembylas, M. (2003). Interrogating "Teacher Identity": Emotion, Resistance, and Self-Formation. *Educational Theory*, *53*(1), 107–127. https://doi.org/10.1111/j.1741-5446.2003.00107.x

Conclusion

It is not possible to understand mobile knowledge work (MKW) without attending to the myriad strands of *corollary work* that enable this work to take place. Corollary work consists of all those worklife practices beyond what might be commonly designated MKW tasks and unfolds together with MKW in everyday life. It is precisely this simultaneous unfolding that contributes to its particular elusiveness. So, despite its centrality in materialising the conditions necessary to and through which MKW is *made to work*, corollary work tends to go unnoticed. The evidence presented in this book draws attention to the growing pervasiveness of corollary work and how it is accounted for by workers themselves.

We give texture and liveliness to this work via the detailed accounts of MKWrs across three different sectors of the knowledge economy (digital creative, ICT management and academia). The accounts of these workers demonstrate the creative ways in which MKWlives are made and remade. Although we artificially divide corollary work into specific sociomaterial practices of worklife; i.e. placing, time work, the imperative to narrate productivity, and identity work, these strands are always emergent and mutually entangled. They are deployed for heuristic purposes in this book to give more concrete reality to those elusive practices that constitute corollary work.

Another key contribution of the book is its attention to the intimacy of the relationship between work and life. Our use of the term *worklife* reflects these MKWrs' accounts of how work and life are conjoined in the conduct of MKW. But this conjoining of worklife via entanglements of place, technologies, temporal orientations and sensibilities also involves differentiation. Work and life, in Ingold's terms, 'go along together' (2016, p. 13), joining together in ways that are mutually transforming even as, in the joining, an interstitial differentiation is created at particular moments of everyday life and across the lifecycle. Differentiations between work and life arise at specific moments, most acutely in relation to childcare/family, work burnout, and when younger workers speculate on their potential to make or sustain a family life in the future. It is the palpable close identification with work and productivity as sites of self-fulfilment and happiness that both shapes these moments of differentiation and propels the conjoined flow of worklife at others.

The continual regeneration of conjoined worklives is nourished if not impelled by an investment in work as the primary site of happiness and self-fulfilment. This affective investment in the joining of work and life goes beyond the cool and transitory alliance implied by the notion of assemblage (Mason, 2018). Rather the sociomaterial practices and relations that conjoin worklife take on an affective quality. This means that any attempt at the unjoining of worklife is accompanied by a sense of loss, because this would involve the unbinding of those sociomaterial relations that become bound together through a confluence of affective efforts and investments. As many of the accounts attest, it is through this confluence of efforts and investment that attachment to worklife is (re)produced. We show how the promise of happiness through work is propelled by the idea of an authentic merging of work and life. This authentic work-identified life relies on its repeated performance through identity work. Thus, the promise of happiness and self-fulfilment through an authentic, work-identified self justifies and sustains the extensification of the corollary work that these workers describe.

The placing of work is just one of corollary work's many aspects. Via the location of our study in an Irish city region, the book starts out by identifying some of the specific emplaced challenges and opportunities relating to this location. However, as a region that is integrated in a global circuit of MKW practices and post-Fordist work arrangements, we expect these workers' accounts to resonate with and speak to patterns of worklife across other such advanced economy locations. We illuminate the corollary work of placing worklives at the scales of cities and regions and of everyday place scapes. Numerous relational and reflexive practices underpin these placings. The relational, reputational and symbolic agency of place also comes into play. For example, the city and region are made to work through: their *reputational* capital; their becoming in relationships of *connectedness*; their value in relation to *imagined alternative emplacements*; the sense of *rootedness* (cultural and geographical) they afford in relation to families, networks, local and global knowledge; and their centrality to the crafting of particular *worklife styles*.

The mobility of work and workers means that places and practices are constantly being decoded and recoded such that both place and worklife become hybridised. The hybridisation of worklife environments requires reflexive management and the constant (re)configuring of emplaced resources, connections and relationships. Yet, processes of hybridisation are differentiated. For example, the data suggest that while myriad places are mobilised primarily for work, life migrates into designated workplaces less often. Similarly, the blurring of the public/private binary by the conjoining of work and life appears to have little impact on gender relations and practices. As homes become increasingly significant sites of MKW, gender shapes how worklives are placed and practiced there. For example, home and childcare combine unevenly with MKW in the accounts which suggest different patterns for mothers and fathers. Third places are also sought out as either work ambient or pragmatic sites in which work time is best managed. The 'bundling' of MKWlife places is a continuous sociomaterial accomplishment that often works smoothly. However, when different interests come into play regarding how places are used and for what purpose, conflictual relations arise. It is precisely because of the mobility of work and workers that the issue of emplacement takes on such visceral importance, and demands reflexivity with regard to the self-place[ing] relationship. Thus, the corollary work of placing worklife (be it conventional workplaces, third places or homes) has relational, processual and reflexive dimensions.

Corollary work is also deeply implicated with time and time work. ICT managers and digital creatives describe temporal practices of constant readiness and sensitivity to ever-shifting configurations of knowledge, information, technologies, environments, customer demands and economic conditions. We characterise their temporal orientation as that of 'anticipatory availability' – a temporality that prioritises ever-readiness for work. This future-oriented temporality requires specific performances of time work through sociomaterial practices of anticipation and availability. It is driven by uncertainty and involves pre-empting change, vigilant updating and the agility to act at short notice. With only a few exceptions, and perhaps by way of compensation, this is accompanied by a very tight scheduling of non-work activities and family time. The differences in how anticipatory availability is practiced emerge in shifting configurations of gender, worklifecycle stage and differential access to financial, digital and other resources.

We introduce the notion of 'reflexive rhythmicity' to capture the temporal orientation and time work of academics. The diversity of stakeholders and work tasks that constitute academic work produces a rhythmic workday and work year and puts reflexivity at the centre of academic worklives. Most centrally, the temporal orientation of reflexive rhythmicity emerges in the movement between the promise of a hybridised, organic worklife flow and those turbulent or arrhythmic flows that undermine this promise. Arrhythmia arises most acutely in the emergent norms of the student-lecturer relationship as mediated by constant connectivity and email communication in particular. It also surfaces when academic autonomy, or work's meaningfulness is compromised. Overall, the time work engaged in by academics relates to sustaining the personal and professional meaningfulness of the work itself, which is always in danger of being lost.

By conceiving of corollary work as a sociomaterial 'doing' that is repeatedly enacted to enable and normalise MKW, this book engages with CSCW and STS debates about the role of digital technologies and infrastructures in the knowledge economy. While positivistic takes on digital technology and connectivity as enabling of MKW have been critiqued and the values ascribed to digitally-enabled mobility questioned by other scholars, we illuminate the imbrication of digital technology and technological infrastructure with all those sociomaterial corollary practices of identity, productivity, time and placing. Our analysis considers the agentic role of technologies in the sociomaterial entanglements that (re)make MKWlives. Although technology might not be central to how corollary work is described, it plays a significant agentic role via the infrastructural assumptions that shape everyday worklife. The rise of 'platform economy' models that put machine-learning algorithms and digital-task managers at the centre of anticipating and channelling worklife practices give these considerations even greater urgency. Moreover, more sophisticated technological signalling of availability, 'busyness' and relationality is likely to deepen the grooves of corollary work.

As the close link between technologies and reputational work (Gandini, 2016) tightens, social media platforms play an increasingly central role in conveying work outputs and personal 'brands'. Work surveillance implications open up another set of concerns that are only recently becoming evident to workers. These trends and their implications fall outside of the remit of this book. However, future analyses might usefully address the ways in which corollary work figures in and may be reproduced by these developments. It is likely that as workers become more attuned to them, they will factor more visibly in their corollary work. Although issues of technology design also fall outside the remit of this book, our close analysis of MKWlives potentially challenges those assumed worklife boundaries (and their gendered patterns) that shape and get built into the design of technology and interactivity.

While different sectors focus on different products and productivity indicators, all of the MKWrs taking part in this study construct and subscribe to narratives of productivity. They describe journeys of becoming and staying productive despite distractions and interruptions. The imperative of productivity requires the narration of personal productivity stories variously shaped by managerial narratives of company and employee productivity and productivity as the outcome of autonomy, creativity, drive and individual 'talent'. It is through these narratives that sectorial cultures, expectations and benchmarks of success are reproduced. Workers describe the ways in which they work and rework themselves and their products simultaneously in the context of all-encompassing productive lives. Achieving and maintaining productivity for MKWrs requires self-awareness, reflexivity and constant improvisation. Indeed, the imperative of productivity requires the repeated narration of accomplishing tasks and delivering outputs. It is also evident in the cultivation of productive subjectivity through narratives of self as always-improving, driven and efficient. Constantly evolving sociomaterial environments and practices demand alertness to work and productivity opportunities, and excite investment in work as a personalised creative pursuit and a labour of love. But work attachment and a constant quest for productivity have their costs. In Berlant's (2011) terms, these narratives are framed by an optimistic attachment to promises of happiness and fulfilment through all-encompassing productive worklives. When they don't deliver, the costs are borne personally, often by reinvesting or redoubling efforts.

The worklives of mothers in particular involve endlessly creative (re)entanglements of place, time and technologies to sustain their work orientation alongside the demands and expectations of motherhood. While expressing a strong duty 'to be there' for their children, this is articulated mainly in terms of ensuring physical presence, while at the same time, protecting continued mental connection to work. Physical presence for children is worked at through flexible place making and nifty time work, while at the same time managing high levels of anxiety and precarity. There is a sense that despite the many signals of virtual and physical presence actively sent out, these are always in danger of failing – the danger is primarily in relation to failing as a mother, either in the present, or in the future. While these tensions between the demands of work and motherhood might be more acute in the accounts of the digital creatives, similar tensions are expressed across all three cohorts.

In contrast, the accounts of fathers suggest a relatively seamless confluence of work and fathering practices with some middle-aged fathers in well-established careers combining fatherhood and work to their satisfaction. With nuanced differences across sectors, younger men and women who see themselves as potential fathers and mothers, express concern that their all-consuming worklife practices in the present potentially prevent the establishment of a family in the future. Shifting gears, slowing down, even 'settling down' are distant dreams. As such, gender and worklife stage emerge as tenacious factors in defining the worklife practices of these workers.

Our focus in this book has been on providing insights into the textures of contemporary MKWlife in an advanced capitalist context. By doing so, we have identified the subtle workings of contemporary capitalist work arrangements in these three sectors, and the imbrication of exploitation in the very texture of worklife and worker aspirations. Although the workers' accounts do not explicitly raise issues of exploitation, or the structural conditions that are shaping these worklives, they give texture to these everyday worklife conditions and the corollary work they engage in. Perhaps it is the level of investment in work and depth of work identification that pushes exploitation beyond the consciousness of contemporary MKWlives (Gill, 2014). Nonetheless, their descriptions of proliferating corollary work suggest exploitative effects and implications, not least in how the costs of work infrastructuring are increasingly borne by workers themselves. This is more than 'self-exploitation'. This is the effect of closely-knit exploitative conditions across place, time, subjectivity, devices, infrastructures and affect. These conditions are elusive. But they are made all the more elusive via their framing as personalised quests for productivity and happiness. The more personalised and pleasurable work is made, the more difficult it is to articulate its costs. The effect is that the corollary work described in the foregoing chapters tends to elude definition and grounding. In this book we corral these elusive sociomaterial conditions and practices into a more concrete form via the term corollary work. By doing so, we hope to contribute to emergent debates on how these forms of exploitation might be named, resisted and/or subverted, not least because these working conditions are increasingly prevalent across the labour market with even more pernicious effects in less privileged sectors.

We are conscious that the focus of our concerns in this book serves to elucidate only one layer of the conditions that make MKW possible. There are multiple other layers of global and local working conditions and associated corollary work that have not been addressed in the foregoing chapters. Indeed, the emphasis on individual choice and 'noble self-betterment' that characterises MKWlives often comes at the expense of attention to 'the working conditions of others' (Duffy, 2016; Tokumitsu, 2014). This book does not address those forms of work dispersed across the world, and closer to home, that are part of the wider landscape of global capitalist relations, and that underpin both MKW and its corollary work. For example, the worklives of MKWrs rely on the marginalised and often invisibilised work of cleaners, childcarers and delivery services. Yet, these are generally not factored into how worklife is described by middle-class MKWrs. Domestic and caring labour, but also other kinds of manufacturing and service labour, shape the everyday material maintenance and reproduction of MKWlives. Moreover, as Adkins and Dever observe, 'the need to employ a domestic and/or caring worker brings global inequalities into the very heart of affluent households' (2016, p. 134).

Although only a minority of the workers taking part in our study employed carers or domestic workers in their homes, many of those who did, employed migrant workers. Sara's account below captures this well. As the only one across the three sectors to reflect on the working conditions of those other workers that make up the knowledge economy, she notes:

> I do not buy into my own self-importance as, you know, a knowledge provider or whatever the wanky term for that is this week (…) if the work dried up, I would happily turn around and clean toilets to keep a roof over my head (…) the person who collects my rubbish, look, the people who keep a society running are not the people sitting at the top of the knowledge economy (…). You cannot run a hotel if you don't have somebody to clean the rooms, and you cannot have a restaurant empire if there's nobody to cook in any of the kitchens or deliver the food to any of the tables. So I think that Ireland has a big problem coming up where we have educated the snot out of every fucker to crawl out of diapers.
>
> (Sara, DC)

She continues by referring to the domestic arrangements that support her worklife and the exclusion of her migrant Polish housekeeper from the Irish knowledge economy:

> My housekeeper is literally an astrophysicist from Poland (…) she has a PhD and speaks six languages and cleans my bathroom. And then she and I sit down and read the paper and have huge arguments about, you know, the Irish economy. But she can't get a job here because, as my husband points out, she may speak six languages, but one of them isn't really English. And there's also no nuclear industry here, you know. And that's what she did, she worked in nuclear power plants in Poland and the former Soviet Union. So you know, you still need people to do the manual labour or do the blue-collar work that keeps, it's actually really what keeps your economy running.
>
> (Sara, DC)

The knowledge economy and MKW is cross-cut by complex layers of differently valued work taking place in diverse social conditions and cross-cutting relations of inequality and power. In this book we unravel only those aspects of corollary work undertaken by MKWrs in order to make MKW possible. This work is increasingly normalised as a way of life but deserves attention if we are to understand the shifting working conditions of some of the most privileged workers in the contemporary economy. It is because of the ways in which it makes work central to life that it must be factored into the productive economy as work. Corollary work falls into the interstices of the production/social reproduction binary with wide implications for how we come to understand contemporary MKWlives and their relationship to the restructuring of worklife arrangements more generally. Yet, it is through this work that MKWrs are made to work above all else.

The contemporary growth of crowd work marketplaces can only lead to the intensification and extensification of the sociomaterial practices outlined in this book and render the conditions of exploitation even more elusive. Moreover, faster and more capacious digital infrastructures, the drive towards outsourcing, and the cultivation of internal labour markets within organisations is likely to further normalise corollary work (as non-work). These conditions are giving rise to much debate about the kinds of resistance or protest that might be effective in response to the workings of contemporary capitalism (Hardt & Negri, 2000; Lazzarato, 1996; Weeks, 2007). While some pose 'anti-work', 'slow work' and a general 'slow movement' as a means of resistance, such tactics seem inadequate given the pervasive and systematised nature of contemporary MKW and its corollary work. As well as continuing to make worklife the responsibility of the worker, even adding additional burdens and built-in failures, these tactics do little to challenge the pervasive sociomaterial conditions that imbricate workers in the ceaseless (re)making of their worklives in the service of MKW. Our contribution is to unpack the elusive corollary work through which MKW is made possible and through which workers are 'made to work' from the perspectives of MKWrs themselves.

References

Adkins, L., & Dever, M. (2016). *The Post-Fordist Sexual Contract: Working and Living in Contingency*. London: Palgrave Macmillan UK.

Berlant, L. G. (2011). *Cruel Optimism*. Durham, NC: Duke University Press.

Duffy, B. E. (2016). The Romance of Work: Gender and Aspirational Labour in the Digital Culture Industries. *International Journal of Cultural Studies*, *19*(4), 441–457. https://doi.org/10.1177/1367877915572186

Gandini, A. (2016). Digital Work: Self-branding and Social Capital in the Freelance Knowledge Economy. *Marketing Theory*, *16*(1), 123–141. https://doi.org/10.1177/1470593115607942

Gill, R. (2014). Unspeakable Inequalities: Post feminism, Entrepreneurial Subjectivity, and the Repudiation of Sexism among Cultural Workers. *Social Politics*, *21*(4), 509–528. https://doi.org/10.1093/sp/jxu016

Hardt, M., & Negri, A. (2000). *Empire*. Cambridge, MA: Harvard University Press.
Ingold, T. (2016). On Human Correspondence. *Journal of the Royal Anthropological Institute*, *23*(1), 9–27. https://doi.org/10.1111/1467-9655.12541
Lazzarato, M. (1996). Immaterial Labor. In P. Virno & M. Hardt (Eds.), *Radical Thought in Italy* (pp. 133–146). Minneapolis, MN: University of Minnesota Press.
Mason, J. (2018). *Affinities: Potent Connections in Personal Life*. Cambridge: Polity.
Tokumitsu, M. (2014). In the Name of Love. *Jacobin*. Retrieved from www.jacobinmag.com/2014/01/in-the-name-of-love/
Weeks, K. (2007). Life within and Against Work: Affective Labor, Feminist Critique, and Post-Fordist Politics. *Ephemera*, *7*(1), 233–249.

Appendix

Demographic information on the study participants

Appendix– Demographic information on the study participants

Cohort	*Pseudonym*	*Age*	*Gender*	*Nationality*	*Job Title*	*Relationship*	*Children*	*Education Level*
Academics	Aoife	Mid-30s	Female	Irish	Lecturer, part-time	Married	A newborn baby	PhD
Academics	Bridget	Early 50s	Female	Irish	Lecturer, full-time	Married	None	PhD
Academics	Cathal	Mid-40s	Male	Irish	Lecturer, full-time	Married	A 7-year-old daughter and an 11- and a 12-year-old son	PhD
Academics	Claus	Mid-30s	Male	Bulgarian	Lecturer, full-time	Single	None	PhD
Academics	Elaine	Mid-30s	Female	Irish	Lecturer, part-time	–	A 12-year-old daughter	PhD candidate, part-time
Academics	Gabriel	Mid-30s	Male	Italian	Lecturer, full-time	Single	None	PhD
Academics	James	Mid-50s	Male	Swedish	Lecturer, full-time	Married	–	PhD
Academics	Jenny	Late 30s	Female	North American	Lecturer, full-time	In a relationship, *not* cohabiting	None	PhD
Academics	Josh	Early 50s	Male	Irish	Lecturer, full-time	Married	–	PhD

continued

Appendix continued

Cohort	*Pseudonym*	*Age*	*Gender*	*Nationality*	*Job Title*	*Relationship*	*Children*	*Education Level*
Academics	Kate	Mid-30s	Female	Irish	Lecturer, full-time	Married	A nursery-school-age baby	PhD candidate, part-time
Academics	Lucy	Mid-30s	Female	Italian	Lecturer, full-time	In a relationship, cohabiting	None	PhD
Academics	Maeve	Mid- to late 40s	Female	Irish	Lecturer, full-time	Single	With children	PhD candidate, part-time
Academics	Marc	Early 40s	Male	Irish	Lecturer, full-time	Single	None	PhD
Academics	Philip	Late 30s	Male	Irish	Lecturer, full-time	Married	Two early teenage children	PhD
Academics	Shannon	Early 50s	Female	Romanian	Lecturer, full-time	In a relationship, cohabiting	Two adults over 20 years of age, not cohabiting	PhD
Academics	Tom	Mid-40s	Male	North American	Research Assistant, full-time	Single	None	PhD
Digital Creatives	Seamus	Late 30s	Male	Irish	Entrepreneur	Single	None	Bachelor's degree
Digital Creatives	Arthur	Early 30s	Male	Irish	Entrepreneur	Married	None	–

Digital Creatives	Betty	Late 30s	Female	Swedish/ Chilean	Owner of an online parenting magazine	Married	Two 5-year-old twin daughters	MBA
Digital Creatives	Dean	Late 30s	Male	Irish	Web developer/ internet marketing	Married	A 4-year-old daughter	Master's degree
Digital Creatives	Earl	Late 20s	Male	Irish	Owner of a digital design start-up	In a relationship, *not* cohabiting	None	Graphic design degree
Digital Creatives	George	Late 50s	Male	Irish	Enterprise Ireland official	Married	Two grown-up children	–
Digital Creatives	Kathy	Early 30s	Female	Irish	Entrepreneur	In a relationship, *not* cohabiting	None	Graphic design degree
Digital Creatives	Lily	Early 30s	Female	Irish	Start-up owner	Married	A 1-and-a-half-, an 8- and a 14-year-old child	Master's degree
Digital Creatives	Leo	–	Male	–	Enterprise Ireland official	–	None	–
Digital Creatives	Sharon	Late 30s	Female	Irish	Start-up owner	Married	A baby son and two primary-school-age daughters	Bachelor's degree

continued

Appendix continued

Cohort	*Pseudonym*	*Age*	*Gender*	*Nationality*	*Job Title*	*Relationship*	*Children*	*Education Level*
Digital Creatives	Noel	Late 20s	Male	Irish	Entrepreneur	Engaged, cohabiting	Expecting a baby	Master's degree
Digital Creatives	Peggy	Mid-30s	Female	Irish	Owner of a software development start-up	Married	A 3-year-old son	Law degree
Digital Creatives	Rita	Mid-40s	Female	Irish	Start-up owner	Married	Three children – 4, 10 and 12 years old	–
Digital Creatives	Steve	Late 30s	Male	Irish	Owner of a start-up for development of mobile apps	Married	A 5-year-old daughter and a 7- and a 1-year-old son	–
Digital Creatives	Zara	Mid-40s	Female	Slovak	Unemployed	Single	None	Art student
Digital Creatives	Sara	–	Female	American	Web designer, self-employed	Married	None	Master's degree
ICT Managers	Charles	Mid-40s	Male	American	CEO of software firm	Married	Two children under 10	Bachelor's degree
ICT Managers	Jerry	–	Male	Irish	CEO software distribution firm	Married, second marriage	Two school-age children	No university degree

ICT Managers	Jared	–	Male	Irish	Technical director of scientific software development firm	Married	Four grown-up children	PhD
ICT Managers	Jonathan	–	Male	Irish	CEO of measurement software firm	Married	Two teenage children	Bachelor's degree
ICT Managers	Damien	30 years old	Male	Irish/British	Managing director, software development and consulting start-up	Engaged, *not* cohabiting	None	Bachelor's degree
ICT Managers	Jill	–	Female	Irish	Accounts payable for American manufacturing software developer multinational	In a relationship, cohabiting	A 13-year-old daughter	Bachelor's student
ICT Managers	Annabel	Late 20s to early 30s	Female	Irish	Software quality assurance for small intl. telecom software development firm	In a relationship, cohabiting	None	Bachelor's degree

continued

Appendix continued

Cohort	*Pseudonym*	*Age*	*Gender*	*Nationality*	*Job Title*	*Relationship*	*Children*	*Education Level*
ICT Managers	Dominic	–	Male	Irish, recently acquired citizenship	General manager of nano microscope firm	Married	A 3-year-old son	Bachelor's degree
ICT Managers	Séan	–	Male	Irish	Marketing consultant, marketing director for software platform developer firm	Married, second marriage	Two grown-up children and two stepsons	Bachelor's degree
ICT Managers	Martin	–	Male	American	CTO of manufacturing design company	Single	None	Master's degree
ICT Managers	Delia	–	Female	Irish	Financial controller of telecom software firm	Single	None	Master's degree

ICT Managers	Dan	Late 20s	Male	Irish	Founder and managing director of IT network start-up	In a relationship, *not* cohabiting	None	Master's degree
ICT Managers	Angela	–	Female	Irish	Managing director of small programming firm	Married	A 9-year-old daughter and a 14-year-old son	PhD candidate, part-time
ICT Managers	Kelly	–	Female	Irish	Founder and chief engineer of telecom software firm	Married	A 5- and a 12-year-old daughter	Bachelor's degree
ICT Managers	Nancy	Early to mid-30s	Female	Irish	Marketing manager, alternative energy firm	In a relationship, *not* cohabiting	None	Master's degree
ICT Managers	Derek	–	Male	Irish and South African	Entrepreneur, business owner	Engaged, cohabiting	–	No degree

Index

For Product Safety Concerns and Information please contact our EU representative GPSR@taylorandfrancis.com Taylor & Francis Verlag GmbH, Kaufingerstraße 24, 80331 München, Germany